SHIT IS FUCKED UP AND BULLSHIT

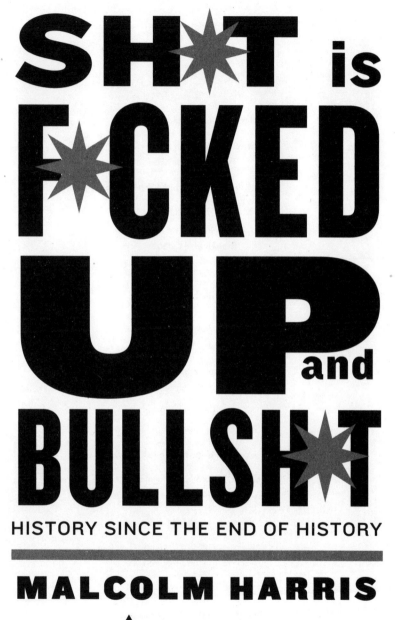

SH✸T is F✸CKED UP and BULLSH✸T

HISTORY SINCE THE END OF HISTORY

MALCOLM HARRIS

🏠 MELVILLE HOUSE
BROOKLYN • LONDON

Shit is Fucked Up and Bullshit

First Melville House Printing: February 2020

Melville House Publishing
46 John Street
Brooklyn, NY 11201

and

Melville House UK
Suite 2000
16/18 Woodford Road
London E7 0HA

mhpbooks.com
@melvillehouse

ISBN: 978-1-61219-836-1
ISBN: 978-1-61219-837-8 (eBook)

Library of Congress Control Number: 2019049424

Designed by Jordan Wannemacher
Printed in the United States of America

1 3 5 7 9 10 8 6 4 2

A catalog record for this book is available
from the Library of Congress

All power to the people.

CONTENTS

SHIT IS FUCKED UP AND BULLSHIT

INTRODUCTION

The earth is extinguished, though I never saw it lit.
—SAMUEL BECKETT, ENDGAME

THE WRITING COLLECTED here spans the period between the summer of 2011 and the fall of 2019, between the birth of the Occupy movement and the midterm survival of the Trump regime. In the first piece (in terms of when it was written), on the rhetoric of the 2011 Ikea catalog, I quote Thomas L. Friedman, who summed up the feelings of that moment: "Things will slowly get better, unless they slowly get worse. We should know soon, unless we don't." Wall Street put a gun to the nation's head in 2008 and threatened to shoot. The government paid up and bailed out the capitalists. It was clear something historical had happened, but not what or why. Plus, historical things weren't supposed to happen anymore.

While the established pundits struggled to make sense of the world, a new cohort of activists and writers emerged with a scavenged explanation: class conflict. The reason no one could figure out if America was in a crisis or out of one is because its effects were uneven, and by design. This was heresy in a twenty-first-century America, where socialism had been disproven. We were taught to locate ourselves near the end of history's long arc toward justice, a "You are here" dot sliding along the asymptote between the way things are and the best we could hope for them to be. And yet, stuff kept happening.

Instead of providing a higher standard of living to everyone for less work, we saw technology and the market generating unimaginable profits for a tiny ruling class, while everyone else struggled a bit harder every year. Americans lost their houses while rents went up and speculator landlords left beds empty. The crowning achievement of the Obama administration was a compromised health care bill that secured the existence of a rage-inducing private system. Higher education, that great equalizer, drove young people and their families into tens of thousands of dollars of average debt and didn't supply the promised good jobs. It became difficult to shake the feeling that most of us were on a trajectory other than "slowly better."

* * *

Being in New York at the end of 2011 was the right place to be geographically at the wrong time historically. After I graduated from the University of Maryland in 2010, I moved back home to California and got a job off Craigslist at a new site focused on the "sharing economy." (I had applied for a full-time gig with health insurance, but in a twist that would become familiar, wound up with a part-time remote contract that paid a few hundred bucks a week.) For some months I spent my spare time reading, watching Netflix DVDs, writing on my blog, and thinking about what to do with myself. When I had told an advisor at Maryland that I hoped to write about ideas professionally but outside academia, he laughed and asked, "Are you independently wealthy or do you plan to live off women?" I resigned myself to grad school.

Not wanting to get too comfortable back at home (and knowing I wouldn't be able to afford to live in the Bay Area), I planned a trip to the East Coast to try and find a place to live. The low level of commitment between remote worker and remote boss excused a move without warning, I figured, as long as I maintained Internet access. At the same time, I had earned my first real publication. I stumbled on a new online magazine that seemed like it would be a good fit for my writing, and I sent the Ikea piece to their submissions email. On the other end of the address was the small crew that made up *The New Inquiry*, principally publisher Rachel Rosenfelt and editor Rob Horning. They liked my piece and more of the material on the blog. When I visited New York, Rachel made me an offer: move to Brooklyn, help edit *The New Inquiry*, and stay in her closet-sized extra bedroom for $400 a month until I found a permanent place. As anyone who's lived in New York in the twenty-first century knows, that's the kind of deal you can't turn down.

I kept my other job, spent most of my time working on *TNI*, and started to get to know the New York writing world. I got my medium-sized break in the spring of 2011 when the magazine *n+1* published an essay I'd written about the explosion of student debt called "Bad Education." Based on research I'd done in college for a presentation I helped develop for a left-wing student group about the financial crisis and its connection to the university, that piece gave me something to point to when I was pitching book reviews or justifying my presence at magazine parties. Though it didn't turn into a bunch of highly paid reporting assignments, the strong reception of "Bad Education" (along with Rachel's insistence) convinced me that I wouldn't have to get another degree to be taken seriously. Plus none of the grad schools to which I had applied chose to admit me, which made it hard to attend any of them.

* * *

The first Occupy Wall Street general assembly was August 2, 2011. Occupation was the preferred tactic of the ultraleft student movement, which I had been a part of at Maryland. I had childhood friends who joined building occupations as part of the fight against tuition hikes at the Universities of California and I watched videos online of them being beaten and pepper sprayed by police. Students at the Rio Piedras campus of the University of Puerto Rico took over their school for real, leading the fight against austerity on the island. Some of us wanted more, bigger occupations, outside the schools and into the public squares. "Occupy everything" was the slogan, and the plan was to never give it back. We didn't quite get to world revolution, but we got a lot further than almost anyone expected. Sometimes I fear that the most important thing I'll ever do with my life is fake a rock concert or lose a court case about my Twitter account—more on that soon.

My Occupy case lasted longer than the occupation, but it didn't stop me from working. At the beginning of 2012, *The New Inquiry* launched as a two-dollar-a-month subscription (digital) magazine, and I left my job to edit full-time. Well, I didn't leave so much as I informed my boss that he had neglected to renew my contract and therefore I didn't work for him anymore and was going to do something else. The first issue of *TNI* was, fittingly, based on the topic of precarity—the weak connections that increasingly characterize the employment relationship. *TNI's* readers paid my rent for three years, and it was an immense privilege (as well as a ton of work). I got to edit an incredible set of writers, and I'm proud of the material we put out, including especially prescient issues on drones, cops, weather, weed, consent, and borders.

When it came to my own writing, *TNI* was a great place to grow, and a lot of the pieces collected here are from that period. I had the freedom to pick my own topics, and a top-rate editor in Rob who was always willing to be patient and open-minded with me. Plus, publishers had started to send us review copies of forthcoming books. When I could, I sold reviews and essays to other magazines and sites, and I started to build the relationships that could sustain me as a freelancer. My first dependable writing gig came in 2013 when an editor I'd worked with at *Boston Review*, David Johnson, got a job at the newly launched *Al Jazeera America* and found a place for me there. For the first time since college I had a regular column, which allowed me to respond to current events quickly and write the occasional low-stakes piece about redheads or sex robots.

Over the course of 2014, I wrote the first draft of the manuscript for what would become my book *Kids These Days: Human Capital and the Making of Millennials*, which expanded on the research behind "Bad Education" into a broader analysis of my generational cohort. (Though it wouldn't be published until November of 2017.) At the same time I kept doing columns for *Al Jazeera* and freelancing where I could. That was going well enough that in 2015 I could step back from paid work at *TNI* and focus exclusively on my own writing. In the spring of 2016, I found out at the same time as everyone else that *Al Jazeera America* was folding. I was living check-to-check when, with no warning, my job disappeared. I panicked. The line between making it and not felt incredibly thin, and suddenly I was on the wrong side. I reached out to other editors and planned to leave New York City, which was getting more expensive faster than my wages were increasing—a process I had contributed to by moving there in the first place and paying those ever escalating rents for as long as I could. Luckily Ted Scheinman at *Pacific Standard* came through with some steady work, but I still moved to Philadelphia in the summer of 2016.

Selling my book and moving to a cheaper city gave me the breathing room to work on longer, more substantial pieces, which are the ones that pay better anyway (provided you can afford to work for a month or two before getting a check). I got to report some stories, and I placed my first real feature with the *New York Times Magazine*. It was about furniture startups that targeted millennial buyers, and it was published on November 10, 2016. I'm not even sure I read it. At least I don't have to blame myself: I may be a communist, but I still voted for Clinton.

* * *

The situation has gotten much worse since a guy called Mickey Smith brought a sign that said SHIT IS FUCKED UP AND BULLSHIT to Zuccotti Park and the whole world knew what he meant. Like everyone who cares at all, I've struggled with the question of what the hell I'm supposed to be doing if I can't stand the few continuing to ratchet up their exploitation of the many. It has been amazing as a leftist in America over the past decade to see so many people shift in that direction, and at the same time we have to know it's in large part because things have gotten harder for more of them. By any metric you want to use, the exploiters are tightening their grip on the exploited at an astonishing rate. How much is there left to squeeze? For how long?

After Occupy, I didn't stop doing political work, but I did separate it from my writing. I joined politically oriented volunteer childcare collectives, first in Brooklyn, then in Philly. There's a whole network of them it turns out, and there's very little ego or debate involved in the work, which was a relief. But here I'm less interested in what it means for us to do our part than where we are, how we got here, and what it is that needs to be done. This collection pulls together my best attempts to process and understand the events of this period as they occurred. I want to put this writing in its proper context—personal, historical, political—but there's never just one. Perhaps the most important thing I can say is that I wrote most of the pieces for money, most of which I spent on rent.

I'm starting the collection with an essay about what I see as an acute emergency situation for caring people in America, a breaking point. Then I jump back to 2011, the beginning of the Shit is Fucked Up and Bullshit era, when it started to become clear to more Americans that the twentieth-century narrative of progress unto the end of history was, itself, more history. If the title of this book speaks to a phenomenon you already recognize intuitively, then I hope the contents help clarify how and why, and maybe even point to a way for things to be otherwise.

And if the title doesn't make sense to you yet? It will.

THE NEW NORMAL

AND INTO THE FIRE:
A LETTER TO THE LEFT
(2018)

True he had broken the law, true he had struck for a despised people, true
he had crept upon his foe stealthily, like a wolf upon the fold, and had dealt
his blow in the dark whilst his enemy slept, but with all this and more to
disturb the moral sense, men discerned in him the greatest and best qualities
known to human nature, and pronounced him "good."
—FREDERICK DOUGLASS, "JOHN BROWN"

THOUSANDS ARE DEAD in Puerto Rico, stranded by ruling elites. American companies profit from bombs they know are going to be dropped on busloads of Yemeni children. Our border policy is evil in ways most of us lack the depravity to imagine, as concentration camps always are. Republicans have settled on rape and white power as wedge issues. The President of the United States is, without exaggeration, one of the worst people in the country. A coordinated axis of fascists rises to power around the world. The law is a mockery, the civil service a joke. And that's just a small selection of what we can't avoid hearing in the news.

What are we to do about all of this?

Since Trump's ascension, "The Resistance" has become a brand name, a content category. Middle-aged suburban liberals have boosted MSNBC to record audience numbers, and they've spawned a group identity to rival the Fox News infotainment cult. Together, The Resistance pores over every detail of the president's internal affairs investigation, waiting for the day the cops finally throw the cuffs on Trump and his whole wicked cabal. A sizable portion of the audience is fully in earnest and is probably responding to the only call that's been addressed to them, but the money behind the performers is cynical and The Resistance is not a resistance movement.

Resistance is a political mode of engagement that is outside the liberal democratic model envisioned by the American Constitution. In a 1968 column, the left-wing German writer Ulrike Meinhof paraphrased Student Nonviolent Coordinating Committee (SNCC) representative Dale A. Smith's words as they struck her at a Berlin conference about Vietnam: "Protest is when I say I don't like this and that. Resistance is when I see to it that things that I don't like no longer occur. Protest is when I say I will no longer go along with it. Resistance is when I see to it that no one else goes along with it anymore either." (The quote is often erroneously attributed to Meinhof.)

Here are some examples from recent symbolic debates: holding a demonstration against Confederate statues outside the mayor's office is protest, while pulling down the statues is resistance. Sending a petition to the dean about an offensive window in a university dining hall is protest, breaking it is resistance. Protest occasionally involves getting arrested on purpose; resistance is something you try to get away with.

It's worth preemptively examining the meaning of "violence." We must distinguish the violence of an assassination, say, from the violence of a toppled statue. In the first case, we're talking about intentionally inflicted harm on a person. In the second case, if we're talking about violence at all, we're talking about a conceptual violence that breaks down a state of things on which a class of people had grown dependent—in this case, the white-supremacist symbolic order that racist constituencies installed the statues to glorify. When Slavoj Žižek made the trollish claim that Gandhi was more "violent" than Hitler, he was comparing these two kinds of violence. When Karlheinz Stockhausen called 9/11 "a great work of art," he was trying (and failing) to pull apart the types of violence from their entwinement in terrorism.

Nonviolence is complicated as well, more than we might think. The paradigmatic model in the US is the civil rights movement, where, we're told, nonviolent direct action (grounded in Christian morality) integrated the south and won the day. But most Americans at the time saw the sit-ins as a form of violent criminality. As SNCC field coordinator Charles E. Cobb Jr. writes in his book *This Nonviolent Stuff'll Get You Killed: How Guns Made the Civil Rights Movement Possible*, even the most committed Christian pacifists (including MLK) were armed and ready to defend themselves from white marauders. Nonviolence for most of the activists, Cobb told me in an interview, was a tactical choice, and a limited one: on all the famous marches, people still flung rocks at the police. "Nonviolent" just meant they weren't trying to start a war, though most Americans didn't even believe them on that point. To the powerful and privileged, symbolic violence can be just as menacing as the interpersonal kind, often more so.

My first nonviolent direct action (NVDA) training was at a Quaker meeting house, I think in 2002, when I was thirteen. One of the first exercises they put us through involved arranging ourselves in a line according to how violent we thought a suggested tactic was. When they offered the chant of "Fuck Bush!" I found myself on the far end with my friend Max and two Vietnam vets. It sounds silly compared to the Trump-driven discourse, but mere protest chants can still appear violent. According to firsthand accounts (including the police report), protesters at Fox News hatemonger Tucker Carlson's DC-area house knocked on the door and chanted from the sidewalk. A single circle-A graffito was sprayed on Carlson's driveway, an act the police announced they were investigating as a hate crime. Yet, as soon as the noted-liar Carlson yelled, "Antifa!" commentators from the center-left all the way to the president called for an armed crackdown, as if they had been waiting for the opportunity. Our symbolic violence, protected though it might be by the Constitution, is met with guns.

A bomb may seem intrinsically violent, but if it's successfully deto-nated without risk to people, its violence is the second kind. Describing the activities of, say, the Weathermen or the Animal (ALF) and Earth Liberation Fronts (ELF)—whose bombs and fires never killed an enemy, intentionally or via negligence—as mere protest wouldn't be right, but the way our TV cop procedurals recapitulate these histories, the well-meaning militants always go too far and carelessly off some innocent bystander. Using the logic of legal liability, this narrative erases the whole category of action between permitted protest and insurrection. Either you obey the commands of the police and pack up your protest whenever they tell you to, or you might as well be murderers. That's a narrow, legalistic division applied to a category of action (resistance) that is meant to be a check on the law itself. There is, empirically, territory between protest and bloodlust.

We have seen some strong protest moments under the Trump regime. On the first full day of his presidency, the Women's March made clear that gender conflict would feature on the national stage. The Muslim ban and child separation policies spurred liberals, immigrant communities, and leftists around the country into the street. And yet, we've seen no sustained resistance movement. Despite the chants of "shut it down," the biggest threat to the Trump administration has been the Trump administration's own petty incompetence. In the 1970s America witnessed domestic political bombings every day, usually from the Left. They hit police stations, army barracks, even the Pentagon, all to try and halt the racist war machine, even if only in one place, for one day. Since Trump took power, I can't find evidence of a single coordinated action of this type.

What happened? Did Americans get more peaceful? (Doubt it.) Are we less angry or polarized? (That's not what I hear.) Is our present situation less desperate? (Climate scientists say definitely not.) Are weapons harder to get? (Not too hard, judging from the news.) Have we, as a country, learned from history? (All evidence is to the contrary.) Publics around the world—notably of late, the French—fight much more aggressively against ruling cliques that are far less culpable than America's. In the face of an illegitimate government run by bigoted crooks, what accounts for the lack of resistance?

* * *

Trump was inaugurated on January 20, 2017, and if Americans remember it for anything in particular, it's probably the lackluster crowd shots, the indefensible lies about which discredited administration mouthpiece Sean Spicer (and the president behind him) from day one. But it wasn't just Trump's unpopularity in DC that kept the National Mall sparse, at least not the way you might think. The Left was ready, and for more than protest.[1] Different formations organized to block the various entrances: a feminist bloc, a queer "Qockbloc," a Movement for Black Lives bloc, a climate bloc, a labor bloc, and a classic antifa/anti-capitalist black bloc. It was like a social justice *Avengers* movie: everyone united, overlapped, and coordinated to fight in our common interest and defense. Organizers framed the day as a "festival of resistance," and it worked. The inauguration was inaccessible for much of the day.

I was in DC for what became known as the J20 protests, and it was just luck that I wasn't with the black bloc when the police hit them with tear gas and stun grenades, corralling hundreds before subjecting them to frivolous felony prosecution for over eighteen months. The police actions surprised experienced organizers because activists have considered DC's MPD to be relatively well-behaved with respect to our First Amendment rights, at least since a 2002 mass arrest at an Iraq War protest that led to huge civil fines against the authorities. Their overreaction was compounded when the prosecutor's office charged felony riot across the board, even though there was no evidence that almost anyone had directly participated in lawbreaking. The DA's office dropped whatever charges were left after it became obvious they would never achieve convictions at trial and that police and prosecutors had hidden exculpatory evidence and lied about it.[2] A class action on behalf of the arrested is ongoing.

---

1. It's worth noting that anarchist DC organizers had been preparing for an inauguration day of action since well before Election Day, regardless of the winner. Without that decision, the blockades would not have been ready in time.

2. The trial judge dismissed a number of J20 cases when it came out that the key piece of evidence—an undercover video recorded by the far-right group Project Veritas—had been edited, while a number of other Veritas videos had been withheld from the court. Despite her malfeasance, the *Washington Post* reported in June that lead prosecutor Jennifer Kerkhoff had been promoted to chief of the Felony Major Crimes Section of the US Attorney's Office for the District of Columbia.

Far from a disunifying obstacle, so-called identity categories helped structure the lines of attack on J20. Our problem was not the existence of distinct black and Black blocs—they fought side-by-side against the cops and MAGA hats—our problem was a militarized police force dedicated to order regardless of the law. Since 9/11, all left-wing dissent has run smack into a homeland security apparatus that was built in significant part to repress us.

Under the George W. Bush administration, it was common to hear versions of the decontextualized Ben Franklin quote: "Those who would give up essential Liberty, to purchase a little temporary Safety, deserve neither Liberty nor Safety." I had the bumper sticker on my childhood dresser. But that equation didn't have much to do with what was happening. Americans weren't purchasing any real safety with the post-9/11 security state, and in retrospect few of us were involved in those purchases at all. They were imposed on the country and the world by a greedy, brutal coterie of liars.

When Republicans and Democrats formed the Department of Homeland Security (DHS), leftists warned that the new focus on terrorism would be used to suppress domestic dissent. "The long-term goal is a modern, massive, and highly invasive electronic policing system in which government and corporate databases are merged; information gathering is extensive and speedy; and the activities, backgrounds, and beliefs of noncitizens and citizens are easily tracked," Candace Cohn wrote of DHS for *International Socialist Review* in 2002. That quote could have been a slide on a Palantir pitch deck, and it's hard to find anything so prescient in the mainstream media of the time, especially with regard to corporate/government cooperation. Those of us who talked about fascism in America were called "crazy children," and though some of us were one or the other, and some of us were both, if anything, our verifiable predictions turned out to be conservative.

The anti-terror complex's first target was, of course, the *ummah al-Islam*: the Muslim community, abroad (as targets for the American-led Global War on Terrorism and as subjects of US-backed regimes), as well as at home. In a detailed report from Human Rights Watch and Columbia Law School's Human Rights Institute, interviewers talked to hundreds of key players in dozens of post-9/11 terrorism prosecutions. What they found was egregious: racial profiling, the entrapment of people with mental and intellectual disabilities, use of a confession extracted from a US citizen through torture in Saudi Arabia, undercover FBI agents radicalizing disaffected teenagers, and extremely long sentences for nonviolent offenses. In one case, a man named Shukri Abu Baker received sixty-five years in prison based on the theory that his contributions to charitable works in Palestine would, by improving the life of the people, improve the popularity of the Hamas government. Overreach was the plan; laws would not be allowed to interfere with law enforcement.

Starting in 2002, the scope of the counter-terrorism agenda expanded. In a period that activists call "the green scare," the feds devoted anti-terror resources to cold case property damage investigations of environmental groups from the 1990s. As reporter Vanessa Grigoriadis wrote at the time for *Rolling Stone*, "In a post-9/11 world where every FBI agent wants to catch a terrorist, an 'eco-terrorist' is better than nothing." It didn't matter that, unlike other terrorists, no environmentalists were accused of even trying to hurt anyone; terrorism enhancements meant decades-long sentences. "Investigating and preventing animal rights and environmental extremism is one of the FBI's highest domestic terrorism priorities," FBI Director Robert Mueller said after the 2006 arrest and indictment of Earth and Animal Liberation Front members in "Operation Backfire." "We are committed to working with our partners to disrupt and dismantle these movements." There is no way to calculate how many lives will be wasted because the government dismantled rather than heeded the radical environmental movement in the 1990s, but the number is on the order of war, not accident. The count includes Avalon Rodgers, an ELF leader who suffocated himself in his holding cell two weeks after his Backfire arrest.

Over the last five years, "occupy" has become a generic sort of modifier, an "artisanal" for antiestablishment progressives (or rather, another one), but at the beginning of Occupy Wall Street in 2011, it was the exclusive province of the far left. Occupy sprung up in loopholes in the urban landscape, where public-private partnerships made administrative and regulatory authority ambiguous, and though a full-scale national uprising didn't emerge, the movement's rhetorical goals were largely achieved: class language returned to the American conversation in the form of the 99 vs. the 1 percent, and occupiers established student debt as a generational political concern. But Occupy also served as a lesson about the limits of protest. We were at the mercy of cops who were held back not by the magical power of the right to assemble, but by optics and confusion. When justifications were in place and the calls came down, mayors and police in all jurisdictions were willing (and often eager) to deploy chemical weapons in their city centers to disperse decidedly nonviolent assemblies. Documents obtained by the Partnership for Civil Justice Fund showed that DHS and the FBI had mobilized the full breadth of the counterterror infrastructure to monitor and, hiding behind local authorities, dismantle the movement.

Where we have seen resistance over the past decade, much of it has come from what might be reasonably described as a second-wave Black Power movement. Police murders of Michael Brown and Freddie Gray triggered uprisings in Ferguson, Missouri, in 2014 and in Baltimore, Maryland, in 2015, respectively. In both cases, governors called up the National Guard in order to maintain order and protect the local governments. In Ferguson's case, it's not clear whether the apartheid-white city authorities would have been overthrown by force had the military not intervened. To match the new wave of Black Power, the FBI introduced a new wave of Cointelpro (counter intelligence program). A 2017 FBI intelligence assessment found it "very likely" (80 percent–95 percent certain) that "Black Identity Extremists" are planning to kill police officers in revenge, which authorized treating them as threats to national security.[3] "The FBI and Department of Homeland Security are at war with Black activists," said Rashad Robinson, executive director of Color of Change, which sued for access to unredacted accounts of the government's surveillance. Despite the state monitoring, somehow Ferguson activists Darren Seals, DeAndre Joshua, and Edward Crawford have all been shot to death under suspicious circumstances.

---

3. "Intelligence assessments"—which allow agents to investigate law-abiding Americans under the incredibly loose standard of possible connection to a possible threat—were authorized by a 2008 Attorney General's guidance which was presented as "the culmination of the historical evolution of the FBI and the policies governing its domestic operations subsequent to the September 11, 2001, terrorist attacks on the United States."

When we look at the recent history of counter-resistance in America (and the unceded territories it occupies), Trump seems less a break than a smooth transition. In 2016, leaders of the Standing Rock Sioux Tribe established a resistance camp to support a blockade of the Dakota Access Pipeline—which was to push oil from North Dakota down to Illinois—and it became a cause célèbre that linked indigenous land rights to environmental sustainability and global warming. Along with private security operators, the federal homeland security system kicked into gear, spying on activists, infiltrating their organizations, and training local police in electronic surveillance and mass-arrest techniques. That fall, coordinated by the feds, authorities attacked demonstrators with water hoses (in subzero temperatures), dogs, concussion grenades, chemical weapons, and sound canons, injuring hundreds and rounding up hundreds more in the process. Days after Trump's inauguration, the Department of Justice filed federal charges against six of the water protectors, seeking more than a decade in prison for each of them. When the American Civil Liberties Union (ACLU) recently feared for the future of environmental activism under Trump, their concern was not that he'd change things, simply that he'd continue past practices that make dissent difficult and resistance riskier still.

The horrible void that we have right now in place of a resistance movement is properly contextualized within this history. The issue is not that the people are too apathetic or too distracted by Netflix. Movements that might have grown big or militant enough to pose a threat to the order we've seen built since 9/11 have been repressed by the state, even when they only comprise Americans peacefully exercising their right—duty—to influence the path of their society. It does not seem to matter whether the activists in question are law-abiding or not. US authorities are increasingly indiscriminate in their tactics (mass arrest, tear gas, chemical sprays), and eliminative in their strategy, preemptively dismantling any resistance from the Left regardless of the law's protections for dissent. They have been steadily backing us into a corner for over a decade. It's getting cramped, and they're not stopping.

* * *

What about antifa? The black-clad hooligans have made a name for themselves (ourselves) alongside the rising tide of the alt-right, and filled in as the Fox News left-wing bogeyman. But although antifa is mostly made up of leftists and anarchists, its hope is to get liberals and even the odd conservative to join the fight. The tactical end goal of today's antifa strategy was realized when, in August of 2017, one week after Heather Heyer was murdered in Charlottesville, Virginia, tens of thousands of people flooded the streets of Boston to halt a fascist rally before it started. So far, antifa has had our hands full combating elements on the self-described fascist right, never mind the American government—fascist as we might justifiably characterize it.

In an ostensibly democratic society like ours, anti-fascism becomes defensive. We try to keep Nazis out of the marketplace of ideas, whether that's playing concerts, recruiting, holding rallies and conferences, or spreading literature. And yet, we know damn well that the contradictions at the heart of the liberal order—between our color-blind laws and our white-supremacist living history—will sprout Nazis and Klansmen perennially. All of society should be mobilized against insurgent fascists, but the difference between the antifa action we've seen so far and the deeper resistance that's required by the current situation is the difference between antibiotics and amputation.

What about the Democratic Socialists of America (DSA)? The DSA is a national left organization with members in Congress, something that hasn't happened in seventy years. The organization has also built hotels on "democratic socialism," a valuable brand at a post-Occupy time when "capitalism" is increasingly unpopular with the Democrat base. And yet, the DSA is hampered by its foundational ethic and organizational culture. In reaction to 1968's "*Soyez réaliste: demandez l'impossible*," the DSA was built to represent "the left wing of the possible." Their program has been and remains a takeover of the institutions of the Democratic Party, followed by electoral victory, culminating in a Polanyian barrier between basic needs and the market's caprices.

The DSA, then, has little organizational desire to lead a resistance struggle against a fascist Trump regime, even though the necessity of that fight is where much of their momentum is coming from. As leftists of all stripes try to find our crisis footing, the DSA has been struggling to structure its own bureaucracy for the slow road ahead. When the organization raised hundreds of thousands of dollars for anti-fascists injured in the Charlottesville battle, they found themselves trapped mime-like inside the tax code's tiny checkboxes, unable to disburse funds to the wounded. I've spoken with left-wing DSA members around the country who complain they spend much of their time and energy on internal conflicts with conservative elements in their chapters, particularly around the kind of legalism that tripped up the organization's Charlottesville fund.

I expect the DSA's influence to grow within the Democratic Party and wane on the Left. If they are able to rebrand the party's progressive caucus and secure the S-word on the national spectrum, then they will have been more successful than any group of American democratic socialists in generations, and they're already close. Godspeed. But to what end? A fairer distribution of resources is mostly moot when the mode of their manufacture is making the planet uninhabitable. I fear that the degree to which countries elect democratic socialist governments in the coming years is the degree to which we'll see the limits of national sovereignty: think Greece's election of Syriza in 2015 and its subsequent strong-arming by the global bondholder class, or the 2017 legal coup in Brazil against Dilma Rousseff's government.

This is not to say I don't vote. I do, and for the Democrats I can't stand. I also attend protests, volunteer, and even occasionally engage in conscious consumption. Americans will continue to use a diversity of progressive strategies and tactics, and that is the reality, regardless of any calls from me or anyone else. These are the practices of citizens. But what confronts us now is not the question of citizenship, i.e., how to conduct oneself in a democratic society as a recognized member of the polity. It's not a question at all. The Greeks called it *Ananke*—necessity—the primordial goddess who crushed the cosmos into existence, a faceless snake coiled around an egg the size of the universe. Thucydides used a verb form when he wrote of peoples forced into war by threat of death.

* * *

During the semester of college debate I did before I gave it up for politics, I learned one useful argument, and it was called "*status quo.*" It works like this: if I make a proposal, you can't complain that I'm risking a harm that is already occurring independent of what I'm suggesting. If I say we should fill all the public swimming pools in town with lemonade for one day a year in June, and you argue this could lead to the spread of childhood diabetes, I can complain that you're using a *status quo* argument. *That's already the way things are.* Childhood diabetes is widespread and my lemonade proposal makes no substantial difference. You're not really fighting childhood diabetes, you're just being conservative.

At a time of economic, political, and ecological crisis, moderating concerns start to sound merely conservative. Worried about delegitimizing the American government and its various institutions? *Status quo.* Concerned we will accidentally wreck the biosphere, such that in the near future Earth will fail to sustain human life? *Status quo.* When debaters want to really go off, they construct a narrative in which whatever the opponent's proposal is, it leads to minority groups rounded up and put in desert concentration camps. *Status quo.*

We are currently being led by the worst of us down a clearly marked road to hell. Every day we watch life cheapen, like a stock that's being successfully shorted. Whether the system is broken or functioning the way it's supposed to for the people on whose behalf it functions, some of us find it acutely intolerable. It is intolerable. But what is the actionable form of that intolerance? That is a question about resistance.

But meaningful resistance comes with serious risk. A confederation devoted to, say, disrupting the Department of Homeland Security and halting the enforcement of immigration laws is guaranteed to be treated like a terrorist group, even though its purpose and methods would have nothing to do with terrorism. It's the conceptual violence more than any threat to the safety of its personnel that DHS would find unacceptable: both the general idea of people organizing to resist the law, and the specific resistance to the government's ethnic cleansing program. If lawbreaking alone constitutes a kind of violence, then the political use of lawbreaking *is* terrorism, at least as far as the feds are concerned. Anyone who involves themselves in this kind of activity could be risking significant prison time for themselves and their uninvolved loved ones. And that's if a government that many of us recognize as well within the fascist tradition limits itself to standard practices for dealing with political prisoners, which is not something that fascists are known for.

American institutions are used to measuring risks only to bury them under a pile of equations and hedge bets that are supposed to synthesize certainty. The risks one accepts to engage in acts of resistance can't be offset, but if it's any consolation, the risk management models haven't worked very well anyway, certainly not for carbon emissions or the housing market. And if we're not shielded from those risks—ecological catastrophe, economic collapse, etc.—the way we thought we were, then the equation changes. There is no safe baseline for comparison. Life becomes a question of what kind of risk we'd rather take: the frying pan or the fire.

Count my vote for the fire. I can think of no life more cowardly and dishonorable than one spent shoving and piling other, poorer people between me and the rising tide. Compared to the certain knowledge that that is what is required from Americans in the twenty-first century, what is there to risk? *Status quo.* "Out of the frying pan, into the fire" makes the first step to liberation sound like a pointless exercise, but there's no other route on offer, and the alternative could easily be just as bad depending on who you are, even in the short term. Better to risk it.

* * *

Where are the Bikers for Trump? Where are the police? Where are the military? Where are the ICE? Where are the Border Patrol? . . . These are bad people. These are people causing problems . . .
—PRESIDENT DONALD TRUMP, ON ANTI-FASCISTS

One of the last conversations I had with the hacker activist Aaron Swartz, before he chose death over prison, was at some downtown bar during Occupy Wall Street. We were having a friendly debate about our self-perceptions of the movement: Aaron argued that we were the good guys, while I said the opposite, that the Goldman Sachs execs were the good guys in America and that they always would be because they owned the place. I was trying to get him to embrace the role of the evil insurrectionary hacker genius—Ben Kingsley in *Sneakers*—partly because I thought it was cool and partly because I thought it was true. He had been indicted earlier that year by a federal grand jury on a long list of felony charges related to his use of an MIT system to download academic journal articles that he intended to release for free in the name of common knowledge. It didn't matter that Aaron, precocious until his suicide at twenty-six, worked within the law's loopholes and never for personal gain; the prosecutors treated him not just like a criminal, but like an enemy. He was the kind of brilliant, harmless gadfly that liberal democracies are supposed to celebrate, and the state bullied him to death.[4] I don't expect better treatment than Aaron got, I don't think any of us should.

We are the bad guys, for now. Despite how self-evident it appears that Donald Trump—the literal human model for villain archetypes in this country going back decades—is the enemy of the people, anyone who's seen their name on a criminal charge knows better. If the Left can't break rules or handle being demonized in the press, then the Left is insufficient to its task. We must leave behind the desire to act within the American law and maybe more importantly the American narrative of debate and protest and voting and reform, for they are incompatible with resistance to the Trump regime, which is metonymic for a politico-ecological, global-historical crisis that is elapsing on a much quicker timeline than almost anyone expected. The ultimate morality of our actions will be decided in retrospect, against the backdrop of a boiling planet.

Fuck it. Gather a small group of people whom you'd trust with your life and who see the situation the way you do. Meet in person, without your phones, somewhere outside. Talk about who your collective friends

---

4. The woman who directed Aaron's prosecution, Carmen Ortiz, appears to have ended her public service career when Trump cleared out the US attorneys' offices. In 2017 she joined the firm of Anderson & Kreiger, where the *Boston Globe* reported she would be handing internal investigations, corporate compliance, and litigation, as well as "expanding the firm into white-collar defense."

and enemies are, and what your capacities are to help your friends and to frustrate your enemies. Name your group after one of our martyrs; there are too many from whom to choose. Discuss your own morality and rules because you need both and you can't use the government's. Prepare to defend yourselves and each other by whatever means are necessary. Be careful, and practice, and be careful while you practice, and practice being careful. The Resistance will be patchwork at first, but we'll find each other quickly, a constellation flickering to life.

Being backed into a corner doesn't leave us with no way out, it leaves us with one: through. Ready or not, see you in the fire.

THE EKTORP SOFA
(2011)

I **WAS ABOUT TO** recycle the *Harry Potter*-length 2011 Ikea catalog when the copy on the cover caught my eye: "Hooray for the everyday." Next to a shelf of decorative Scandinavian literature and a child of indeterminate ethnicity, the white words hang like an inexpensive piece of Ikea art—a sort of postmodern crocheted plaque, only instead of "Bless this home," there is a cloying embrace of the quotidian. In the midst of economic crisis and sinking uncertainty, what is Ikea trying to say? When Ikea shouts "Hooray for the everyday" from its catalog cover, I fear today's everyday is different than yesterday's.

One of the consequences of crisis is that the everyday ceases to exist as such. No one knows what will happen tomorrow or the next day. These kind of conditions make it hard to shop or construct your new Scandinavian furniture in peace. Thomas L. Friedman, in a 2010 *New York Times* column, summed up the present moment well: "It's like this: things are getting better, except where they aren't. The bailouts are working, except where they're not. Things will slowly get better, unless they slowly get worse. We should know soon, unless we don't."

He concludes with a plea for an answer—any answer!—from the Obama administration. With all this uncertainty and sky-high unemployment, it's a tough market, even for cheap-and-stylish furniture businesses. Orthodox economic theory tells us that people who don't know if they'll have a job in six months are less likely to buy couches. Even cheap and stylish couches.

Considering the threat of falling consumer demand, Ikea and the federal government find themselves engaged in the same task: convincing us that things have returned to normal, even if that normal isn't the one we are used to.

This idea of the "new normal" has entered popular discourse, mainly through the work of Nobel laureate economist and *New York Times* columnist Paul Krugman. In his August 1, 2010, column "Defining Prosperity Down," Krugman predicts that authorities could declare current levels of unemployment "structural" and make no further effort to deal with the problem. He attacks the Federal Reserve—an organization that has the distinct honor of attracting the ire of Congress's only open socialist (Senator Bernie Sanders) and its fiercest Randian (Rep. Ron Paul)—for failing to aggressively pursue full employment. The counterargument Krugman critiques, that unemployment is due to the business community's fear of coming regulations and therefore not the Fed's responsibility, reeks of the same conservative ideology that left former Fed chair Alan Greenspan apologizing on the House floor to the Committee on Oversight and Government Reform. New chair Ben Bernake has proven less "change we can believe in" and more Greenspan with a cool beard.

In ocean ecosystems, heavy metal contaminants concentrate in the upper trophic levels as predators accumulate toxins from their prey. The new normal is the inverse, limiting the effects of the demand crisis to a swelling class of unemployed. The 2011 Ikea catalog contains a short essay called "We're all from Småland."

> We've come a long way from being a one-store company in the stony fields of Småland. At the same time, nothing at all has changed. It's still about doing more with less, challenging convention and not letting a single thing to go to waste (good for prices and the planet) . . . We've found people all over the world who hate to throw money down the drain. People who know that value doesn't come from big price tags and are willing to work a little harder. People who are Smålanders at heart, just like us.

There is no language of crisis here: "nothing at all has changed." Even though that phrase ostensibly refers to the company's founding, it has a menacing firmness to it that sticks in my throat. "Nothing at all has changed" is an injunction as much as a history, as if followed by "Am I understood?"

We Ikea customers have been under this injunction all along: The crisis acts as a reminder of our true selves, and we are—despite all evidence to the contrary during the boom—thrifty at heart. The new normal is thus positioned as a comforting return to the Protestant work ethic, to harmony with nature. Chris Farrell describes this "new frugality" in his book of the same title in almost aesthetic terms. Being thrifty, he argues, shouldn't be about poverty, but about feeling good in your relation to the Earth and your possessions. Farrell answers the pressing question of what to do with all the extra money you will have left over—he suggests yoga lessons. This kind of optional frugality not only hides those most affected by the recession, but presents itself as a commodity. While the actual consequences for the demand crisis fall on the growing ranks of the unemployed, Ikea shoppers pay to simulate thrift, just as they always have.

The perfect example of the new normal may be the Ektorp three-seat sofa. The catalog explains that the sofa is now a "customer assembly" piece—also known as a "you have to build it yourself, with only tiny Allen wrenches that will totally break" piece—which has made the Ektorp more environmentally sound and cheaper. It's listed for $599 in the new 2011 issue. In the 2010 catalog, though, the same couch without the self-assembly was listed for $499. Even though the Ektorp really is less expensive in 2011 (online, the base model is listed for $399; it's an extra $200 for the pictured gray cover), Ikea doesn't bother to list the cheaper price. One might think customers affected by a recession would be more enticed by a $200 price differential than a handsome gray cover, but the catalog isn't for them. In the new normal, frugality isn't a simple function of cost, but an independent product feature. Despite all the rhetoric about their customers being thrifty Smålanders, the Swedes know you don't really remember last year's price. The guy who goes to shopping excited to pay only $599 for an Ektorp and the chance to Allen-wrench his way to environmental sustainability isn't a sucker, just normal.

OCCUPY

RADIOHEAD PLAYS OCCUPY WALL STREET
(2011)

IT STARTED LIKE this: An autonomous group of Occupy Wall Street activists were sitting around brainstorming ways to get more people out to Zuccotti Park over beer and pizza. This was a little over a week into the occupation, before the mass arrests on the Brooklyn Bridge, and it still wasn't clear whether the whole thing would catch on. Someone suggested we should get Radiohead to play a free concert—they were in town for a couple small shows and fans were ready to sell pounds of flesh for tickets. The band wouldn't even have to play the thing, people just had to think they were going to.

The first move was extremely low-risk. In a post about Occupy Wall Street for the blog at *Jacobin* magazine, I claimed I had "heard unconfirmed reports that Radiohead is planning a concert at the occupation this week, which if true could make it uncontrollable and attract more folks to a relatively uninhabited part of the city." Bound by blogger ethics I would never fabricate a story, but that's a claim that really doesn't mean anything at all. *Gawker*'s Adrian Chen saw my post and figured (correctly) the rumor was almost certainly bullshit.

> **Adrien Chen (@AdrienChen):** Dude on the ground hears a rumor that Radiohead will play #OccupyWallStreet. I'm going to say no.

Malcolm Harris (@destructuremal): @Adrianchen You never
know, man. I hear they're really political.–Dude on the Ground

This was the opening I was hoping for, actually better than that.

He bit just a little. It did sound plausible, after all. Radiohead is an out-
spokenly left band; with the good they could do for the demonstrations, it
seemed wrong of them not to play the occupation. The seed of truthiness
was big enough that when I sent him a Direct Message with a contrived
story about an editor who wouldn't let me run an unconfirmed rumor
that the OWS Radiohead concert was on, even though this time (I told
Adrian) I knew it was true. He posted it on *Gawker* right away.

I had figured there would be some fact-checking involved, at least a little
bit, so I had looked up the name of Radiohead's manager and, using a riff
on an April Fools prank I played on my dad in middle school, reserved a
Gmail account under the manager's name, Bryce Edge. It's amazing what
people will believe when it comes from a clean-looking Gmail account. My
friend Vicky Osterweil, who was involved since the early planning of the
prank and knew much more than I did about the OWS bureaucracy, suggested I notify the Occupy Wall Street Arts and Culture Committee. She
found the email address, and I sent a friendly email from "Bryce."

Radiohead @ Occupy Wall Street
Bryce Edge
To: arts_culture
Sep 29
Dear Occupiers,
My name is Bryce Edge, and I'm one of the managers for
the band Radiohead. The guys are really impressed with
what you have managed to pull off, and they wanted to stop
by and play a couple songs in support before leaving New
York. I don't want to create a big media circus that might
worry the police or endanger what you've built, plus the
band wants to play for the people who have been camped

out, not everyone in New York who didn't get a ticket for
Thursday's show. I was told this was the committee to
email—do you think this would be possible? They have
some unscheduled time Friday afternoon between 4 and 6,
would that work? I read that the police aren't allowing sound
equipment, but they could do acoustic. Let me know.
Best,

Bryce Edge
Courtyard Productions, Inc.
8383 Wilshire Boulevard # 528
Beverly Hills, CA 90211-2425

The Arts and Culture committee bought it completely, and the prank
was helped along by their concentrated authority. Had we tried this
stunt on a larger group in which individuals weren't empowered to speak
for the collective—like the General Assembly, which operated through
consensus—they probably would have left the media to figure it out for
themselves. Instead, the Arts and Culture committee very quickly held a
press conference. When Vicky called me from the park to tell me about
the press conference, I thought the jig was up. We and Russell Simmons,
who had excitedly tweeted the Radiohead rumor to his million-plus followers, would be made to look like fools, or even worse, saboteurs. But
organizers used the press conference to "officially confirm" the scheduled
performance based on the email above.

Now I want to say that it was never the goal to troll the OWS bureaucracy; I was honestly hoping they would just keep their mouths shut and
let the gossip mills work. But that didn't stop me from laughing my ass off
when I heard Vicky's incredulous voice on the phone: "They just confirmed
it. Officially. 'It is confirmed. '" What the hell were the words "confirm"
or "official" supposed to mean? It was a pompous exercise in the exact
sort of discourse the occupations are about undermining. I don't know
how much of that conference was a genius exercise in publicity through

Zizekian overidentification on their part, and how much was just rogue organization kids getting bamboozled. Either way, once it was confirmed, there was no stopping.

I sat on my couch staring open-mouthed at Twitter, only snapping out of it when I realized I wouldn't be able to get into the park if I waited any longer. When I arrived, Zuccotti was as packed as I had seen it. People were buzzing, but I never overheard anyone admit to being there just for the concert. There was a lot of "I was looking for an excuse to check it out, this seemed like a good one."

I believe *Pitchfork* published the first official denial from Radiohead's people, the counterrevolutionary bastards. But by that point people were already gathering in the park, and the media wasn't sure what to believe. The supposed wall between speculation and reporting collapsed, with reputable news outlets declaring that Radiohead was spreading false information in an attempt to dampen the crowd, or that they would show up but not play. In the hustle to keep up with high-traffic sites that openly publish rumors, reporters had to find something truer than the truth, even when faced with an unambiguous denial from the band itself.

It might have helped that Bryce reconfirmed in an email sent from inside a noticeably more fashionable Zuccotti Park to a member of the Arts and Culture Committee:

Bryce Edge
to [Redacted]
Sep 30
Dear [Redacted]
They're still coming. Not sure who the press source is, but it's not us. Could hardly back out now!

Cheers,
Bryce

Eventually the rumor died with a whimper, and was eclipsed almost immediately by the takeover of the Brooklyn Bridge and the resulting mass arrests the next day. But what we might call the nascent "occupy spectacle" tactic has taken off in earnest with the occupation of *Law and Order*'s fake occupation. The point of occupying space isn't just to have it, it's also to use it for fun. Now that truth is effectively crowdsourced, it's about time we made up some better ones.

A BRIDGE TO SOMEWHERE
(2011)

OCTOBER 1, 3:00 p.m.: The crowd at Zuccotti Park, larger than any day except the one immediately preceding, starts circling the park in preparation for a march across the Brooklyn Bridge. I've heard that organizers talked to the police and assured them we will be walking peacefully on the sidewalk and the bridge's pedestrian walkway. As it kicks into gear, we lumber down Broadway, a chanting column stretching across blocks. There must be a couple thousand people.

I don't think there's another country in the world where a protest march of thousands of citizens would be expected to confine itself to the sidewalks, where the flow of traffic is so sacrosanct that lines of police scooters guard the gutter like we need an escort. I overhear a couple mustachioed union guys talking about militancy and being gruff and fed up. So far the occupation's direct actions haven't reflected that ambient anger, leaning instead toward the liberal universalist "We are the 99%" rhetoric in which the police and most bankers are on "our side." But dissensus is apparent from the way different clusters are shouting slogans. They both start: "How do we fix the deficit?" but the different answers ("End the wars!/Tax the rich!" and "Start the war!/Eat the rich!") suggest not everyone is feeling as compliant as the organizers may have led the police to believe.

3:30 p.m.: We reach the entrance to the bridge, and the absurdity of the original plan becomes quickly apparent. The crowd is far too big to fit orderly at the entrance to the pedestrian walkway. A large mass of people overflows onto the entrance to the Brooklyn-bound motorway.

There's been a lot of questions as to what exactly happened at this point: whether the police read warnings or not, whether the police enticed protesters onto the bridge with candy or not, etc. Here's what I saw from the front lines: the head of the march fractures at the fork onto the pedestrian walkway and the motorway entrance. The rest of the crowd is behind them and undivided, but the motorway is the bigger of the two outlets. There are a handful of police, mostly senior officers, with a megaphone and only a few zip-ties, blocking it. One of the more senior officers tries to read a warning over his megaphone, telling us to walk on the pedestrian bridge to avoid arrest, but he's drowned out by chants of "Take the bridge! Take the bridge!" The march marshals, who told the police the route in advance, give up trying to wave people back onto the approved path. A few of them shrug and join the chant; others are livid.

This is the moment it's important to understand in terms of the afternoon's narrative. It's hard to find footage that shows the concurrent actions of both the police and the protesters; the cameras all seem focused one way or the other. But if you were standing at the entrance to the motorway, this is what you saw: the chanting reaches the back of the crowd, and now it's a thousand plus yelling to seize the bridge. Protesters on the front lines lock arms and, once they're sure the march will follow, start a slow, purposeful advance on the police and onto the bridge. The police, shouting on their radios at this point, turn and walk briskly toward Brooklyn.

As it becomes clear we have taken the bridge, marchers who had already entered the walkway jump over the railing and onto the street. I see two teenagers who must be a couple from the rehearsed but nervous "I want to if you want to" look they share before clambering down. The chants are now all about the bridge: "Whose bridge?/Our bridge!" "Occ-Upy!/ Brooklyn Bridge!" There is more joy than I've seen so far at Occupy Wall Street; no one can quite believe what's happening.

When we reach about halfway across the bridge, we see the police have called reinforcements and set up an orange mesh barrier preventing our advance. I can't see the back of the march, but we hear from whispers that we're enclosed at both ends. Unsure whether we're safer sitting or standing, we try both in rapid alternating succession. A Latino teenager turns to me, shakes his head and says, "Man, I've got priors, I can't get arrested." He sighs and pulls out his phone to call his mom. There are a few tense moments. I hesitate, sigh, and pull the small jar of pot out of my bag and drop it inconspicuously on the ground.

4:20 p.m.: *Later at the jail I will see a handwritten sign that informs the buzzing hive of officers to put this as the time of arrest for all of the seven-hundred-plus protesters. I wasn't looking at my watch.* The police start grabbing people from the center. There's a valiant effort from the front lines to grab them back, but we have nowhere to go. A white-shirted officer extends and collapses his metal baton. One by one the police snatch the protesters, and it dawns upon everyone that they have enough zip-tie cuffs for all of us, that they probably have one for each person in the city. One guy resists and a handful of officers slam him headfirst to the asphalt.

As we're cuffed, they line us up on either side of the street facing the middle. We're separated into groups of five and assigned official arresting officers. Mine is a young woman, maybe late twenties or early thirties, named Jimenez. She seems cheerful and distracted. The tied rows cheer and whistle for the new arrestees, who in turn smile and strut like they're on a catwalk. Each shouts their name to legal observers taking notes on the walkway above. Spirits are surprisingly high; everyone is aware that we're still occupying the bridge in one way or another. Transport vehicles appear on the other side of the mesh: large prison buses, paddy wagons with their sealed trunks, and even city buses driven by our union allies. I'm loaded into one of the aforementioned wagons with fourteen others. We fill the benches and are forced to take turns standing in the middle.

5:00 p.m.: As soon as the officers shut the heavy metal doors, I slip my right hand out of the plastic cuffs. As it gets incredibly hot, sweat lubricates wrists and ten to twelve of us are out of our constraints. I have a few bottles of water in my bag and we pass them around, pouring it into the mouths of those of us still cuffed. We do about five minutes of ideological infighting before laughing it off and sharing names. I've never seen a collection of mostly strangers so gracious in doling out and accepting help. Less than an inch of plastic separates the freer from the bound; it only took a few minutes for care to become a collective responsibility.

After about an hour, a trip into Brooklyn and back into Manhattan, we can tell that we have arrived at One Police Plaza and were being stored in the wagon awaiting processing. Fifteen people in an unventilated metal box for hours get really hot, and a few started to get faint. We shifted them to the cooler floor, and tried to conserve water. *It wasn't until later that I thought about what it would have been like had our restraints been tighter.* I use my phone to tweet: "We're considering calling 911: 'Help, me and 14 other people have been kidnapped and put into a van by a gang of armed men! Send help!'" Our escorting officers enter and exit the car, but won't answer any of our yells. We all distinctly hear one on a radio say, "But I still have fifteen bodies in the trunk . . . ." I scream back, "We're not bodies yet!"

But it isn't all bad. A college student pulls out her phone and plays the classic Against Me! sing-along "Baby I'm An Anarchist." We talk about Occupy Wall Street and tactics and who we know in common. It's like some kind of experimental sauna party.

7:00 p.m.: We're out of the wagon and into a courtyard where we're lined up against a wall and our zip-ties (which we've slipped back on) are cut. We go one by one in new groups of five, and we take Polaroids with our new official arresting officers. Mine is named Po Manning, and he's not much older than the majority of us. His uniform doesn't have any of the adornments that come with time served, and his cop haircut seems like it could only be the result of a hazing ritual. Officer Manning smirks when he realizes I had leaned in to faux-kiss his cheek in the photo: "That's fucking cute." They take our cigarettes, keys, phones, and such, put them in our bags, and throw them in a big pile, unsearched. I start to regret ditching my weed on the bridge.

Processing is a slow shuffle from space to space, and the station is packed. We're drenched with sweat and enjoying the relatively open air. When an officer sneers at my group of fifteen, "What's with you people and not showering?" I could have punched him in the face. They have us sign receipts saying they didn't steal the cash in our pockets, which must have been a frequent problem before this practice. An officer pats my legs for a concealed shotgun and leads me and four others to a cell in the back. I start to regret not sticking my phone in my underwear.

7:40 p.m.: My cell mates are my two friends and roommates, and two guys we don't know. One is a recent transplant to New York, a structural architect in his midtwenties who works restoring historical buildings, the other is a buff and jocular finance student from Ontario visiting New York for the first time. None of us has been in a cell before, but no one is regretful. During the whole trip through processing, I didn't hear one person complain that they were tricked or arrested unjustly.

We use my roommate Max's unintentionally smuggled pen to write out playing cards on the back of our receipt slips. It turns out crazy eights is no more fun behind bars, so we quit without finishing a game. The cell is the classic 8x10 with a nonfunctional sink, a bench with a pad, and a plain toilet bowl. Fitting five guys in this space is a little tricky, especially since we're all antsy. An officer comes by with sealed peanut butter or cheese sandwiches and milk cartons for each of us, although the former (from the famous "Rikers Island Bakery") strain the definition of "sandwich" to its breaking point. From a cell over we hear laughing suggestions that we should reject the 1% milk in solidarity with "the 99%."

We had heard from our DJ friend in the wagon that a call went out for jail support on the email list for the New York SlutWalk, which had happened earlier that day. Apparently the news had gotten around, and the cell on the other side of us is developing an out-loud collective fantasy involving walking out of jail to a crowd of cheering, self-described sluts. For a while we attempt to entertain and exercise ourselves; four of us sit on the bench counting while the fifth does twenty push-ups. Then we rotate. Everyone but the Canadian quits after three cycles. We stop counting.

Officer Manning comes by and takes our IDs, and our push-up champion nervously confesses that he's a Palestinian, born in Saudi Arabia. We look at each other and hope that there are too many of us arrested for the police to bother causing more hassle, which ends up being largely the case. The engineer didn't bring his license, which Manning explains will necessitate holding him overnight. He gives us his brother's number and we promise to call as soon as we get out.

1:00 a.m.: Manning comes by and tells us that we're almost out, maybe another thirty minutes.

The hour from 1:30 to 2:30 is the worst part of the day.

2:30 a.m.: Manning comes by and tells us it will be a little longer. The police have to share computers.

It's getting late and we try and put ourselves to sleep. Our tallest member (roommate Will) stretches out on the unpadded bench, while the rest of us scrunch horizontally, our heads on the pad stuffed under the bench. Roommate Max suggests that from an aerial view we look like a sow and her piglets. Sleeping curled up in the literal corner of a packed cell right next to the toilet is actually easier than I would have thought, and for a second I almost pull it off.

3:00 a.m.: Our officer finally returns with the key, and lets four of us out. We give our man-left-behind salutes and promise again to get in touch with his people. Shuffling into a line near the door, our backs once again to the wall, we wait. Manning is standing with us, and knowing we're about to be released more or less without long-term consequences, asks us, "Was it worth it?" We don't even look at each other, everyone agrees. "Good," he says, "good work then. And I guess we'll see you again next week. It works so smooth it makes you wonder why we arrest you in the first place." I do wonder that.

We move like penguins into a small anteroom before the courtyard where sergeants sign our summonses. One by one we sign forms saying we will appear in front of a judge before a date in mid-November. Our Canadian friend turns to Manning, panicked: "I'm going back to Canada tomorrow. What should I do?" "Are you coming back to New York any time soon?" "Hell no!" "Then just don't show up. What're we going to do—get you extradited for a ticket?"

3:30 a.m.: We finally exit the building, grab our bags from the pile, and head for the street. I smoke the best cigarette of my life. Will texts the brother as promised. Across the street we're met by fellow occupiers who tell us to call the National Lawyers Guild so they won't be searching the jails for us, and point us to a corner store where we can grab free coffee and fruit. Instantly the night's anxiety peels away and the whole ordeal becomes retrospectively romantic. We chatter back and forth about everything, still incredulous about the bridge—*The Brooklyn Bridge*! A tall clean-cut guy walking home from a party interrupts, "I couldn't help but overhear . . ." and asks us all about the day's events and the occupation, which he's been hearing so much about. He walks with us and listens, asking questions, but mostly just enjoying our now boundless energy.

Walking back toward occupied Zuccotti Park, the four of us run into the rest of the Canadian delegation. Our cellmate joins his friends and starts telling our stories; we say our goodbyes and promise to stay in touch. As we reach the park, we see that even with over seven hundred arrests, the encampment is still going strong. We drop off our new pre-dawn friend at the occupation, and catch a cab back to Brooklyn. As we pass the entrance to the bridge, I see that to my surprise the lanes out of Manhattan are still closed.

THE RIGHT TO HAVE REMAINED SILENT

(2016)

A FEW YEARS AGO, I accidentally set a bad legal precedent. In October 2011 I was arrested along with hundreds of others during an Occupy Wall Street march across the Brooklyn Bridge. Like everyone else I was charged with "disorderly conduct," and *People v. Harris* was totally unexceptional until I got an email from Twitter. At first it looked like spam, but my filter didn't flag it. The New York district attorney's office had subpoenaed my account information, and Twitter was giving me a heads-up and a chance to try and stop them.

What had been little more than a parking ticket turned into a heavyweight bout. Twitter filed its own motion to quash the subpoena. The ACLU, the NYCLU, the Electronic Frontier Foundation, and Public Citizen joined in on an amicus brief defending my right to dispute the search and asserting the state's need for a warrant. Judge Matthew Sciarrino was not buying it, even though he had had his own troubles with imperfect digital hygiene. (Two years before the Brooklyn Bridge arrests, Sciarrino was moved from the Staten Island Criminal Court to Manhattan after attorneys complained he had been friending them on Facebook before hearings, according to the *New York Post*.)

The prosecutors said there was something in my tweets that incriminated me, and the judge believed them. When Sciarrino started threatening Twitter with major fines, the bird squawked. Twitter's official policy continues to be that authorities seeking user data require a warrant, but the company turned mine over without one. With the prosecutor seeking jail time—unusual for disorderly conduct—I pleaded guilty on the advice of my attorney and did some community service. I was thinking of how worried my mother would be, and how I really did not want to go to jail, even just for a couple weeks.

Privacy became a central question in the case, and though my tweets were public, having them brought to bear against me in a courtroom felt like a violation. The Fifth Amendment protects us from self-incrimination, and without Twitter's cooperation or my testimony, the tweets would have been hard to authenticate. But the prosecutor claimed that because I tweeted them, my words ceased to belong to me—except insofar as they could be used to undermine my defense. Twitter didn't think that was true, and their user agreement said as much. But that's what the judge decided.

Even more galling was that the prosecutor, Assistant District Attorney Lee Langston, was young, five or six years older than me (I was twenty-three at the time). He is only a few connections removed from me socially, and I heard through the grapevine that he considered himself "really liberal" and that he "supported" Occupy Wall Street. I did not feel supported. Here he was, arguing that everything you post can be used against you in a court of law, while as a young American living in part on the Internet he knew damn well that there are different kinds of public information. If he's going to argue that social media posts are totally public, then he shouldn't have gotten mad at me when I tweeted out unprotected Facebook photos of him dancing silly at a Harvard Law prom.

Objectively speaking, you should not troll prosecutors. Objectively speaking, I should not have tweeted that Langston and the editor of a prominent feminist blog were dating. But why shouldn't the messy public-private divide cut both ways? I knew Langston was reading my tweets, and his whole "trying to put me in jail" thing felt very personal. What's off-limits when someone wants to lock you in a cage? What could be a greater privacy violation than jail? It's not like I tried to cavity search him. Besides, I was scared. Humanizing the state in the person of this prosecutor made me feel safer, even though it may have just put me at greater risk.

* * *

When so much of our communication, shopping, even thinking happens on the record, how (and how much) can we achieve any meaningful privacy? Do we surrender our information in perpetuity to the public, to the press, to corporations, and to the government when it goes online? Is it naive to expect anything less?

My weird experience at the intersection of these and more digital-privacy questions is what prompted me to read Meg Leta Jones's *CTRL+Z: The Right to Be Forgotten*. Jones, a professor of communication, culture, and technology at Georgetown University, explores what could be called the regime of digital-past management, comparing the US's laissez-faire model with the European Union's varied and more active policies. While the First Amendment puts almost everything up for grabs, the Europeans believe individuals should have tools to defend themselves from their pasts.

Central to the author's questions about private data is the length of time we're tied to the information we shed. Information never dies, but a lot of it is much harder to reach than you might imagine. The average web page doesn't last forever; it might not even last a few months. Jones quotes a few studies that put the half-life of information on the Internet—the time at which 50 percent of it will have vanished—at three years. And this is really vanished, like you couldn't find it if you tried.

Depending on your perspective, this "URL death" is either like torching the library of Alexandria every week, or one of the Internet's most essential features. In terms Jones borrows from Sumit Paul-Choudhury, the "preservationists" on one side fear a world unwound by link-rot entropy, while the "deletionists" on the other worry that the Tetris blocks of information are stacking far faster than our ability to handle them responsibly. Yet most people fall somewhere between these poles, due to a paradox in privacy that Jones points out: we want it for ourselves, but we still want to peek at others.

This is one of the reasons Jones doesn't put a lot of faith in approaches to digital-past management that call not for new laws but new attitudes about privacy, like legal scholar Jeffrey Rosen's case for "new norms of atonement and forgiveness." From Rosen's point of view, we need social solutions to social problems. If we're all more exposed, then we need to do a better job accepting nudity. A village of glass houses should cut it out with the stone throwing.

Jones sees the effects in the meantime—harassment, shame, cramped lifestyles, paranoia—as too damaging to allow. People need a legal recourse, she argues, when past bad or even just embarrassing acts threaten to overwhelm a person's present and future. The EU's answer is Title 17 of the "Proposal for a Regulation of the European Parliament and of the Council on the Protection of Individuals With Regard to the Processing of Personal Data and on the Free Movement of Such Data," which provides for a "right to erasure" for EU citizens. Essentially, you fill out a request form asking Google to detach embarrassing but publicly inconsequential search results from your name. The information stays online, but it doesn't show up when someone looks for you. There's a way for the individual to escape their past, at least on Google.

Beyond individual well-being, collectively our privacy rights constrain institutional actors. You can't, for example, elect to have the government monitor your sex life. Individual choices—malicious or forgiving as they may be—can't protect society, especially when our choices are gameable. For example, individuals will click "accept" on anything you put between them and a new tool or toy, but that doesn't mean we want companies to use that knowledge to obviate any and all rights we have over our personal data. We want to use Google Maps and Amazon and all the rest, but that doesn't mean we want them to have the information our usage generates.

With full access to the average person's data trail, you can know a lot: where they've been when, what they talk about and with whom, what they wear and eat, the pills they take, whom they love, whom they hate, where they'll be, and so on. With that knowledge and all the computing power companies can buy, people are reduced to infinitely manipulatable input-output functions.

American law is badly suited to deal with these questions, perhaps uniquely so. In denotation, the Constitution is much more afraid of governmental interference with the press than of the press interfering with privacy.

The US's press privacy regime is based on the idea that there are two kinds of people who can reach the public as such: journalists and the people they write about. American journalists are broadly protected from government action both when it comes to the good-faith pursuit of news and prurient gossip. Scrutiny is, by design, the price for fame or power in America.

But with social media, we can all theoretically reach everyone at once. Tweet the wrong (or right) thing, and no one can become a someone in a minute. One time some offhand joke I made was retweeted by Justin Bieber and suddenly that joke was the most popular thing I had ever said in my life. We may not know whether we're now journalists or celebrities, but we're all very suddenly public. In this environment, US law isn't set up to be any help.

The First Amendment's protections for speech and the press aren't unlimited, but they're very broad, and stronger than the EU's. Whereas the UK press is governed by stricter libel laws, the American approach to speech and public information is norm-based. If celebrities sued every time an American tabloid printed lies about them, they'd never have time to be famous.

Rather, reader norms delegitimize tabloids. With few exceptions, when the *National Enquirer* publishes a bombshell story, nothing happens. If publications want to be taken seriously, if they want to affect the world, they don't print lies—and apologize when they do. Other norms include respecting the division between public and private people (your neighbor being an asshole isn't news) and the division between public and private behavior (a celebrity's beach body isn't news either).

Given that the First Amendment singles out American journalists for trust, journalists' first responsibility is to be accountable for the trust placed in the profession. Journalists need to do more than just tell the truth; they are supposed to abide by a set of standards and practices that may exceed our individual appreciation of their usefulness. Maybe it's not immediately apparent why a newspaper might on ethical grounds refrain from printing a photo of a kid breaking the windshield of a police car—*It's public! It's news!*—but editors are called to balance benefits to the public against the costs to their subjects. An exposed corrupt congressman gets what he deserves, but does the publicly incriminated rioter? Is that what the First Amendment is for? Restraint is one of journalism's cardinal virtues; the profession serves the public by not saying things too.

Online platforms did not sign up for journalism's responsibilities any more than the ink producers did, but they've always walked a murky line. If you post your content on Google's servers and YouTube makes money on the ads they sell against it, Google fulfills the function of a publisher or a broadcaster but without any of the voluntary responsibilities. And when American courts allow Google to comply with French privacy laws by delinking people from unflattering information on the .fr domain and nowhere else, for better or worse they project around the world our quirky Constitution and its emphasis on unlimited speech over personal privacy.

US courts generally don't hold online platforms liable for any illegality with respect to content users post unless the platforms know it's illegal beforehand. This is usually only an issue when it comes to intellectual property. The copyright holders to the old cartoon *Fillmore!* can't successfully sue YouTube just because someone posts full, infringing episodes. When it comes to libel on platforms, American law is not much help. A defamed individual is probably better off trying to change the narrative.

Compared with the costly responsibilities of journalism, being a platform looks appealing, especially when you have to compete with them for attention. *Gawker* is not unique, but its synthesis of British journalism norms and Cayman Islands liability made Nick Denton's project a trailblazer. The site has famously transgressed both public-private divides, outing a relatively unknown corporate executive's texts with an escort and publishing a Hulk Hogan sex tape. It is playing a version of the privacy paradox: people will still click on things they think shouldn't have been published. And if *Gawker* publishes these things, other sites will too, or at least write about *Gawker* doing it. Self-restraint works only if everyone does it, and though *Gawker* built a bridge between legitimate news and tabloid gossip, it's now the so-called legacy media companies who walk it every day.

Supervillain Peter Thiel, with his many lawsuits against *Gawker*, claims to be playing white knight for the American press norms of yesteryear, but whether he wins or loses, that fragile deal is definitely over. Is that so bad? Privacy norms shift over time. Allegations of Bill Cosby's repeated sexual assaults were public and well-founded, but for a long time they fell into the media void of "private behavior." A university professor of no particular public profile might be considered a private person and his sexual harassment of graduate students not newsworthy, but exposing this behavior can go a long way toward creating a social environment of accountability. Privacy norms, in part, protect the locally powerful, and journalists who abide by them aren't always serving the public after all.

Which brings me back to *People v. Harris*. It's flattering to think the district attorney's office picked me out of a crowd of hundreds because they thought I was important, but I'm pretty sure that's not what happened. Rather, I'm almost positive that the assistant district attorney saw a tweet of mine quoted in a *Guardian* article about the march. The tweet was public, but I didn't expect it to be *that* kind of public. My audience, though potentially limitless, was practically limited to my fewer than two thousand followers at the time. And if *The Guardian*'s writer had contacted me, I wouldn't have given the same quote for fear of getting myself in trouble. Do I want a law that would have prevented *The Guardian* from publishing the tweet? I do not. Do I wish the reporter had asked me anyway? Hell yes.

I was lucky that I didn't face more serious consequences; someone in a different situation could have had their life ruined. Allen Bullock, a Black teenager from Baltimore, faced possible life in prison and a $500,000 bail after dramatic photos of him breaking a cop-car window with a traffic cone during a 2015 riot led coverage around the world. It's impossible to know if Bullock would have felt compelled to turn himself in if the pictures had never been disseminated. Punishing their subject is probably not what the photographers intended, but it was a predictable outcome of their actions.

America is not Europe, and national content producers and platforms are not likely to see their lawful speech regulated any time soon, not for privacy. In *CTRL+Z*, Jones doesn't get into regulatory capture, but American multinationals have a lot of influence on the laws they have to follow. Even if regulators were able to navigate the First Amendment challenges, it's hard to imagine getting strong digital rights to privacy past Silicon Valley lobbyists. This Wild West approach makes the Internet we have possible, but it also makes the Internet we have hard to manage.

Jones thinks the process of changing norms is too slow for the immediate harm reduction we need, but norms are all we have. Whether most
editors and journalists have ever lived up to the special trust our system
puts in them, I don't know, but they're not so special anymore. In the
age of data, regular folks can't rely on the impotence of their words, and
there's no one to stop us from broadcasting whatever dumb—or allegedly
incriminating—shit we think up. No law restricting information will save
us, from ourselves or each other. If we want to live networked in safety,
dignity, and respect anyway, we'll all have to be professionally thoughtful.

MILLENNIALS

BAD EDUCATION
(2011)

THE PROJECT ON Student Debt estimates that the average college senior in 2009 graduated with $24,000 in outstanding loans. In August of 2010, student loans surpassed credit cards as the nation's single largest source of debt, edging ever closer to $1 trillion. Yet for all the moralizing about American consumer debt by both parties, no one dares call higher education a bad investment. The nearly axiomatic good of a university degree in American society has allowed a higher education bubble to expand to the point of bursting.

Since 1978, the price of tuition at US colleges has increased over 900 percent, 650 points above inflation. To put that number in perspective, housing prices, the bubble that nearly burst the US economy, then the global one, increased only fifty points above the Consumer Price Index during those years. But while college applicants' faith in the value of higher education has only increased, employers' has declined. According to Richard Rothstein at the Economic Policy Institute, wages for college-educated workers outside of the inflated finance industry have stagnated or diminished. Unemployment has hit recent graduates especially hard, nearly doubling in the post-2007 recession. The result is that the most indebted generation in history is without the dependable jobs it needs to escape debt.

What kind of incentives motivate lenders to continue awarding six-figure sums to teenagers facing both the worst youth unemployment rate in decades and an increasingly competitive global workforce?

During the expansion of the housing bubble, lenders felt protected because they could repackage risky loans as mortgage-backed securities, which sold briskly to a pious market that believed housing prices could only increase. By combining slices of regionally diverse loans and theoretically spreading the risk of default, lenders were able to convince independent rating agencies that the resulting financial products were safe bets. They weren't. But since this wouldn't be America if you couldn't monetize your children's futures, the education sector still has its equivalent: the Student Loan Asset-Backed Security (or, as they're known in the industry, SLABS).

SLABS were invented by then-semipublic Sallie Mae in the early 1990s, and their trading grew as part of the larger asset-backed security wave that peaked in 2007. In 1990, there were $75.6 million of these securities in circulation; at their apex, the total stood at $2.67 trillion. The number of SLABS traded on the market grew from $200,000 in 1991 to near $250 billion by the fourth quarter of 2010. But while trading in securities backed by credit cards, auto loans, and home equity is down 50 percent or more across the board, SLABS have not suffered the same sort of drop. SLABS are still considered safe investments—the kind financial advisors market to pension funds and the elderly.

With the secondary market in such good shape, primary lenders have been eager to help students with out-of-control costs. In addition to the knowledge that they can move these loans off their balance sheets quickly, they have had another reason not to worry: federal guarantees. Under the just-ended Federal Family Education Loan (FFEL) Program, the US Treasury backed private loans to college students. This meant that even if the secondary market collapsed and there were an anomalous wave of defaults, the federal government had already built a lender bailout into the law. And if that weren't enough, in May 2008 President Bush signed the Ensuring Continued Access to Student Loans Act, which authorized the Department of Education to purchase FFEL loans outright if secondary demand dipped. In 2010, as a cost-offset attached to health reform legislation, President Obama ended FFEL, but not before it had grown to a $60 billion-a-year operation.

Even with the Treasury no longer acting as cosigner on private loans, the flow of SLABS won't end any time soon. What analysts at Barclays Capital wrote of the securities in 2006 still rings true: "For this sector, we expect sustainable growth in new issuance volume as the growth in education costs continues to outpace increases in family incomes, grants, and federal loans." The loans and costs are caught in the kind of dangerous loop that occurs when lending becomes both profitable and seemingly risk-free: high and increasing college costs mean students need to take out more loans, more loans mean more securities lenders can package and sell, more selling means lenders can offer more loans with the capital they raise, which means colleges can continue to raise costs. The result is over $800 billion in outstanding student debt, over 30 percent of it securitized, and the federal government directly or indirectly on the hook for almost all of it.

* * *

If this sounds familiar, it probably should, and the parallels with the pre-crisis housing market don't end there. The most predatory and cynical subprime lending has its analogue in for-profit colleges. Inequalities in US primary and secondary education previously meant that a large slice of the working class never got a chance to take on the large debts associated with four-year degree programs. For-profits like the University of Phoenix or Kaplan are the market's answer to this opportunity.

While the debt numbers for four-year programs look risky, for-profit two-year schools have apocalyptic figures: 96 percent of their students take on debt and within fifteen years 40 percent are in default. A Government Accountability Office sting operation in which agents posed as applicants found all fifteen approached institutions engaged in deceptive practices and four in straight-up fraud. For-profits were found to have paid their admissions officers on commission, falsely claimed accreditation, underrepresented costs, and encouraged applicants to lie on federal financial aid

forms. Far from the bargain they portray themselves to be on daytime television, for-profit degree programs were found to be more expensive than
the nonprofit alternatives nearly every time. These degrees are a tough sell,
but for-profits sell tough. They spend an unseemly amount of money on
advertising, a fact that probably hasn't escaped the reader's notice.

But despite the attention the for-profit sector has attracted (including
congressional hearings), as in the housing crisis it's hard to see where
the bad apples stop and the barrel begins. For-profits have quickly tied
themselves to traditional powers in education, politics, and media. Just
a few examples: Richard C. Blum, University of California regent (and
husband of California Sen. Dianne Feinstein), is also through his investment firm the majority stakeholder in two of the largest for-profit colleges.
The Washington Post Co. [now Graham Holdings Co.] owns Kaplan
Higher Education, forcing the company's flagship paper to print a steady
stream of embarrassing parenthetical disclosures in articles on the subject
of for-profits. Industry leader University of Phoenix has even developed
an extensive partnership with *GOOD* magazine, sponsoring an education
editor. Thanks to these connections, billions more in advertising, and
nearly $9 million in combined lobbying and campaign contributions in
2010 alone, for-profits have become the fastest growing sector in American
higher education.

If the comparative model is valid, then the lessons of the housing crash
nag: what happens when the kids can't pay? The federal government only
uses data on students who default within the first two years of repayment,
but its numbers have the default rate increasing every year since 2005.
Analyst accounts have only 40 percent of the total outstanding debt in
active repayment, the majority being either in deferment or default. Next
year, the Department of Education will calculate default rates based on
numbers three years after the beginning of repayment rather than two.
The projected results are staggering: recorded defaults for the class of 2008
will nearly double, from 7 to 13.8 percent. With fewer and fewer students
having the income necessary to pay back loans (except by taking on more
consumer debt), a massive default looks closer to inevitable.

Unlike during the housing crisis, the government's response to a national wave of defaults that could pop the higher-ed bubble is already written into law. In the event of foreclosure on a government-backed loan, the holder submits a request to what's called a state guaranty agency, which then submits a claim to the feds. The federal disbursement rate is tied to the guaranty agency's fiscal year default rate. For loans issued after October 1998, if the rate exceeds 5 percent, the disbursement drops to 85 percent of principal and interest accrued. If the rate exceeds 9 percent, the disbursement falls to 75 percent. But the guaranty agency rates are computed in such a way that they do not reflect the rate of default as students experience it; of all the guaranty agencies applying for federal reimbursement last year, none hit the 5 percent trigger rate.

With all of these protections in place, SLABS are a better investment than most housing-backed securities ever were. The advantage of a preemptive bailout is that it can make itself unnecessary: if investors know they're insulated from risk, there's less reason for them to get skittish if the securities dip, and a much lower chance of a speculative collapse. The worst-case scenario seems to involve the federal government paying for students to go to college, and aside from the enrichment of the parasitic private lenders and speculators, this might not look too bad if you believe in big government, free education, or even Keynesian fiscal stimulus. But until now, we have only examined one side of the exchange. When students agree to take out a loan, the fairness of the deal is premised on the value for the student of their borrowed dollars. If an eighteen-year-old takes out $200,000 in loans, he or she better be not only getting the full value, but investing it well too.

* * *

Higher education seems an unlikely site for this kind of speculative bubble. While housing prices are based on what competing buyers are willing to pay, postsecondary education's price is supposedly linked to its costs (with the exception of the for-profits). But the rapid growth in tuition is mystifying in value terms; no one could argue convincingly the quality of instruction or the market value of a degree has increased tenfold in the past four decades (though this hasn't stopped some from trying). So why would universities raise tuition so high so quickly? "Because they can" answers this question for home-sellers out to get the biggest return on their investments, or for-profits out to grab as much Pell Grant money as possible, but it seems an awfully cynical answer when it comes to non-profit education.

First, where the money hasn't gone—instruction. As Marc Bousquet, a leading researcher into the changing structures of higher education, wrote in *How the University Works* (2008),

> If you're enrolled in four college classes right now, you have a pretty good chance that one of the four will be taught by someone who has earned a doctorate and whose teaching, scholarship, and service to the profession has undergone the intensive peer scrutiny associated with the tenure system. In your other three classes, however, you are likely to be taught by someone who has started a degree but not finished it; was hired by a manager, not professional peers; may never publish in the field she is teaching; got into the pool of persons being considered for the job because she was willing to work for wages around the official poverty line (often under the delusion that she could 'work her way into' a tenurable position); and does not plan to be working at your institution three years from now.

This is not an improvement; fewer than forty years ago, when the explosive growth in tuition began, these proportions were reversed. Graduate students are highly represented among the newly precarious; with so much available debt, universities can force graduate student workers to scrape by on subminimum wage, making them a great source of cheap instructional labor. Fewer tenure-track jobs mean that recent PhDs, overwhelmed with debt, have no choice but to accept insecure adjunct positions with the new crop of graduate student-workers keeping wages down. Rather than producing a better-trained, more professional teaching corps, increased tuition and debt have enabled the opposite.

If overfed teachers aren't the causes or beneficiaries of increased tuition (as they've been depicted of late), then perhaps it's worth looking up the food chain. As faculty jobs have become increasingly contingent and precarious, administration has become anything but. Formerly, administrators were more or less teachers with added responsibilities; nowadays, they function more like standard corporate managers—and they're paid like them too. Once a few entrepreneurial schools made this switch, market pressures compelled the rest to follow the high-revenue model, which leads directly to high salaries for in-demand administrators. Even at nonprofit schools, top-level administrators and financial managers pull down six- and seven-figure salaries, more on par with their industry counterparts than with their fellow faculty members. And while the proportion of tenure-track teaching faculty has dwindled, the number of managers has skyrocketed in both relative and absolute terms. If current trends continue, the Department of Education estimates that by 2014 there will be more administrators than instructors at American four-year nonprofit colleges. A bigger administration also consumes a larger portion of available funds, so it's unsurprising that budget shares for instruction and student services have dipped over the past fifteen years.

When you hire corporate managers, you get managed like a corporation, and the race for tuition dollars and grants from government and private partnerships has become the driving objective of the contemporary university administration. The goal for large state universities and elite private colleges alike has ceased to be (if it ever was) building well-educated citizens; now they hardly even bother to prepare students to assume their places among the ruling class. Instead we have, in Bousquet's words, "the entrepreneurial urges, vanity, and hobbyhorses of administrators: digitize the curriculum! Build the best pool/golf course/stadium in the state! Bring more souls to God! Win the all-conference championship!" These expensive projects are all part of another cycle: corporate universities must be competitive in recruiting students who may become rich alumni, so they have to spend on attractive extras, which means they need more revenue, so they need more students paying higher tuition. For-profits aren't the only ones consumed with selling product. And if a humanities program can't demonstrate its economic utility to its institution (which can't afford

to haul "dead weight") and students (who understand the need for marketable degrees), then it faces cuts, the neoliberal management technique par
excellence. Students apparently have received the message loud and clear,
as business has quickly become the nation's most popular major.

When President Obama spoke in the State of the Union of the need to
send more Americans to college, it was in the context of economic competition with China, phrased as if we ought to produce graduates like steel.
As the near ubiquitous unpaid internship for credit (in which students pay
tuition in order to work for free) replaces class time, the bourgeois trade
school supplants the academy. Parents understandably worried about their
children make sure they never forget about the importance of an attractive
résumé. It was easier for students to believe a college education was price-
less when it wasn't bought and sold from every angle.

If tuition has increased astronomically and the portion of money spent
on instruction and student services has fallen, if the (at very least comparative) market value of a degree has dipped and most students can no
longer afford to enjoy college as a period of intellectual adventure, then
at least one more thing is clear: higher education, for-profit or not, has
increasingly become a scam.

* * *

We know the consequences of default for lenders, investors, and their
backers at the Treasury, but what of the defaulters? Homeowners who
found themselves with negative equity (owing more on their houses
than the houses were worth) could always walk away. Students aren't as
lucky: graduates can't ditch their degrees, even if they borrowed more
money than their accredited labor power can command on the market.
Americans overwhelmed with normal consumer debt (like credit card
debt) have the option of bankruptcy, and although it's an arduous and
credit score-killing process, not having ready access to thousands in pre-
approved cash is not always such a bad thing. But students don't have
that option either. Before 2005, students could use bankruptcy to escape
education loans that weren't provided directly by the federal government,

but the facetiously named "Bankruptcy Abuse Prevention and Consumer Protection Act" extended nondischargeability to all education loans, even credit cards used to pay school bills.

Today, student debt is an exceptionally punishing kind to have. Not only is it inescapable through bankruptcy, but student loans have no expiration date and collectors can garnish wages, social security payments, and even unemployment benefits. When a borrower defaults and the guaranty agency collects from the federal government, the agency gets a cut of whatever it's able to recover from then on (even though they have already been compensated for the losses), giving agencies a financial incentive to dog former students to the grave.

When the housing bubble collapsed, the results (relatively good for most investors, bad for the government, worse for homeowners) were predictable but not preordained. With the student-loan bubble, the resolution is much the same, and it's decided in advance.

In addition to the billions colleges have spent on advertising, sports programs, campus aesthetics, and marketable luxuries, they've benefited from a public discourse that depicts higher education as an unmitigated social good. Since the Baby Boomers gave birth, the college degree has seemed a panacea for social ills, a metaphor for a special kind of deserved success. We still tell fairy tales about escapes from the ghetto to the classroom or the short path from graduation to lifelong satisfaction, not to mention America's collective college success story: the G.I. Bill. But these narratives are not inspiring true-life models, they're advertising copy, and they come complete with loan forms.

POMP AND EXCEPTIONAL CIRCUMSTANCE

(2012)

IF THERE WAS going to be major action to reduce the $1 trillion in student debt—or at least the rate at which it's increasing—it probably should have happened by now.

The conventional wisdom going into the election was that President Obama and the Democrats would have to galvanize the youth vote if they wanted a repeat of 2008. With nearly 20 percent of families, and 40 percent of young families, owing a slice of the education debt, the issue affects a large and growing constituency. And because existing student loan policy is so anti-student and pro-bank, Democrats could have proposed a number of commonsense, deficit-neutral reforms, even reforms that would have saved the government money. The stars were aligned for a major push.

Remarkably, it didn't happen. Instead we saw dithering, half measures, and compromises meant to reassure voters that politicians were aware of their suffering and that something was going to be done. The moves that were implemented did not address the core problem: the amount of money debtors will have to pay. For example, President Obama claimed credit for delaying a doubling of interest rates on federal loans from 3.4 to 6.8 percent, while, at the same time, ending interest grace periods for graduate and undergraduate students. The first measure is temporary and is expected to cost the government $6 billion; the second is permanent and will cost debtors an estimated

$20 billion in the next decade alone. Despite his campaign rhetoric, President Obama has overseen an unparalleled growth of student debt, with around a third of the outstanding total accruing under his watch.

Neither major party offered a credible plan to reduce the student-debt burden. While Obama assured voters ("Let me be perfectly clear . . .") that he understood the importance of supporting students who wanted to go to college, the Romney campaign spouted free-market platitudes. The real difference between the two sides was ultimately more about who debtors would owe—the Treasury or private lenders—than about how much. Not a single policy proposal on the proper scale was offered, and so the true size of the problem fell out of the national debate. Obama won reelection with a smaller majority than in his first election—the first time that has happened to an incumbent president since 1944—and the Republicans retained control of the House of Representatives.

There's nothing accidental about a student-debt discussion that veers between insubstantial and nonexistent. An intricate web of government and financial interests and the laws that protect them have kept the fixes cosmetic while allowing the outstanding total to grow. Policy failures reveal the conflicts of interest that characterize the day-to-day business of governing and unmask the incentives that reduce "hope" and "change" to advertising copy. The challenge of student debt, like climate change and other urgent needs, threatens to exceed the capacity of our current political and economic systems.

* * *

Shortly after taking office in 2009, President Obama demanded an end to the Federal Family Education Loan (FFEL) Program, which guaranteed student loans made by private industry. Funding loans through middle men meant that the government was paying a premium on credit it could be funding directly.

"Well, that's a premium we cannot afford—not when we could be reinvesting that same money in our students, in our economy, and in our country," Obama said.

He got his wish with the 2010 passage of health care reform, which included the cancellation of FFEL as a cost-offset. However, the step was not retroactive, and by that time, the damage had already been done: students had taken on crippling debt from private lenders that they had little prospect of repaying, thanks to the moribund job market in the wake of the financial crash.

Enter Senator Sherrod Brown of Ohio. The Democrat proposed the Student Loan Debt Swap Act, which would allow students caught in the old lending scheme to move their debt into a direct deal with the federal government, which would in turn pay off the private obligations ahead of schedule. When officials at the Congressional Budget Office scored the 2009 version of the bill, they found it would save the government more than $9 billion in lender subsidies and payments.

Yet Senator Brown's bill failed in the Committee on Health, Education, Labor, and Pensions and has languished there ever since.

For banks, the FFEL program was the best of both worlds while it lasted: private loans, government guarantees. And they made the most of it, relying on the government to backstop a huge amount of risk. In 2008 testimony before the Senate Banking Committee, Tom Deutsch, then deputy executive director of the American Securitization Forum (ASF), a trade and lobbying association for the securitization industry, claimed that a startling 85 percent of loans issued under the program were financed on the global market.

To securitize student loans, holders combine them into diversified tranches and sell them to investors as highly rated financial products. Combining a bunch of different loans into one investment commodity is supposed to allay the risk of individual defaults; the thinking is that even if some debtors can't afford to pay, the securities will reflect successful overall repayment. And with the government guaranteeing at least 97 percent repayment in the event of catastrophe, the diversified tranches are rated AAA—as safe an investment as possible. It's the exact same logic that governed the production and rating of mortgage-backed securities in the run up to the housing crisis.

Securitization is about pulling future value into the present through aggregation and prediction, and college students seemed liked a perfect source of future value. As long as wages increase for graduates—surely as safe an assumption as ever-rising housing prices—then they will (in aggregate) pay back the loans. Which means, in the language of global finance, that we can assume they *already have*. Thus teenagers' promissory vouchers for tens of thousands of dollars were pooled into Student Loan Asset Backed Securities (SLABS) and became legal tender.

When the program proved a loser for anyone but the lenders, Brown's bill offered a way out for those left behind: it would have paid off private loans made under FFEL from 1994 through 2010, effectively delivering on the government guarantee ahead of schedule—100 percent of principal plus interest and fees. You might think investors would be thrilled to collect their bets early and see students successfully access lines of educational credit (since this is, they stress, what securitization is for). But turning SLABS into money at its nominal value wasn't enough for investors.

The ASF has consistently lobbied against the bill, warning the Senate Education Committee that the debt-swap program would inflict "extraordinary losses" on institutional investors, who "purchase SLABS . . . with the idea that the repayment of these securities will match their capital return objectives." In other words, investors were counting on the vouchers being worth more than face value.

How can investors lose interest that hasn't accrued yet? Are they bluffing to preserve a sweet deal? Chances are we'll never know. The federal government has shown little appetite for fights with bondholders who make these kinds of threats. And the ASF knows the feds particularly well.

* * *

The ASF represents 350 firms on both sides of securitization deals—including Sallie Mae, the premiere student lender and SLABS issuer. ASF's purpose is to "achieve consensus among the various segments of the securitization markets to determine the best approaches to the important legal, regulatory, and market practice issues facing the markets," which only *sounds* like a violation of the criminal conspiracy statute. But as Yves Smith has detailed at her blog Naked Capitalism, the ASF is most interested in representing the interests of its sell-side members, the firms that package and sell securities, not the Little Old Ladies Union buyers the organization uses for cover. When these interests conflict, such as when banks robo-sign loans then certify them as high-quality financial products, the ASF backs the salesmen. In February of 2012 the world's biggest bond manager, Pimco, withdrew from the association, citing ASF's unwillingness to reflect investor-side concerns. But this conflict hasn't stopped the ASF from justifying its positions with frequent references to retirement accounts.

Although ASF may have lost Pimco, we can be confident it will still have the ear of the Senate Committee on Banking, Housing, and Urban Affairs. On March 27 of 2011, James Johnson, senior counsel to ranking Republican Richard Shelby, stepped down from his post. The very next day, ASF announced that Johnson would be heading its new lobbying operation. You might think that Johnson would be subject to the one-year cooling off period before being eligible to lobby his former colleagues, but when Congress passed the Honest Leadership and Open Government Act of 2007, it defined senior employees as those making at least 75 percent of a congressperson's salary. At the time of this writing, that amounts to $130,500 per year. From April 1, 2010, to his final day as a federal employee, Johnson was paid $124,937.66 annually. He thus narrowly dodged the designation, job title notwithstanding. Johnson effectively walked out of a senior position with the Senate on Friday, and walked back in on Monday with a new boss. It's exactly the kind of situation the law was ostensibly designed to prevent.

Spring 2011 happened to be a crucial period in the development of postcrisis financial regulations. Referring to the signal piece of Wall Street–constraining regulation passed in the wake of the downturn, Shelby told the Senate, "For lobbyists, lawyers, and government bureaucrats, Dodd-Frank is proving to be a goldmine." That was February 17, 2011, only five weeks before Johnson started at ASF. His office soon got busy making sure there would be as many holes as possible in the law's two-hundred-plus rules left to regulators, and he's been overwhelmingly successful.

But Dodd-Frank wasn't the only target on Johnson's radar.

Nestled near the end of his 2012 first quarter lobbying report is a mention of S. 1102, or the Fairness for Struggling Students Act of 2011—the only item not obviously tied to the securities industry. S. 1102, sponsored by Illinois Democrat Richard Durbin, makes an exception to current statutes and allows debtors to discharge private student loans in bankruptcy. At present, student loans are one of a few types of debt that can't be discharged. The others are criminal penalties and child support. This nonsensical and dangerous treatment of student debt began with a false panic in 1976 about doctors and lawyers shrugging off their loans and continued through three decades of tweaks to the bankruptcy code. This turn against student debtors culminated in 2005, when congress classified all education debt as nondischargeable. Durbin's bill in effect repeals the 2005 law as it applies to exclusively private loans, which comprise only 15 percent of the existing total. But the new bill promised a meaningful step toward a fair system. Or at least it would have, had it been passed. It didn't even get a vote, dying in committee in 2010 and again in 2011.

We don't know whether ASF's lobbying against the bill was decisive. But we can be confident that Johnson got a fairer hearing than the struggling students the act was meant to help.

* * *

Not only has Congress failed to create new legislation to aid student debtors, but existing law and the courts have offered inconsistent protection. Nondischargeability is one of many things that make student debt an especially crippling type of debt to have. Student debt never expires, and most loans are subject to tax-refund and government-benefits withholding. Creditors can garnish student debtors' wages. And courts haven't been clear on whether the vast majority of student debts are meaningfully subject to restrictions on abusive collection practices.

The Fair Debt Collection Practices Act (FDCPA) is the chief legal protection against the abusive conduct of debt collectors. But the law's definition of debt collectors has many exceptions, including one for government agents, and the Department of Education (DOE) has fought to extend these exceptions to its private contractors. In *Brannan v. United Student Aid Funds, Inc.* (1996), the Ninth Circuit Court of Appeals ruled against the DOE's intermediaries: private guaranty agencies that refund lenders and continue to collect from defaulted student loans on behalf of the DOE did not fall under FDCPA's exception for government collectors. Twenty days after the ruling, however, the Department of Education issued notice that it considered student loan guaranty agencies to be acting in a trustee capacity for the government. Two years later, The US District Court for Kansas followed the DOE's guidance and officially exempted guaranty agencies again under a different provision in the FDCPA, this one excluding firms pursuing debts as part of activity "incidental to a fiduciary responsibility." Since then, lower courts have continued to apply the fiduciary-responsibility exception to dismiss harassment claims (see *Rutz v. Education Credit Management Corporation* [2012]).

If the rules governing the implementation of the FDCPA are murky, its spirit and intention still read clear. Collectors are not allowed to call after 9:00 p.m. or before 8:00 a.m.; collectors are not permitted to show up at a debtor's place of work or talk about the debt to a third party; collectors are not allowed to make harassing phone calls or threaten arrest. The FDCPA specifically protects against "misrepresentation or deceit." The law's various provisions send the unambiguous message that, in this country, owing someone money doesn't give them or their agents the right to make your life a living hell. But according to the Department of Education, that rule doesn't apply to you if you happen to be a student.

Even whistle-blowers who have attempted to alert the public to shoddy student-loan practices have failed to get a fair hearing. In 2005 an employee in the Las Vegas collections division of Sallie Mae alleged a wide-ranging pattern of fraud by a corporation supposedly acting on behalf of the federal government. Michael Zahara filed a suit under the whistle-blower provision in the False Claims Act (FCA) on behalf of the US government, accusing Sallie Mae of abusing forbearances, a repayment option in which debtors are allowed to cease monthly installments for up to five years without defaulting. During this period interest accumulates and compounds, building on itself and pushing the total owed ever higher. In his suit, Zahara said Sallie Mae encouraged collectors to falsify oral agreements from debtors putting their loans into forbearance, thereby keeping default rates artificially low while inflating eventual interest totals.

Despite earning his own PBS special, Zahara saw his counsel withdraw after it was revealed that Zahara had a previous arrest, and his suit was dismissed. Fired for his cooperation, Zahara sued for false termination, but a judge also dismissed that suit after Sallie Mae buried him in discovery motions. The judge cited the case's slow progress and his "inherent authority to do so in order to manage and control my docket."

Two years after the first filing, another collector reported the same pattern of forbearance fraud, this time in Sallie Mae's New Jersey office. Loan collector Sheldon Batiste's allegations were so similar to Zahara's that they should have lent credibility to Zahara's original claims. But instead the similarities put Batiste right in the middle of another loophole. The FCA only allows one blow per whistle, which means Zahara's complaint—though it was dismissed on procedural grounds without any judgment on the case's merit—will be the last word on Sallie Mae's allegedly fraudulent use of forbearances, at least as far as the government and debtors are concerned. In June 2012 a federal district court judge in New York gave the preliminary okay to a $35 million settlement of a suit brought by Sallie Mae's shareholders against the company's leadership alleging, among other malfeasance, "Forbearance became a means for Defendants to remove loans from delinquent status, without regard to the borrowers' ability to repay the loans, for the sole purpose of reducing reported loan delinquencies and defaults and recording additional interest income." The settlement did not require Sallie Mae to admit any wrongdoing. Defrauded borrowers will get nothing from the deal, despite a March 2012 report from the New York Fed that found an unsettling 47 percent of student debtors in deferment or forbearance. None of them are counted among defaults.

* * *

To see why legal safeguards have apparently failed student debtors, it helps to understand the fears around the student loan bubble. The bubble has been a valuable metaphor for illustrating the way finance creates the illusion of value that may not actually exist; the housing bubble popped when markets could no longer sustain the fiction of ever-increasing real estate prices, and suddenly there was nothing to fill the void vacated by all that hot air. The rate of student debt growth over the same period (the last thirty to thirty-five years) dwarfs even the rate of housing price increases. All the hallmarks of a bubble are there, including massive securitization and seemingly risk-free financial products. But, as the financial analysts are quick to remind us, the vast majority of this debt is government-backed. What's the worst that could happen?

As far as investors are concerned, this line of thinking works just fine, but it should look less rosy for the Treasury. If it turns out the subsequent work of student debtors isn't worth as much as the markets figured, another trillion-dollar bailout may be required, and the taxpayers can hardly afford it.

Yet neither investors nor the Treasury seem particularly concerned. In March the ratings agency (and ASF 2013 conference lead sponsor) Fitch reaffirmed its AAA ratings for student loan–backed securities, despite the news that 27 percent of borrowers categorized as in repayment are actually more than thirty days late. Congress's turn to student loan reform has singled out private loans and for-profit colleges for regulation, but mostly ignored Treasury lending practices. The assumption is that the government guarantee renders any bailout unnecessary, since the value of the securities is ultimately a referendum on the functional solvency of the United States. You can't pop a red-white-and-blue bubble.

This understanding is partially true. But the part that's gone largely unnoticed is what the government and markets expect to happen to defaulted loans. Defaulted loans don't just disappear into a government loss column—in fact, they never disappear anywhere. The idea of defaulting implies that the debtor is unable to, and therefore does not, pay off the loan. But that's not exactly how it works. The Department of Education releases default projections a year in advance, so the latest numbers at time of writing are for loans issued in fiscal year 2013: the government expects to originate, across three major categories, a staggering $121

billion in student loans, of which more than $20 billion, or 17 percent, is
projected to default.

Twenty billion dollars in defaulted loans sounds like a lot of money
for the government to back, but that doesn't take into account the money
defaulted debtors will pay on these loans *despite defaulting*. Of the $20
billion in dud loans the government guarantees, it expects to recover $22
billion from debtors. If you subtract the $3 billion the feds will pay in col-
lection costs, they still recover around 95 percent of principal from loans
that default. When you default on your mortgage, you can walk away
from the house, but when you default on a student loan, you can't give
your degree back. All you can do is work and pay. There's no escape from
student debt, and the government and markets both know it.

This is, then, the real plan for the education bubble: student debtors
will be forced, in one way or another, to fill it in. Not only are student
loans not a burden on the federal government, they're a good investment.
In 2012 the DOE estimated its subsidy for student lending at -17 percent.
In other words, the DOE "subsidies" actually represent money *coming in*.
Including all expenses, from losses on defaults to debt collection to program administration, the DOE will pull in more than $25 billion in profit
from student lending *in 2012 alone*—billions more dollars than the IRS
will assess in gift and estate taxes combined, and more than enough to pay
NASA's whole budget. The DOE explains the negative subsidy through
a divergence between "the Government's borrowing rate and the interest
rate at which borrowers repay their loans." After all, no one can borrow at
lower rate than the US Treasury, certainly not college students and their
families. Bondholders aren't the only ones who think student debtors—
including defaulters—will pay back every cent they owe, with interest. The
government is literally counting on it.

* * *

There are consequences to imposing a trillion-dollar deductible on generational prosperity, and they're just beginning to emerge. In 2011 Gallup
released a disturbing report titled, without exaggeration, "In U.S.,

Optimism About Future for Youth Reaches All-Time Low." The poll-sters found that for the first time since they started measuring, less than half of surveyed respondents think today's young people will live better than their parents. There's considerable evidence Americans aren't just being pessimistic; a Pew study found that between 1984 and 2009, real net wealth for households headed by someone under thirty-five declined 68 percent. Over a third of young households owe more in debt than they own in assets. Considering that tuition costs are still increasing, and nei-ther lenders nor the Federal Government have an incentive to make any changes, there's no reason to think these trends won't continue.

At the end of the day, all the numbers, all the loopholes, all the sto-ries of jobbery don't tell us anything we didn't already know. That the financial system manufactures value that doesn't exist isn't exactly news any more, and government-industry collusion is a campaign talking point (not to mention funding mechanism) for both parties. Everyone knows that banks have stables of lawyers on call to suffocate small-fry complain-ants with paperwork and that debt collectors find ways around the rules. To treat these as revelations would be to do everyone a disservice. All the legal intricacies can't camouflage the fact that, in the search for more things to sell, investment banks priced and auctioned a sizable portion of college students' anticipated future wages, all with, to put it charitably, the government's cooperation. And when the bills inevitably come due, the laws ensure that there's no choice but to pay.

Meanwhile, reformers are outgunned by a powerful financial lobby and a pro-business Congress and White House. The most heartening recent piece of student loan–policy news was a report from the Consumer Financial Protection Bureau (CFPB) and the DOE on private loans that concluded, "It would be prudent to consider modifying the [bankruptcy] code" to allow debtors to discharge private loans in bankruptcy "in light of the impact on young borrowers in challenging labor market conditions." But not only would the change affect just the small minority of debtors who have private loans and no cosigner, but Congress also has already con-sidered this same modification the last two years in the form of Durbin's bill (with corresponding legislation in the House) and has been content to watch it twist in the wind. After the CFPB-DOE report was released, Fitch felt compelled to reaffirm its SLABS evaluation, describing the CFPB's proposed policy change as "unlikely" to come about. Given that Congress is predominantly composed of the same members who expanded nondischargeability to private loans in 2005, it's unsurprising they haven't changed their minds.

Congress nibbling the edge of the problem may give the public the impression that someone is looking out for them, but when it comes to student loans, there's not a single piece of legislation that would have a meaningful impact on the most important number: the large and rapidly increasing amount debtors will have to pay. And even the relatively meaningless pieces of legislation don't stand a chance of passing. There's not a single proposal on the table that might decrease the cost of tuition, and there's a solid chance Democratic plans to shift the lending burden to the Treasury will only exacerbate the problem by spurring universities to raise prices disconnected from even the pretense of a conventional demand structure. The government trumpets flexible repayment plans that end up extending both the lifespan of a loan and its interest period. Besides, no interested party cares if student debtors pay up soon; they will have to someday, and the longer it takes them, the more interest accrues, the bigger the haul. In the meantime, markets and investors are empowered to just pretend the money is there anyway.

The problem with the bubble metaphor is that everyone is waiting for a bang when they should be listening for the splash of value accumulating at the bottom. As long as the public is focused on the education bubble and whether or not it will pop, they won't notice it filling in slowly. Record-high youth unemployment and stagnant or declining pay even for college graduates (at least in part due to the downward impact on wages caused by a desperately indebted workforce) make it harder for borrowers to pay back their loans with any expediency. Assuming current rates of repayment and issuance (which is, admittedly, lowballing it), the $1 trillion outstanding total will double within a decade. And short of suicide, expatriation, or revolt, there's not much thirty-seven million American student debtors and counting can do about it.

ARMS AND LEGS

(2012)

*The riots provided a long-sought opportunity for
settling scores; rioters spoke of "payback."*

**—INVESTIGATIVE REPORT ON THE 2011 LONDON
RIOTS CONDUCTED BY *THE GUARDIAN* AND
THE LONDON SCHOOL OF ECONOMICS**

SOMETIMES IT'S IMPORTANT to start with numbers. When
it comes to intergenerational conflict, tied as it is to stories
about Oedipus and Hamlet, numbers help ensure we're speaking of a particular relation rather than a mythic archetype.
These are some numbers:

- A 2010 congressional report put youth unemployment at 20 percent,
  "the highest rate ever recorded for this age group." The same report
  noted that young workers are severely overrepresented among the
  unemployed, making up 13 percent of the labor force and 26 percent
  of those out of work.
- Between 30 and 40 percent of Americans will be arrested before they
  turn 23, a significant increase from the 1965 rate of 22 percent. This
  despite a large drop in victimizing crime generally, and victimizing
  crimes attributed to young people in particular, over the same period.
- Among those surveyed who could name an age group hit

hardest by today's economy, 45 percent said "young adults" rather than middle-aged or older. In 2011, for the first time since Gallup started asking respondents the question in 1983, less than half of Americans said they believe the next generation will be better off than they have been.

- Since 1978, tuition at US colleges has increased 650 points above inflation, dwarfing the rates of increase for housing and healthcare over the same period and leading to over $1 trillion in student debt held disproportionately by the young.

This is an actually existing generational war, and it's not over the aesthetics of hair length, uptight social conventions, or even the dream of economic mobility. For young people, it's a tooth-and-nail scrap for survival in a world system they recognize as not simply cold, but antagonistic and draining.

* * *

When Roosevelt Institute economics expert Mike Konczal digitally parsed the information from Occupy Wall Street's "We Are the 99%" Tumblr, on which participants and sympathizers explain the personal circumstances surrounding their involvement, he found a heavily skewed age distribution: the one thousand or so posters had a mean age of twenty-nine and a median age of twenty-six. This distribution is especially striking considering there are only two submitters under the age of twelve. Among their central complaints were debt (specifically student debt) and employment, but their concerns were tied to the basic reproduction of their lives more than to the achievement of any status or material goods. The word "body" appears more in the set of terms than "house," "home," or "car." Konczal doesn't see in these laments the desire for a classic American "good life," but something older:

> *They aren't talking the language of mid-20th century liberalism, where everyone puts on blindfolds and cuts slices of pie to share. The 99% looks too beaten down to demand anything as grand as "fairness" in their*

distribution of the economy. There's no calls for some sort of post-industrial
personal fulfillment in their labor—very few even invoke the idea that a
job should "mean something." It's straight out of antiquity—free us from
the bondage of our debts and give us a basic ability to survive.

When Konczal writes of the "99%" he doesn't mean the literal aggregate, but the people who have chosen to identify with the collectivity, a group with a very uneven age distribution. This isn't because the young are American society's most oppressed, but because a confluence of factors beyond being made miserable (including but not limited to extremely low rates of unionization, a common proficiency with electronic communications technologies, a tenuous relationship to the job market, culturally imbued entrepreneurial aspirations, and a sophisticated spectacle industry selling them anarchy) provide the conditions for the occupations' decentered organization. None of these factors is a particularly progressive sign, but together they determine new sensible lines of resistance, new stories about how people can change what it is they see and feel around them every day.

Class politics have become intelligible as a generational politics, the forces of what is and what has been arrayed against what else could be. For some the divide is the result of a promise betrayed, whether that promise was that they could maintain their inherited class positions or improve them. For others it's a recognition that existing institutions are so riddled with predation and corruption, or tied inextricably to ecological devastation, that even their maintenance is unthinkable work. For still others it's the trauma of service in the latest set of American wars, always declared by the old and fought by the young, or the accumulation of years of police harassment. Some occupiers hardly know why they're there. If there's one thing the 99 percent rhetoric got right it's the 1 percent thing; there's a serious conflict not between the percentages (such an uneven fight would already be over), but between the two sets of associations. This is politics: a vision of division, a line of conflict.

As the statistics have demonstrated, young Americans don't just imagine themselves as beaten down: 37 percent of households headed by someone under thirty-five have *less than zero dollars* in net worth. And this metric heavily underestimates young Americans' desperation by excluding those still counted as dependents.

But how could this be the case? If such a high percentage of young Americans were literally destitute, there would be homeless encampments in every major city in the country.

Leaving aside the fact that *there were* homeless encampments in every major city in the country before police violently intervened, the household poverty numbers from Pew reveal the extent to which debt distorts young people's economic picture. Since a person's net worth includes both total assets and debt, high rates of student loans and low rates of home-ownership push a large proportion of young Americans into the red. Whereas other measures treat debt as unreal, in net worth it's the rest of a household's assets that aren't really there when the collectors come calling. The measure treats every household as if repo men had just come and settled their outstanding loans. The numbers mean that at least 37 percent of young families couldn't cover their debts with all their possessions combined. Of the young people living with their parents who go uncounted in the household numbers, over 45 percent are in poverty when measured as individuals. No matter how you slice the numbers, the central dilemma is hard to avoid: a dangerous portion of young Americans owe more than they reasonably expect themselves to be worth in the future.

It isn't a stretch to call the recent wave of American occupations a youth movement. Originating from student struggles against high tuition—in California, New York, and most militantly, Puerto Rico—the occupations channeled young Americans' fear and insecurity into often inchoate action. The desire for a chance to live with one's head above water doesn't translate neatly into policy offerings. Massive debt relief could make a dramatic difference, but it's hard to imagine a policy that would be less popular in America than forgiving $1 trillion in student debt on the grounds that it was totally unreasonable to charge students so much in the first place. Sitcom audiences laugh at every arm-and-a-leg tuition joke.

Perhaps this sense that debt has reached absurd and unimaginable proportions is why Occupy Wall Street cleared 50 percent approval in national polls. This despite being largely composed of a bunch of groups (anarchists, communists, socialists, homeless people, punks, college kids, hippies, conspiracy theorists, drummers) that are much less popular when disaggregated: the resonant slogan "Shit is Fucked Up and Bullshit" makes sense to a lot of people, not least of all because it doesn't suggest any kind of obvious answer. By now it's clear that the purpose of the camps and marches wasn't to convince someone in charge to fix something. The debate about whether or not to issue demands to those currently in power was settled in California and New York, before Zuccotti Park was occupied, where insurrectionary left-communists set the agenda. In "Communique from an Absent Future," a pamphlet out of the California student occupations that helped popularize the tactic, the group of anonymous authors wrote,

> As the unions and student and faculty groups push their various
> "issues," we must increase the tension until it is clear that we want
> something else entirely. We must constantly expose the incoherence
> of demands for democratization and transparency. What good is it
> to have the right to see how intolerable things are, or to elect those
> who will screw us over?

It's this language that found purchase nationally, despite (and no one should be confused, it is *despite*) finding its direct antecedents in fringe radical theory. No matter what the pseudo-official pronouncements out of the occupations say, the encampments haven't been about prefiguring a better society. Few occupiers are so naïve as to really think a ramshackle group of tents in a corporate non-park in the middle of New York City's financial district could or should function like a postcapitalist biodome. Occupation is one kind of action a group with no self-perceived leverage takes. It's a tactic based on a tension at the very root of governmental power: bodies take up space, and if those limbs are determined not to move, it takes force to move them.

The sort of hopeless debt sketched out earlier reduces its holders to bodies stripped of assets, including the agency that is supposed to come with being a free laborer. For a sizable portion, these bodies don't even own their own bodies insofar as the products of their future work are already promised.

Massive debt spread widely over the cohort makes its individual payment increasingly more difficult, which, due to interest, increases the size of the collective total owed. Because young workers perform under virtual indenture, their labor is less valuable on the market. High unemployment, along with the debt, renders them always vulnerable to replacement by an equally educated, equally hopeless peer. It's only one of the harmful self-perpetuating cycles into which the economy has thrust young workers. As for the potential benefits of collective bargaining, four times as many American workers under twenty-four are officially unemployed as belong to trade unions, and that ratio is not likely to improve.

President Obama sold himself so successfully to young Americans by mirroring our hopes for post-Bush reform that the resulting disappointment is directed more toward the hope itself than the man who never stood much of a chance of fulfilling it. It's in this situation, when reform in the government and in the workplace feels exhausted, that the framework of liberal aspirations and demands collapses. And Occupy Wall Street is the most palatable instantiation of this post-hope politics by process of elimination that we're likely to see.

* * *

Bodies take up space, and young bodies don't own much of their own. Fiscal austerity, whether it's in New York or Madrid, involves tightening racist and ephebiphobic restrictions on public spaces. When the police fire shots across the generation gap, it's often in the course of managing this territory.

- Zyed Benna, seventeen, and Bouna Traoré, fifteen, electrocuted while fleeing police in the Paris suburbs. The teens had been playing soccer at a public park after closing hours and were afraid of being interrogated.
- Alexandros Grigoropoulos, fifteen, was shot and killed on an Athens

street by Greek Special Guards, the police division responsible for patrolling public spaces.

- Oscar Grant, nineteen, was executed face-down on the ground of an Oakland train station, his arms behind his back, a transit officer astride his legs.

All of these deaths provoked significant civil disturbances, and the fires still smolder and flare in Athens and Oakland. But these aren't twentieth-century style race riots. These days when disorder runs rampant, it's the young doing the running. Sometimes we see these eruptions partially compartmentalized by different identifications, as in France when the crippling protests by young workers followed the unrest in the largely immigrant Paris *banlieues* by four months in 2005–2006, or in the UK where aggressive anti-tuition actions preceded the Tottenham riots by eight months in 2010–2011. At the Oakland occupation, where the critique has placed a major emphasis on racialized police violence, the lines have blurred.

The international business press has been quick to connect the dots and note both the rise in intergenerational tension and the risk of civil unrest. In February 2011, well before the riots rocked London, *Bloomberg Businessweek* ran a major article comparing UK youth unemployment to the rates in prerevolutionary Tunisia and Egypt. The cover reads "THE KIDS AREN'T ALRIGHT" in block caps, superimposed over a young man hurling a brick.

It isn't worth the breath to ask whether anyone should advocate riots, how politically conscious they are, or whether the generational lens obscures class divisions. The die—or better yet, the mold—is already cast. As the writer Evan Calder Williams put it in his "Open Letter to Those Who Condemn Looting" after the riots in London,

> One doesn't defend a riot. It is not "good" or "bad." A riot is a scrambling of positions of belonging and of judgment. Often, it is an internal dissolution of what might have appeared common lines of class.

It involves situations the likes of which we are sure to see more, the turning of the hopelessly poor against the poor-but-just-getting-by, between shop-owners and looters, between workers and rioters, between those breaking the windows and those who clean them, and, internally, between individuals themselves, who cannot always be split into one or the other.

Violence isn't an answer, it's the question's premise. Debt and austerity don't just happen, they must be imposed upon a population, and one of Occupy's greatest contributions has been to reveal the kind of instruments the state expects to use. As the California student movement puts in, "behind every fee increase, a line of riot cops." Across age demographics, Americans expect the worsening that has already begun. There have been casualties, and the body count will only rise.

Like the miller's daughter in the fairy tale, asset-less student debtors had to spin gold out of straw—gold that's somehow always already owed to someone else. All the Rumpelstiltskin market asked in return for pulling this amazing sum out of thin air was nine months of her labor, slaughtered, weighed, and priced to sell before it's ever performed. Not even the living labor of indenture, but value stillborn, birthed cold.

But a global economy can only rest on straw for so long. Capitalism, and any other system premised on unending growth, will always produce intergenerational tensions, for each further set of workers must be more productive than the last. The conflict between succeeding modes of production emerges as a generational clash.

But when decades of growth is spun out of straw, conjured through speculation, pulled forward in time through student debt, and appropriated by a tiny elite, we're approaching a set of limits. The shock of 2008 hasn't subsided like the governments promised it would, and we all know it. Banks bet on nations collapsing in a sort of penultimate accumulation; if it's all coming down, better strip the place on the way out. If this *is* a phase in capitalist history, then it's going to take bigger changes than we've seen so far for the system to hold on. Increased inequality over time means more people made poor and indebted, which means more fences protecting fewer houses, more arms in fewer hands.

Today's young people will be the ones to adapt to this new normal and stabilize it, or to reject it in a stumbling search for something else. We should understand the demand for the "basic ability to survive" counterposed not just against literal death, but also the social death of life-on-loan. The possibility of falling short is implicit in the demand, but is there anything more dangerous than a mob wielding bodies they don't own, swinging for their lives with rented arms?

If this generational debt will be enforced by armed guards—and it will—then it will be paid, one way or another, in blood. Exactly whose, it is too soon to tell.

WHERE SHOULD A GOOD MILLENNIAL LIVE?

(2015)

IF AMERICA IS going to keep existing, then young people are
going to have to form households. You can't sleep on Twitter or
take a shower on Instagram or raise a child on Facebook. At least not
exclusively. A generation often characterized by its digital connections
still has to go somewhere. So how should a good millennial live?

There are three main options, though very few people have all of them.
A third of eighteen-to thirty-four-year olds live in households headed by a
parent or other family member, according to a Pew Research survey from
July. A smaller portion, 14 percent, own their own home, many of whom
received help from their parents with the down payment. For the plural-
ity there's renting, and paying half their income is normal, especially in
high-cost cities where young adults are concentrated.

In the public imagination, all of these millennials are worth mocking. Whether they're stuck in their parents' basement watching YouTube,
blowing all their money on a room the size of a closet just to play hipster
and ruin some city, or living the homeowner's dream on Mommy and
Daddy's largess, there's a joke there. A smart, innovative young person
should be able to come up with a shelter solution that's affordable and
sustainable. And, since young workers should be flexible, so should their
housing. Why can't this disruptive generation create a new paradigm?

In October, the media found the millennial housing icon we had all been waiting for. Not only was this pseudonymous twenty-three-year-old ("Brandon") so smart he landed a coveted job at Google, he was too smart to rent an apartment in the notoriously expensive Bay Area. "I realized I was paying an exorbitant amount of money for the apartment I was staying in—and I was almost never home," *Business Insider* quoted him glowingly. "It's really hard to justify throwing that kind of money away. You're essentially burning it—you're not putting equity in anything and you're not building it up for a future—and that was really hard for me to reconcile." With millennial student loans to pay back and a Baby Boomer desire to invest, he didn't have money for housing. What's a smart kid to do?

These are the sort of stories of personal adversity that usually end in the millennial creating a new app or web service that solves his problem. It's a well-worn narrative of innovation, where an unconventionally creative mind runs up against a seemingly unsolvable problem. From the media reaction, you might think this young Googler invented something. Brandon earned a laudatory shout-out on the Today Show, and *Refinery 29* jealously announced he was saving "SO MUCH MONEY." How exactly did this hero disrupt housing? He lives in a truck.

Since Google offers him twenty-four-hour access to the building, as well as showers and food, this enterprising employee decided to do the closest thing he could to living at his desk: he moved into a 128-square-foot box on the back of a 2006 Ford in the company parking lot. Recognizing Brandon's clever thinking, Google has allowed him to go on crashing, and he chronicles his day-to-day on his blog, "Thoughts from Inside the Box." Far from calling him deranged, with the exception of a few jokes about sex, the media thought it was a good idea. "Saving on rent has allowed him to dine at nice restaurants and enjoy San Francisco more than if he opted for living in an apartment," *Business Insider* nodded approvingly, as if living inside a small box were a wise choice.

Brandon isn't the only millennial getting applauded for living in a parking lot. In March, Toronto Blue Jays pitching prospect Daniel Norris earned an ESPN profile and a short Vice Sports documentary for the van where he spent spring training. Despite signing a $2 million deal, the twenty-two-year-old Norris lived in a 1978 VW camper that he parked at a twenty-four-hour Walmart after the police kicked him off the beach. Like Brandon, Norris's media attention was laudatory, framing him as a free spirit and deep thinker. "There he is each evening, making French press coffee and organic stir-fry on his portable stove," Eli Saslow wrote for ESPN. "There he is at night, wearing a spelunking headlamp to go with his unkempt beard, writing in his 'thought journal' or rereading Kerouac." Norris sounds like a millennial superhero.

The best place a millennial can take shelter, according to the media reaction, seems to be in a car near work. In both of these stories the main characters are, of course, homeless. It's important that in both cases that the young men in question are not poor or desperate. In fact, they're both employed and quite well-off. There are plenty of young homeless people, but no national news outlets are covering the clever ingenuity they use to survive. Instead, municipal ordinances against sleeping in cars are on the rise, up 119 percent between 2011 and 2014. Norris and Brandon both could afford conventional housing if they wanted to, they have simply thought better of it. A model millennial has to be both rich and homeless.

To pull off homelessness in a way that impresses national news outlets, it helps to have a job almost no one can get, like Google programmer or professional athlete. "Freelance writer lives in a truck" is less attractive. Thankfully there's another innovation that's one step up: tiny houses. These micro-dwellings are just what the name implies: they're entire homes (kitchen, bathroom, bed, desk) that could fit inside a McMansion living room. Sometimes they're on wheels, sometimes not, but they're supposed to be a millennial-sized answer to shelter.

A few years ago the tiny house movement was just for hard-core hippies and sharing-economy fundamentalists, but as the idea has spread it's been associated with young Americans. "Will Millennials Be The Tiny-House Generation?" *Slate* wondered. *Millennial Magazine* was a little more ominous with "Are Millennials Destined For Tiny Houses?" Their central appeal is cost: tiny houses are cheap, usually under $50,000, making them affordable for a larger percentage of young workers. But there's also something nice about not taking up more space than necessary or paying for rooms you then need to fill with more stuff you have to buy. Since young people are waiting longer to couple and reproduce, a tiny lifestyle sounds smart.

In November of 2015 we saw the first attempt at tiny house public policy. A Washington, DC, councilman introduced a proposal that would see the city build one thousand of these structures throughout the city and sell them exclusively to millennials and low-income buyers. The *Washington City Paper* reported that the initiative probably violates fair housing law and "almost certainly" won't pass, but the idea itself is interesting. Rather than push for higher wages or to keep current housing stock affordable, it's easier to innovate a reduction in average living space.

The model tiny houses do look cool, in a Scandinavian prison cell sort of way, but it's important to take a step back and think about what's going on. The Millennial Housing Lab, a project of Harvard business, law, and design students, dedicated their first project to expanding the tiny house movement. They were trying to build something that made for "reduced cost, reduced environmental impact and a healthier lifestyle." And what they come up with are 160-foot wooden boxes they've located in the forests of Massachusetts. The future of millennial housing, according to Harvard's best minds, is a shack in the woods.

What are we to make of this strange thinking? What's so exciting about the idea of millennials living in boxes? Part of the appeal is ecological; suburban living with its high carbon emissions and water-wasting lawns has been an—if not the—ideal form of American shelter for many decades, but young people see it as increasingly unsustainable environmentally. Higher population density is a sensible urban planning solution. If wealthy older Americans don't plan to change their lifestyles, then they at least appreciate the idea of younger people taking it upon themselves to fix things. Like vegetarianism, small living is thoughtful, responsible consumption.

Meanwhile, not everyone is forsaking indoor plumbing. Corporate profits have grown nearly twice as fast as national productivity since 1990, and they are well recovered from the 2008 crisis. While most people make do with less, a lucky few are cleaning up the surplus. It shows in the housing market too; ownership rates for young workers may be down, but the National Association of Realtors reported that 1.13 million vacation homes were sold in 2014, a new record that tops even precrisis 2006. "Affluent households have greatly benefited from strong growth in the stock market in recent years," the association's chief economist Lawrence Yun said. "Furthermore, last year's impressive increase also reflects long-term growth in the numbers of baby boomers moving closer to retirement and buying second homes to convert into their primary home in a few years."

If we were really undergoing a social shift toward small, thrifty living, it would be manifesting at the top as well. But while the wealthy plot to ensure decades of low-density retirement life, the vision of millennials sleeping in the backs of cars ready to roll down the road as soon as they're not needed or packed together in minimal-sized pods sounds more like a trap than an opportunity. We would have to be real suckers to fall for the old "Sleeping in your car is cool!" trick.

For millennials, whose generational identity has been crafted by media outlets they don't own, it's hard to differentiate our own desires from what's desired of us. Compared to an apartment or a house, living in a truck or a tiny house, it should go without saying, is a decline in living conditions. As is paying 42 percent of your income for shelter today instead of 25 percent in 1998, like residents of New York City do. By characterizing millennials as lifestyle innovators, the class that owns the media can rebrand living with less as a cool trend for the kids.

From this perspective, a lot of our sparkling innovations are glorified infrastructure for declining living standards. "Gypsy cabs" are a long-standing part of the urban economy, but Uber offers a brand. Tenants have been taking in extra boarders to help pay the rent for centuries, but Airbnb legitimizes the practice in the eyes of regulators. An ad for the app Wallapop shows a young man racing to sell his possessions so he can afford to take his girlfriend on a date. The app letgo does the same thing, and it advertises during the same programs. Clearly the venture capitalists funding these companies think youth desperation is a growth industry. The billion-dollar question is which platforms can make it feel normal.

There's nothing wrong with young people wanting to live well and independently, not at the expense of their parents, low-income long-time residents, or the environment. That's what the fantasy of the model millennial living in a box is about, and that's what makes parts of it very appealing. It would be great if Americans got used to taking up less residential space and filling it with less clutter. Cutting the transportation associated with our way of life may even be essential for the persistence of humans on Earth.

But in a system where every personal sacrifice turns up on some corporate balance sheet, where the workers living in trucks—celebrated and not—create the profits that buy vacation homes, it's impossible to separate innovation and exploitation. When we talk about where good millennials should live, we're ignoring more important questions about who owns land, how much, and why. Young Americans can't allow ourselves to be divided and distracted into accepting a world that continues to award less to more and more to fewer.

ART AND TV

UPPING THE ANTIHERO
(2011)

YOU'RE A GOOD *cop, but a loose cannon. Give me your badge and gun.*

Most Americans could write this scene and probably fill in the rest of the narrative while they're at it. It takes place in the police chief's office; he's the one addressing a rogue cop. The cop is a good cop, he is courageous and resourceful with strong instincts and boundless determination. But the good cop has a problem—the letter of the law, the bureaucracy with its endemic corruption, the miles of red tape—all prevent him from doing his job. In striving to uphold the law, he stumbles over the threshold to the wrong side. The good cop is also a bad cop.

This is the classic antihero and his dilemma as it has played out in movies like *Death Wish* and *Dirty Harry*: Is he justified in using disorderly means to achieve orderly ends when orderly means are unavailable? Movies and TV shows have recycled this archetypal conflict so often that it belongs in the pantheon along with "I scheduled two dates for one night!" and "I'm supposed to marry rich guy, but I love poor guy." As audiences became knowing and jaded, the scripts evolved. Cannons got looser and steps over the line went further and became more deliberate. In the past few years, we've seen a series of TV shows in which upping the antihero has crossed its own line, and the old questions about means and ends have ceased to apply. The old cop who chafed at institutional limits has undergone a neoliberal transformation: the result is a new kind of series that we might call the consultant procedural. A derivative of the cop and private investigator procedurals, the consultant procedural starts with some sort of institutional disqualification and follows the central character as he or she ports unmatched professional skills from job to job.

This shift from career-officer protagonists to mercenary contractors is so prevalent that the USA Network has built its current identity out of it: *Psych*, *Monk*, *Burn Notice*, and *White Collar* all straddle the same public-private line between officially sanctioned law enforcement and guns for hire. The pattern has even spread to the "hot doctor" subgenre ("You're a good surgeon, but a loose cannon. Hand in your scalpel.") with *Royal Pains*. And it's not just USA; other networks' recent shows, like *The Mentalist*, *Bones*, *Lie to Me*, *Numb3rs*, or even the BBC's *Sherlock Holmes* miniseries, use the stability of public institutions to provide a consistent narrative base for exciting episodes that take place in the private sector. The new clichéd antihero can work with the government, but he or she must be entrepreneurial above all.

All these shows draw their narrative energy from the constant search for work. Instead of having cases coming to them in an oppressive deluge, as in the *Law and Order* franchise and other traditional cop procedurals, these protagonists must scrape for work wherever they can find it. This puts them in direct contact with the eccentric moneyed class—whether drug kingpins or TV stars. Rapid case turnover and constant semi-employment provide the structure for the consultant procedural, giving writers a good justification for open-and-shut, single-episode stories.

The genre hasn't arisen by coincidence. Book reviewers at the *Los Angeles Times*, recently fired and hired back as freelancers, can empathize with *Burn Notice's* Michael Westen, who risked his life for seasons to reveal a conspiracy and reclaim his CIA job, only to be taken back as a consultant in the latest season. It's no surprise that television writing can reflect—or even predict—changes in American labor.

Although there are other examples, I'm going to focus on three shows that stretch the definition of the consultant procedural: *Breaking Bad*, *Dexter*, and *Psych*. The three differ widely in tone and content, but their protagonists all trace their lineage back to the rogue cop–cum–independent consultant. Of the three, *Breaking Bad* is influenced most by the old antihero's moral transformation, with cancer-diagnosed, public high school chemistry teacher Walter White (Bryan Cranston) taking a second job as a meth cook for hire—a quality consultant. *Dexter's* titular character (Michael C. Hall), a crime-scene analyst with an uncontrollable urge to murder, is a serial killer who generally limits himself to other serial killers. His coworkers don't know where he gets his insights, but Dexter is a murder consultant, using experience from his nocturnal profession to inform his day job. *Psych*, as the only real comedy on the list, may seem an odd entry, but the underachieving cop's son (James Roday as redundantly fake psychic Shawn Spencer) conning his way into a job as a police consultant using phony powers is a self-aware version of this same story. Police consultant is the perfect job for a cop who doesn't want to play by a cop's rules.

As with the archetypal antihero of old, the audience doesn't want to see any of these protagonists caught or returned to stable work, not only because they're likable, but also because it would likely involve some shark-jumping. But unlike the traditional antiheroes, whose drama hinges on whether they will cross the line and use unlawful means, the protagonists in my examples have each forsaken ethical means from the beginning and hardly look back. Dexter accepts that he's a murderer; whether or not it's okay to cut up serial killers isn't really a valid question for him. *Psych's* Shawn doesn't trouble himself much over his fraud or flouting of police procedure and regulations.

Instead of the traditional ends-means-ends conflict, the motives question becomes central in consultant procedurals. Is *Breaking Bad's* Walter really cooking because he wants to help his family or because it finally allows him to get the respect he deserves? Is Shawn working with the police because he cares about people, or is it another adolescent prank designed to get him attention and an adrenaline fix? The difference between Dexter's acceptable and unacceptable kills isn't in what he does, but why he does it.

Traditionally, this sort of motive question has belonged to the villain. The villain, after all, often justifies himself with twisted reasoning, which, the hero is usually left to point out, is only a cover for greed or the lust for power. But with the consultant procedural, the antihero arms race has displaced the hero altogether and left an anti-villain, a bad guy with a good motive.

But the old-style antihero isn't absent from the consultant procedural, he has just been reduced to a supporting role. *Breaking Bad*, *Dexter*, and *Psych* all have secondary cops with means-ends conflicts. In *Breaking Bad*, it's Hank (Dean Norris), the brother-in-law who is (in)conveniently a DEA agent. A jocular boor who rejects promotion to remain comfortable in his familiar Albuquerque office rather than serve on the regional front line in El Paso, Hank is a skilled cop who gets closer than any other character to catching Walter. As the only DEA agent who seems to appreciate the significance of the premium meth Walter makes, Hank pushes himself over the line and beats up Walter's hapless partner Jesse (Aaron Paul). Shamefaced but honorable, Hank plans to plead guilty and resign from the agency before Walter intervenes behind the scenes to have the charges dropped.

Like Hank, *Psych's* veteran detective, Carlton Lassiter (Timothy Omundson), can't hack it in the big leagues. In keeping with *Psych's* ADD po-mo charm, he's not so much a movie antihero cop as a cop who models himself on movie antihero cops. But amid Shawn and his partner Gus's (Dulé Hill) buddy-comedy hijinks, the show never develops "Lassie" and his conflicts with his partner Juliet (Maggie Lawson)—young, female, gorgeous—and Police Chief Vick (Kirsten Nelson). The series hints at a wrecked marriage and his obsessive need to be the cop archetype he imagines he should be (setting him up for a means-ends crisis), but the writers never give him the narrative space to do much more than hint. Omundson imbues this straight-man role with occasional glimpses of stern sadness that make him a bright point in an already strong cast. In one episode, a visiting fed tells him he could have been an FBI agent, maybe, if he'd gone to college. In another, he finds out that his score on the detective's exam—which he believed to be the highest in the department—wasn't only worse than Juliet's, but also worse than Shawn's, who aced the test as an adolescent. Lassiter's good never seems good enough.

Only one of these shows has sacrificed its antihero to a season finale, and *Dexter* has never fully recovered. In the first season, only one character is on to the titular killer. Bristly Police Sergeant James Doakes (Erik King) keeps Dexter up at night, but his single-minded dedication to the job makes him unpopular around the office when compared with Dexter, the genial psychopath. Doakes sees through his coworker's managed exterior, and his cop's instincts pay off when Dexter gets careless. He's able to solve the case, but since others won't be convinced, Doakes goes off the rails alone and crosses the line. Unfortunately, Dexter is waiting on the other side, where he sets him up to die and take the posthumous blame for the killings. In each case, if the secondary antihero can't accept the liberties consultants must take, then his days are limited.

The central moral question has shifted with the central moral actor. All these characters have to yield to the anti-villain, whether in death, paralysis, or quiet desperation. As a central figure, the antihero is used up, but next to the consultant anti-villain, he gains a critical edge. If employees are now supposed to put their personalities to work, what happens to the cops who are "all about the job?" In *Breaking Bad*, Hank finds out quickly that not knowing Spanish—a language he thought belonged to the enemy—will hamper his chances to move up in the DEA. He's not a model of nativist anger but of the role confusion that comes with changing standards. Lassiter's job (and professional conflicts) have been outsourced to plucky mercenaries wielding supernatural powers—how is he supposed to compete with that? And what use is a loose-cannon cop when there's a perfectly effective serial killer doing his job for him? The good cop was always insufficient, as if questions of obedience and the social contract were only trying if experienced by real citizens. Counterintuitively, it's the shift toward precarious work that makes the antihero's role compelling once more. Confronted with consultants who aren't troubled by the same means-ends line, the tough cop finds himself struggling without stakes. He realizes what was true all along—justice and injustice have very little to do with his individual choices, no matter how agonized.

The villainous turn makes sense in an America where the career public servant is no longer the representative worker. Instead we have the precariat—loosely attached workers cobbling their livings together from broken parts inside and outside the state and law. Consultants Shawn and Gus jump back and forth from public to private clients, operating in the neoliberal gray zone of private government workers. Walter is a school-teacher who at first has to work an after-school job at a car wash where he's mocked by his wealthy students. That is, until he entrepreneurially repurposes district chemistry equipment to cook meth. Dexter doesn't obsessively take his work home like the antihero cops of yore; instead, he spends his taxpayer-funded hours plotting his vigilante escapades, his job no more than a useful cover. All three of these villains, and the new genre's protagonists writ large, embody a fantasy of highly skilled American labor, justifiably "gone Galt" but still willing to do public work for the right price, somehow both forced and eager to leave old moral lines in the dust.

WORKING BEAUTY
(2012)

IN THE OPENING scene of Julia Leigh's debut film *Sleeping Beauty*, Lucy (Emily Browning), our beautiful college-student protagonist, serves as a medical test subject. She leans her head back as the doctor slowly threads a tube down her throat, then fills a balloon in her chest with air while she holds the tube in place. Lucy cooperates excellently and leaves with an envelope of money and a smile.

Her still, submissive choking and gagging lend the scene a heavy erotic charge, an allusion to the sex work the viewer may already know is to come from reviews and trailers. In this first scene, Lucy is already selling her body; the distinction between this and sex work is a symbolic technicality.

What's most off-putting in this scene is Lucy's ability to hold a smile on her face throughout the ordeal. If Lucy's remaining still enough to hold the tube down her airway as her body jerks around involuntarily isn't work, then I don't know what is.

Though she usually wears the uniform of an Anthropologie model and often seems to be doing not much at all—there are a few scenes of her cleaning up a coffee shop after working a closing shift and others of her biding her time in the copy room of the office where she's an assistant—almost all of what we see Lucy do in the film is work. We know she's working, but she hardly looks like a worker.

But what does a worker look like? Even the most traditional economic models, as well as revolutionary countercurrents, had to deal with changes over time in the character of what they called labor. In the introduction to *A Contribution to the Critique of Political Economy*, Marx comments on Smith's use of the term:

> The indifference as to the particular kind of labor implies the existence of a highly developed aggregate of different species of concrete labor, none of which is any longer the predominant one. So do the most general abstractions commonly arise only where there is the highest concrete development, where one feature appears to be jointly possessed by many, and to be common to all. Then it cannot be thought of any longer in one particular form.

An undifferentiated worker isn't just a farmer or a bricklayer or a Slurpee-machine mechanic; labor is a composite picture of different forms of human activity that we group under the term. But this aggregate isn't stable, it exists in thought and appearance. What we come to understand as a general laborer is based on this "concrete development" of bodies in motion, but also on what Marx called the "preexisting abstraction": the way we talk about labor in the first place. In this proudly contradictory formula, we tell the story of labor twice: first with our bodies, but only after we use our words. *Sleeping Beauty* is a film most of all about labor, what it means to work. That category destabilizes as the viewer begins to recognize everything Lucy does with her time as work.

Despite her three paid jobs, Lucy can't make rent. This is what prompts Lucy to answer an ad in the school paper for a sort of catering gig: waiting on private parties while dressed in lingerie. She brings the same perfect submission to the interview that she showed in the first scene with the doctor. She lies about her drug use and submits to being poked and prodded by the madam Clara (Rachael Blake) and her assistant. It is her full body that is to be put to work, her full body that must be examined.

When Clara calls to tell Lucy that she's been hired for some jobs, for which she'll be paid exorbitantly, she cautions Lucy not to treat the income as stable. "Think of it as a windfall," Clara says. "Pay off some student loans."

There's a remarkably open acknowledgment here that Lucy is in debt to a third party. The modern labor relation is not supposed to include employees' consumer debt; whether they have credit cards is not the boss's concern. A worker's indebtedness is supposed to come up as a source of employer leverage only in shady criminal dealings when it's owed to the boss: drugs and immigrant smuggling, or in the sharecropping fields and company towns we learn about in history class. But with student debt so prevalent, young workers are assumed (known) to have loans they're compelled to pay, making them even more vulnerable on the market.

Unlike mortgage or credit card debt, student debt is premised specifically on the value of the debtor's body. The exorbitant size of US college debt is justified by the students' imagined future productivity; if you take out tens of thousands of dollars in loans for school, it's because the debt will enable you to command enough on the labor market to pay it back. But when lots of workers need jobs, employers need any particular worker much less. In a sick twist, the known size of the general debt keeps wages down and young workers desperate, making their personal debt even harder to pay back, making them even more desperate, and so on until the wage goes literally negative in the form of unpaid internships. *Sleeping Beauty* dramatizes this debtor relationship: the old men who sleep with her might as well be the banks holding Lucy's loans, taking payment in time with her flesh.

Lucy's new boss tells her to maintain another dependable job, but which job could be dependable in the way Clara imagines? The cobbling together of part-time contracts leaves the precarious worker without any one thing to fall back on. Under earlier capitalist labor relations, workers' ability to get another job gave them leverage on bosses to extract benefits. But under conditions of precarity, workers need more than one job to survive and to be constantly interviewing for new ones. Employers feel no responsibility to provide the means for workers to get what they need in order to live. With high unemployment and so much of job training moved to colleges, they're easily replaceable.

This change affects workers' ability to organize their lives around their jobs. The elements of the social democratic good-life fantasy—job security, health and retirement benefits, steady hours, a living wage, vacation, weekly nonwork time, among others—are available to fewer and fewer workers even as a realistic aspiration. These features are no longer even "common" (known) to all; many young workers now would have no idea how retirement or health benefits work, having never been offered them.

Not that we'll need to learn. The precarious retort to the classic pro-union bumper sticker "The people who brought you the weekend" is "What the fuck is a weekend?" This insecurity is no longer an exceptional condition, it is a developed set of practices with features of its own. We still use the concept of undifferentiated labor, but precarious conditions come with different rules and different assumptions of what a generic worker can be expected to do. It's more important that a worker know how not to ask for a raise, more desirable that she be adaptable than cutthroat. An employee without an office is always at work. The possibility that a worker might leave at some point due to pregnancy isn't a drawback, it's a good reason not to offer benefits or a path for advancement.

When we look at Lucy, we have a picture of the precarious subject: indebted, insecure, vulnerable. After a few successful nights as a server at parties for the rich, old, and distinguished, Clara asks Lucy to do a different kind of work. She'll be put to sleep with a nontoxic drug, stripped naked, and left in a bed where men will pay to use her. Lucy will wake up with no memory of what happened, but the no-penetration rule will apply. She agrees.

These are the hardest scenes in the movie to stand. Watching the old men strip naked alone in a room with a beautiful young unconscious woman is disturbing enough. We peer beneath the tailored suits to their frames, either frail or bloated, but their dicks always recede into the shadows of impotence. These scenes lack the intersubjectivity of rape. One client just wants to snuggle with Lucy as he would with a giant doll. Another violently slaps her around in a sickening display. During this scene, viewers are acutely aware they are watching a beautiful young actress going through the exact experience depicted, except while conscious and on film. The physicality of these scenes breaks the movie's narrative and exposes Browning's acting as intensive labor. The flexibility that characterizes precarious work becomes literal, passing into limp. Lucy must be as flexible as a rag doll when a client throws her body around the room.

Clara's firm assertion to Lucy that she won't be vaginally penetrated plays with the viewer's preconceived positions, but also has a ring of truth to it. The combination of Craigslist personals, high debt, and the comparatively light stigma on paraphilic sex work has created a supply of mostly young women willing to freelance in the fetish business as long as it's sufficiently distinguished symbolically from traditional "prostitution." It's certainly better paid than the medical testing, and probably less invasive.

It's impossible to write about precarity without writing about gender because undifferentiated labor is reforming along these lines. Lucy's passivity and her eagerness to please, her vulnerability and blank demeanor would look incredibly strange on a young man. Her willingness to keep treading water without the promise of anything better to come, her ability to communicate nonthreateningly and stay quiet at the right times are parts of what Nina Power describes in the chapter "The Feminization of Labor" in *One Dimensional Woman*:

> All work has become women's work, even that of men. No wonder the young professional woman beams down at us from real estate billboards as the paradigmatic image of achievement . . . At this point in economic time, those character traits [of precarious professionality] are remarkably feminine, which is why the pragmatic, enthusiastic professional woman is *the symbol of the world or work as a whole*. [emphasis added]

Sometimes Lucy looks like she could be on one of those billboards, or at least the ones for community colleges, but the film is about the other times as well. It turns out the models in the pictures only own one set of clothing. Lucy persists and survives using what Lauren Berlant describes in her book on precarity, *Cruel Optimism*, as "durable norms of adaptation," repeating the play of control and submission that characterizes precarity but under circumstances of her choosing. Whether Lucy is fucking guys at the bar based on the fall of a coin, taking drugs from strangers, or repeating ironic formalities ("And how are you miss?" "Oh very well, very well. And you sir?") over glasses of vodka with a terminally self-destructive friend, she finds ways to make her being in the world sting less. Or the right amount. This is a nonrevolutionary enduring, a body's holding together in a sea of dismembering tugs.

Lucy shows she can endure, at least for now, but can she do more? Can the flexible resist?

If our conception of what it means to be a worker relies on having a bargaining place at the table with the boss—that is, with certain classical notions of workers' power—then Lucy isn't a worker. She isn't a worker, even though all she ever does is work. She's not going to unionize her coffee shop, nor her fellow sex workers, nor the assistants at her office (from which she's fired), nor the other medical subjects, and certainly not the students. If she tried, she'd be terminated or worse: Clara threatens her with vague but menacing consequences if she misbehaves. And what does the doctor care if she goes on strike? He'll pay someone else and stick a tube down her throat. A strategy of resistance against precarious wage labor can't be "unionize your Starbucks," as valiantly as the Wobblies have tried.

I don't know exactly what a successful strategy looks like, but I think it has something to do with the penultimate shot in *Sleeping Beauty*. Lucy wakes prematurely after a dangerous drug interaction to find an old man's naked corpse in bed with her—a client who paid to die there. She opens her eyes with a kiss of CPR breathing from Clara, and sits up like the princess from whom the film draws its name.

She opens her eyes and she screams and she doesn't stop.

DRAMA FOR CANNIBALS
(2013)

THE ORGANIZATIONS THAT put on Shakespeare plays in prisons claim the sort of distinctions that suggest they're part of a crowded field. They're either "the first-ever Shakespeare program in a solitary confinement unit" or "the oldest North American Shakespeare program contained within the walls of a medium security adult male prison performing exclusively the works of William Shakespeare." There's Shakespeare in Prison, The Shakespeare Prison Project, and Shakespeare Behind Bars. *This American Life* devoted a whole acoustic-guitar-scored episode to a prison production of *Hamlet's* Act V. In Italy, *Caesar Must Die*, the newest film from Paolo and Vittorio Taviani, takes it a step further with a scripted movie about a performance of Julius Caesar with an all-convict cast acting under their own names. In the *Times Literary Supplement* Peter Stothard wondered which play in the English-Arabic collection at Guantánamo Bay is most popular. Where there are bars, there's the Bard. What is it about Shakespeare that's able to carve out this exceptional space in criminal justice?

The programs promise impressive, albeit abstract, results. One organization claims their program is "extremely effective in empowering inmates to think creatively, re-examine decisions they've made, get more in touch with their emotions, and develop life skills such as confidence in creative thinking and speaking in front of an audience." Another is premised on the idea that "human beings are inherently good, and that although convicted criminals have committed heinous crimes against other human beings, this inherent goodness still lives deep within them and must be called forth." Shakespeare's plays enable a confrontation with our individual humanity, with existential choices, with honor and murder and revenge. Taking part in a performance is framed as rehabilitative practice rather than a humane way to pass time under inhumane conditions. There's a pattern here, and the actors aren't the only ones following a well-read script. If Shakespeare isn't officially part of the American justice system, his work is at least an accessory to the crime.

All of these efforts to help Shakespeare speak to prisoners reach outside audiences in more or less the same form. An important step is to frame the production as an opportunity for the inmates, one which they always seize with enthusiasm and gratitude. Criminals without any other qualifiers—especially in maximum security, where a disproportionate number of the performance stories take place—are generally depicted as menacing orange crime machines. A convict who's excited about Shakespeare, the audience imagines, might be worth rehabilitating. And just as important, the inmates have to be participating of their own free will because that's the only way the redemption story works. America wants to see penitent self-improvers, not dancing marionettes.

But there's a big difference between consent and compliance. In a heavily controlled environment like the prison, it's hard to talk honestly about voluntary participation. After all, no one *wants to* be in a prison production of Shakespeare. The *New York Times* in their feature about a performance at Rikers and *This American Life* both mention that actors in productions they covered have previous experience, but there's no analysis as to why Hollywood extra and felon might be overlapping categories. Of course there are actors in prison. The plays they choose are small-scale dramas suited to the security concerns of the hosting institutions. The tragedies aren't ensemble numbers; they don't have roles for anyone who might want to join, like a school play does. That authorities can fill an audition with people who prefer being in Hamlet in prison to just being in prison isn't much evidence of anything except perhaps incarceration levels. Certainly not the indomitable human spirit.

The assumption that the redemption narrative belies is that prisoners are stupid, or rather that they possess uncultivated intellects. Shakespeare, as a traditional barometer of analytical ability, calls forth and translates the prisoner's raw talent into recognizable skill. The director plays the role of teacher/coach who believes in the convicts' worth and goodness when no one else will. And when prisoners do connect with the material—as they inevitably do; there are no stories of Shakespeare prison project failures—the outsider's faith is vindicated.

Laura Bates, author of the memoir *Shakespeare Saved My Life: Ten Years in Solitary with the Bard*, provides a good example of the formula. Though Bates didn't direct Shakespeare, she taught him in a literature class in prisons in Chicago and Indiana. The lessons are much the same. In an excerpt published at *The Huffington Post*, she tells the story of Larry Newton, the maximum-security inmate whose salvation provides the title. At first Newton frightens Bates, but when he responds enthusiastically to her tryout essay prompt, she admits him to the class to watch with satisfaction as he becomes her star pupil. In a tragic final act, despite his accomplishments, Bates reveals that Newton will spend the rest of his life in prison. It's a simple story, and it's the one at the core of all these representations, but it's also premised on the idea that NPR listeners understand what they want to hear from prisoners better than prisoners do.

When Bates says of Newton's work, "Not bad for a fifth-grade drop-out," she underrates the capabilities of elementary schoolers. This isn't to critique his analysis, but even an eleven-year-old knows when they're being given an answer in the form of a question. To screen participants, Bates gave them a soliloquy from *Richard II* that begins, "I have been studying how I may compare this prison where I live unto the world. And, for because the world is populous and here is not a creature but myself, I cannot do it." She then poses the seemingly open-ended "What do you understand from the excerpt?" It's a high-stakes test for a prisoner in solitary. Though there's range of acceptable answers implied, it's clear what the instructor wants him to say. The prisoners have to fulfill their role in the story by identifying with the Shakespearean protagonist.

The syllogism goes like this: if Shakespeare speaks to universal humanity, and Shakespeare speaks to a prisoner, then the prisoner is human after all. The non-incarcerated can rest easier knowing bad guys get rehabilitated and punished. But this instruction isn't just a performance for viewers at home, it is educational. What exactly do jailers want their captives to learn?

Wrestling with questions of choice and responsibility, of betrayal and remorse—in the official American curriculum this is called existential thought. But Hamlet, Lear, and Macbeth aren't everymen. It isn't simply enrichment to dress up a society's captive marginalized as kings and princes and have them rehearse tragedy. Even if it's more fashionable to do postcolonial readings of Shakespeare than write him off as emblematic of Western hegemony, the use of treacherous Nordic royals as exemplars of human interiority is suspect.

In a 1928 radio discussion, playwright Bertolt Brecht went off on this Shakespearean hero and his tragic narrative:

> Shakespeare pushes the great individuals out of their human relationships (family, state) out onto the heath, into complete isolation, where he must pretend to be great in his decline . . . Future times will call this kind of drama a drama for cannibals and they'll say that the human being was eaten as Richard III, with pleasure at the beginning and with pity at the end, but he was always eaten up.

This dramatic arc doesn't belong to humanity writ large. It belongs to a particular personality, born of very particular circumstances, and is generalized to whole populations because it's convenient for an enriched few. When we talk about ideology and propaganda, we should suspect our contemporary media, but also our cultural touchstones. No one has a consciousness more archetypically false than a prisoner who believes he's free. What did Larry Newton realize that so impressed Laura Bates? "I had control of my life. I could be anybody I wanted to be," he writes for her.

At the heart of both the Shakespearean tragedy and the story the American justice system tells about itself is a bad choice. Prisoners, it's nice to think, are people who have made mistakes and are facing the consequences. But this national bedtime story is contradicted on the front page of the paper every day. An alien observer looking at the US prison population would never guess its organizing principle is justice. Rather, the penal system is index and engine of social marginalization, with the groups who most frighten the people who run it—young Black men, trans women—facing the highest incarceration rates. Adam Gopnik is right when he calls the American mass incarceration "a fundamental fact of our country today—perhaps the fundamental fact, as slavery was the fundamental fact of 1850." American prisons are central to defining and maintaining the host of unequal, intersecting relations that make up the national fabric, all while literally acting out tales of human universality in Early Modern English.

If the carceral system is the country's fundamental fact, then its fundamental logic is that of cuffs, bars, and guns. No readings or performances are going to change that, but they can change the way we see it from the outside. Without a story about 2,266,800 bad choices, America is just a country that keeps its underclasses in cages. Shakespeare's drama for cannibals lends a sense of noble inevitability to a prison system that's not only historically and globally specific, but exceptional. It's fitting theater for a society that eats its own.

But solitary confinement within the Shakespearean character is not the only way to be alive. While held at the immigration detention center on Ellis Island, Trinidadian Marxist CLR James wrote a book on Herman Melville's *Moby Dick* and what he termed the "authoritarian personality" in the form of Ahab. He was not content to linger on this ill-fated type, whom he likens to a handful of Shakespearean dramatic protagonists. In *Mariners, Renegades and Castaways*, James contrasts the captain with the ground to his figure: the crew. While Ahab is "either in a state of grim reserve, tragic gloom, or hopeless silence, overwhelmed by his isolation," the anonymous crew is united by their virtuosic free association. Together they're able to accomplish what is without hyperbole a superhuman task.

Where other critics have read Melville's descriptions of whaling as dull or even nonnarrative, James sees in them the sublime harmony of unalienated human endeavor.

They're not übermenschen overcome by "problems which cannot be answered, but which the tortured personality in its misery must continue to ask"; they're free laborers whose concerns are at hand.

The full importance of this comparison isn't evident until the final chapter, when the book takes an autobiographical turn. In a very different story about prison education, James describes where he did his writing and his observations about his fellow detainees. He knows that to the warden and policymakers they're "just a body of isolated individuals seeking charity," but he sees more:

> These men, taken as a whole, know the contemporary world and know it better than many world-famous foreign correspondents. They discuss among themselves their attitudes to the United States, their attitudes to World War III, to Russia, to totalitarianism, to democracy, to national independence . . . With a devastating simplicity they sum up regimes. I have heard a man say in five minutes all that needed to be said about one of the most controversial regimes in the world today. He ended, "I know. I have lived and worked there."

It's easier to guard a million Hamlets than a thousand prisoners like these. No wonder authorities would rather expose inmates to stories of individual agency from the dead and foreign than encourage them to form social analyses based on their common experiences. American culture as a whole has little use for narratives about the intelligence and sophistication of self-organized people acting in concert. When film studies professors need a good example of this phenomenon, they're forced to reach for the Soviets. In a detention environment, this kind of thinking can be downright dangerous; everyone knows what prisoners do when they self-organize.

Recently, two of America's most prominent prison institutions have been rocked by hunger strikes with a discipline that could make any professional organizer in the country blush. In California, a demonstration across prisons compelled tens of thousands of inmates to refuse meals and work. At time of writing, three weeks in, one thousand prisoners continue to make the only choice they're given, at enormous personal cost. And in the detention center at Guantánamo, hunger strikes have brought authorities to brutally force-feed detainees intravenously. Authorities move the leaders to increasingly isolated cells; if the prisoners can't be trapped inside their own heads, then they'll be caged in boxes not much larger. Any outside pacifier who thinks they have something to teach these people about responsibility or consequences is grotesquely mistaken.

There is genius in every prison. Not just because, as Stephen Jay Gould has suggested, it's a near statistical certainty that there are individuals with truly exceptional intellects languishing behind bars. Not because societies tend to lock up adventurous minds, or because we have seen evidence in the brilliance of convicts from Thomas More to Emma Goldman to Malcolm X. There is genius in every prison because there is genius wherever people, never alone, make a world for themselves. In the Shakespeare-in-prison stories, the inmates, like Richard III, are eaten "with pleasure at the beginning and with pity at the end," but always eaten, and always alone. The Bard's tragedies are solitary confinement for the mind. America would rather teach its prisoners that man is most human in isolation than learn from them that the opposite is true.

MARX

TURN DOWN FOR WHAT?
(2014)

COMMUNISTS ARE NOT supposed to like capitalism. If there's one thing everyone knows about communists, it's that we don't like capitalism. Capitalism, as described in the writings of Karl Marx, is an organized system of exploitation in which the many labor for the profit of the few. Capitalism takes human behaviors and personal relations and shapes them into market behaviors and market relations, leveling difference and originality along the way. It is bad, and we are against it.

That's the Marxism for Dummies line, and for most intents and purposes it's not wrong. But Marx has a more complicated relationship to capital than he's usually given credit for. In Marxism, capital is a necessary historical phase that displaces feudalism and rapidly increases human productivity. There's a contradiction in the code: through capital, "the amount of labor necessary for the production of a given object is indeed reduced to a minimum, but only in order to realize a maximum of labor in the maximum number of such objects." From this tendency, Marx deduces a way not out but through capitalism:

> The more this contradiction develops, the more does it become
> evident that the growth of the forces of production can no longer

be bound up with the appropriation of alien labor, but the mass of workers must themselves appropriate their own surplus labor. Once they have done so—and disposable time thereby ceases to have an antithetical existence—then, on one side, necessary labor time will be measured by the needs of the social individual, and, on the other, the development of the power of social production will grow so rapidly that, even though production is now calculated for the wealth of all, disposable time will grow for all. For real wealth is the developed production power of all individuals. The measure of wealth is then not any longer, in any way, labor time, but rather disposable time.

Capitalism reduces the cost of being alive to a minimum, but just to shrink the worker's slice as the pie grows. Eventually through this process "it becomes evident" that the owners are parasites, and the expropriated expropriate the expropriators. If all this is the case, then it logically follows that we shouldn't be trying to slow the expropriation down, but rather we should attempt to speed the system toward its inevitable doom. This dynamic is the premise for the collection *#Accelerate*, new from the radically odd publisher Urbanomic.

Starting with Marx's "Fragment on Machines"—from which I've drawn the quote above—*#Accelerate* is a chronologically arranged attempt at an "accelerationist reader." Accelerationism is the bend of theory that follows Marx through Gilles Deleuze, Jean-François Lyotard, and the 1990s Cybernetic Cultures Research Unit (among others), concluding that it's counterproductive to try to block capital's flows and that revolutionaries ought to increase those flows' number and speed instead. The collection draws its hashtag from a piece near the end, "#Accelerate: Manifesto for an Accelerationist Politics" by Alex Williams and Nick Srnicek, which was extraordinarily popular on Marxist social media in 2013—all the more remarkable considering the manifesto has nothing to do with cats.

#Accelerate (the manifesto, not the reader) was an internal memo of sorts to the Marx-inflected left about our relationship to technology and production. The two London-based academics seek to redeem Marx as the "paradigmatic accelerationist thinker" and argue that a "left politics antithetical to technosocial acceleration is also, at least in part, a severe misrepresentation." At a time when capital's most prominent figures and firms claim to be the embodiment of technosocial acceleration, when leftists are assaulting people wearing Google Glass in the street, this is a controversial position to take. "We do not want to return to Fordism. There can be no return to Fordism," Srnicek and Williams write, positioning themselves not so much against as past the twentieth-century bargain between capital and organized labor and definitely against the deluded democratic socialists trying to keep the New Deal dream alive.

It's too bad that #Accelerate and the reader it led to aren't written for a general audience. Post 2008 economic crisis, Marxist critique has ventured cautiously outside the classroom and the movie theater into mainstream economics. Neither Keynesian liberalism or free-market conservatism has an adequate explanation for why the proceeds of labor are accruing to a smaller number of profiteers. Marxism predicted it, and more and more people across and beyond the conventional political spectrum are willing to listen. Accelerationism takes the restoration of the historical Marxist project seriously, but it's still shaking off the mental shackles of academic philosophy, and its proponents lack the interest, training, or perhaps the ability to communicate outside a small self-selected group.

As a mostly twentieth-century academic reader, *#Accelerate* includes some of the worst examples of self-indulgent left academic frivolity. We can track the evolution of Anglo-French accelerationism through the "Ferment" section, which reads in part like a game of Marxist telephone on acid. Gilles Deleuze and Félix Guattari's daring fusion of Marx and Freud yields Lyotard endorsing the joy of being fucked by capital, which yields Gilles Lipovetsky's foolhardy "acceleration of critique." Class struggle falls out of these accounts, as the authors arrogantly pronounce that capital's blender has abolished such distinctions.

Although these pieces of writing are useful in constructing a genealogy, I wonder what purpose they serve acceleration itself. If we are for technosocial acceleration, then surely one of the things we can leave behind is leftist professors from the 1970s who thought "what is important is to be able to laugh and dance." They laughed and danced into tenure and home loans, and now here we are.

* * *

Compared with Marx, the late twentieth-century accelerationists weren't very accurate in their ideas about the future of work. Lyotard compares work under accelerating capitalism to sex work, which he imagines to be passive, a question of enduring "how many penises per hour, how many tons of coal, how many cast iron bars, how many barrels of shit." Here he sees the "jouissance of anonymity, the jouissance of the repetition of the same in work," the "plugging us in here, being plugged in there." It's a vision of work not unlike *The Matrix*, with humans as batteries for machine-capital, living orifices for plugs. But the twenty-first century hasn't just meant the acceleration of factory work, it has meant displacement by automation, and the growth of the service sector, the centrality of communication technology. If all work comes to resemble sex work, it's because service work requires more personality, imagination, and initiative from laborers, not less.

Part of what these accelerationists believe is that capital is effacing difference of all sorts. "Kapital . . . does away with all privileges of place; hence its mobility . . . its machinery obeys only one principle of energetic connections—the law of value, equivalence," Lyotard writes in "Energumen Capitalism," the same essay where he credits "hairdressers and 'no sex,' women's lib and gay movement clothes stores" with accelerating the abolition of sex difference. With a more nuanced take, Shulamith Firestone's "Two Modes of Cultural History" is the only piece in the collection specifically focused on differences between workers. She opposes two gendered forms of imagination: the feminine fantastic and the male empirical. Through the acceleration of capital, she imagines the two combining, as technology makes possible what had previously been considered magic. "When the male Technological Mode can at last produce what the female Aesthetic Mode had envisioned," Firestone concludes, "we shall have eliminated the need for either."

While *#Accelerate* is totally unconcerned with racial division, Marxist sociologist Eduardo Bonilla-Silva's 2003 *Racism Without Racists* predicted a less rosy but structurally similar dissolution of the Black-white American racial binary and the development of a colorist spectrum. And though the magical tech changes that Firestone imagined are coming true, and though the demographic changes Bonilla-Silva predicted are here, these binaries seem to be sharpening in postcrisis America, not blending. What gives?

While Marxism is often hesitant to "get bogged down" in race and gender divisions, capitalism displays no such compunction. The philosophers in *#Accelerate* are more interested in higher-order abstractions like the "human." In his piece "Labor of the Inhuman," Reza Negarestani rejects what he labels "kitsch Marxism."

> One makes a claim in favor of the force of better reason. The Kitsch Marxist says: Who decides? One says, construction through structural and functional hierarchies. The Kitsch Marxist responds: Control. . . . We say "us." The Kitsch Marxist recites: Who is "us?" The impulsive responsiveness of kitsch Marxism cannot even be identified as cynicism. It is a mechanical knee-jerk reactionism that is the genuine expression of norm consumerism without the concrete commitment to producing any norms.

It's important for Negarestani that we tune out these objections before they name any real social divisions. But these divisions are what lend capital its flexibility and endurance, what has allowed it to keep going despite its core contradictions. Capital can't afford to pretend race and gender don't exist, and neither can communists.

Even though it barely comes up in *#Accelerate*, perhaps the best example of accelerationist political practice put gender front and center. Wages for Housework was a 1970s campaign that sought to bring women's unwaged domestic labor under the wage relation so that housewives could strike and engage in the struggle for free time. "If technological innovation can lower the limit of necessary work, and if the working class struggle in industry can use that innovation for gaining free hours, the same cannot be said of housework," Mariarosa Dalla Costa and Selma James write in the pamphlet "The Power of Women and the Subversion of the Community." "To the extent that she must in isolation procreate, raise and be responsible for children, a high mechanization of domestic chores doesn't free any time for the woman." It's a common misconception that capitalism simply means wages for labor; capital has used women's unwaged labor to bear the costs of reproducing labor power across the board. As Dalla Costa and James write, "the entire class exploitation has been built upon the specific mediation of women's exploitation."

How does capital answer this demand? Much like Negarestani's kitsch Marxist, capital disaggregates. In Barbara Ehrenreich's 2000 *Harper's* essay "Maid to Order," she looked at when capitalism did start paying wages for housework, from inside the cleaning industry. While Dalla Costa and James wanted to claim the wage so they could reject it, Ehrenreich writes about how white American feminists argued—to Congress no less—that paying for housework would allow "women" to leave the home for better jobs outside. They were right, Ehrenreich reports, insofar as there has been a decrease in women's unwaged labor and an increase in women's participation in the waged labor force. But part of that increase has been performed by the women who come in to do their housework, and as moms become employers, they try to decrease labor costs too.

According to the Bureau of Labor Statistics (BLS), there are more than 1.4 million people employed as maids, housekeepers, and cleaners—1.3 million of them women, and over 60 percent of them women of color. This kind of labor is notoriously hard to measure, but Ehrenreich's research suggests that in areas near the US-Mexico border, only one-tenth of paid domestic labor is on the books. The BLS puts the yearly average housekeeping wage at $19,570, which is both below the poverty line for a family of three and no doubt inflated by underreporting. Domestic workers without immigration papers not only lack the so-called protection of the law, they're constantly vulnerable to deportation. So much for Lyotard's "doing away with all privileges of place." As Evan Calder Williams writes, "the days and bodies of humans are still far cheaper than any automation, provided money knows where to look. And it always has." White supremacy and the gender division aren't archaisms that capital will puree into a flow of neutered beige singularities, they're labor relations, and integral ones.

Capitalism doesn't function according to the philosophers' universal terms—or economists' for that matter. It's a reckless structure, but in predictably circumspect ways. The American criminal justice system—which libertarians imagine capitalism could survive without—has focused more on race as productive technology has improved, incarcerating Black people at an increasingly higher rate than whites. Once released, the formerly incarcerated take a record with them, one that marks them forever as a second-class worker, unable to demand the same wages and protections.

Accelerationists couldn't predict this "new Jim Crow" because they're always expecting capital to double down. Instead, the owners split. Capital is not only able but required to maintain a host of different labor relations at the same time. Two million (mostly young, mostly women) Americans work in illegal unpaid internships. Black unemployment is consistently twice as high as white unemployment. More than sixty thousand imprisoned migrants worked in US federal detention centers last year for thirteen cents an hour—less than two percent of the "minimum" wage. And that's just within the US "Who is 'us'?" isn't just a kitsch Marxist knee-jerk, it's exactly the question capital asks and answers over and over a million times a day in order to survive.

* * *

Where does this leave us communists? Firestone's vision of a world with "the full achievement of the conceivable in the actual" is crawling forward, threatening to walk any day now. There's not much analysis of specific firms, innovations, or individuals in the *#Accelerate* collection; the authors display a stodgy Scrabble player's unwillingness to use proper nouns outside citations. I can understand not wanting your philosophy to turn over as fast as popular internet companies do, but there are costs to being contemporary, and one of them is shelf life. Analyzing particular moves and agents can tell us more about accelerating capital than meditations on what constitutes the human.

In his piece about the "disruptive" food substitute Soylent, Bhaskar Sunkara sees both the capitalist and communist potential. Soylent is a powder you add to water to create a hypernutritious shake. The company claims—and so far no one has refuted—that people can subsist on Soylent alone. It's a new product and a major jump in the direction Firestone envisioned: imagine making hunger a thing of the past! Imagine food decommodified, a free flow of nutrition to hungry mouths, whoever, wherever, and whenever they are. Disrupting starvation is a Silicon Valley wet dream, but it's never been the food product that's the problem. Instead, Soylent is more likely to disrupt lunch breaks. If we end up living in a world where we pay per second to kiss the nutritious gruel spigot, we'll know for whom the Soylent pours.

Innovations like this continue to lower the cost of getting workers from one day to the next. The "sharing economy," for example, is a communist-sounding sector of the new economy based on people using their goods and skills in common. There's no need for everyone on a block to own a chainsaw, so if one neighbor owns one, she can go online and lease it to her neighbors. It's the same thing neighbors have always done, but rationalized and better suited for a population that's used to relations mediated through money. Sharing resources is another kind of efficiency, so it can mean one of two things: profit for owners or free time for workers. If you don't need to buy a chainsaw, you can afford to work a little bit less or you can afford to be paid a little bit less.

"The line between dystopia and utopia is a thin one," Sunkara writes about Soylent, and it's just as true about the sharing economy and Google's driverless cars. That line is the difference between smooching in the backseat of a solar-powered robot car on your way to the beach with a cooler full of synthetic burgers, and beginning your workday on the car's integrated video chat, using the screen as a mirror so you can wipe the unsightly glob of Soylent from your chin. As labor efficiency improves, that line between what could be and what is gets thinner, taller, better patrolled. Along with labor efficiency, owners' ability to calculate the divisions they need to make in order to keep the system stable also improve, as does their ability to enforce them.

We can see what that looks like in the accelerated US client state of Israel, where a technologically advanced overclass has built a literal apartheid wall between themselves and a pseudo-stateless Palestinian working class, while simultaneously maintaining a separate though equally threatening labor relation with African immigrants. How do the Israelis see through walls they build? The same way accelerationists do: they read Deleuze. In 2006, Eyal Weizman talked with members of the Israeli Defense Force for *Frieze* about how they use philosophy:

> I asked [paratroop instructor] Naveh why Deleuze and Guattari were so popular with the Israeli military. He replied that "several of the concepts in *A Thousand Plateaux* became instrumental for us . . . allowing us to explain contemporary situations in a way that we could not have otherwise. It problematized our own paradigms." When I asked him if moving through walls was part of it, he explained that "in Nablus the IDF understood urban fighting as a spatial problem. . . . Traveling through walls is a simple mechanical solution that connects theory and practice."

As American police militarize and anti-immigrant fascist parties rise in Europe, we can see a sort of Israelification across the west. Technosocial acceleration means dystopia with a lot of intersecting market and non-market mechanisms of control to keep it that way. Capital can build walls and crash through them too; owners play by their own rules, their own geography. Capital draws, redraws, and enforces lines between workers according to structural necessity: it knows how to fight a class war as a race war and call it a drug war; it knows if you subject women to a culture of physical, psychological, sexual, and emotional abuse, you can pay them less; it knows borders aren't for keeping people out, they're for controlling the wages of the people they let in. What here is worth accelerating?

Unfortunately, there's not much of a choice. No amount of diligent union organizing, tech skepticism, or sharing is going to slow capital down. Saying you're an accelerationist is like taking a picture with the Leaning Tower of Pisa: you can make it look like you're doing something, but it truly doesn't matter whether or not you're even alive. The real accelerationists aren't working on dissertations, they're working at Google or McKinsey or they're designing the massively open online courses (MOOCs) that are putting grad students out of work. It doesn't make any more sense to be for technosocial acceleration than against it.

That doesn't, however, make me a pessimist. I'm not quite blithe enough to repeat Mao's "The situation is excellent," but all that potential free time is looking more and more appetizing by the day, especially as people are ground down to produce it. The easiest means of production to seize, the ones nearest at hand, are inalienable from our bodies. Human capital— our ability to use the productive tools around us—is a vital component of technosocial acceleration. We're getting more capable, faster and faster. A credible communist threat would offer people another use for their accelerating abilities besides creating value for profiteers or trying to become one of them. If Marx was right in his more self-assured moments, then we're nearing the point when it becomes intolerable that all these innovations and efficiencies are hurting more people than they're helping. We won't get there any faster by wishing it so or identifying with the process, but in the mean mean meantime, we can prepare. We can undermine capital's attempts to divide us by cleaving to the underdog every time they try another split. We might even get really good at it.

LEGO MARX
(2016)

HERE **IS ONE** idea of what Marxism is about: There are two main classes—workers and capitalists—and they are in conflict. Proletarians have to sell their labor in order to survive, and the owners exploit that desperation for profit. When workers overcome their false consciousness, stop competing against each other, and organize, they will seize the means of production and operate society in their interest. Since their interest involves not being workers anymore (insofar as workers are defined by their exploitation), the working class's self-expression means the abolition of the class system.

This is not a straw man. This is a good story, an important story, maybe one of the most important stories of all time. But it's also very simple. Society is divided on a single split based on people's relation to waged labor. It's like the end of a *Power Rangers* episode: two big forces smash against each other and with courage and class-consciousness, the workers will be strong enough to win. The story is clarifying and just as importantly it is true. But is it true enough?

In this story about society, we're dealing with a couple large concepts. Two classes, one labor relation. It's a world built of big blocks, of Duplos. Insofar as Bernie Sanders's campaign has a Marxist foundation, it's this kind of Duplo Marxism: the 1 percent and the 99 percent. This is, once again, for many intents and purposes, a good story. But the Sanders campaign ran into serious trouble when it viewed most anything outside this narrative as a distraction. His statements on forced childbearing weren't strong enough, and the campaign basically threw up its hands when it came to white chauvinism. In a bad version of Duplo Marxist thinking, if any of these concerns stop someone from joining up, then these people suffer from false consciousness. They don't know what's good for them.

These days "false consciousness" sounds a little too last-century. Now Duplo Marxists use more specific descriptors: "neoliberalism" or "individualism" or "identity politics." Sometimes they're totally right: liberals (and the corporations they own) oppose worker-owner conflict to racial conflict or gender conflict, as if only one can be true at a time. It's a mystification, one that preys on people's good intentions. If Bernie is for workers but Hillary is for women, then how is a nice progressive supposed to pick?

But other times it's the Duplo Marxists who are doing the mystification. Society isn't made up of Duplos, and there are social conflicts—class conflicts—that aren't centered on the wage-labor relation. Duplo Marxists are occasionally nearsighted, prone to lash out at critics who want to add complexity.

Duplo Marxists occasionally use "intersectional" or "intersectionality" as an insult like "individualist." I figure this is related to the idea that identity can be endlessly subdivided—if almost everyone is on the wrong side of some social conflict, then who will be left to fight on the right side of the class war?! Do we really have to keep fighting until the Earth is scorched and all that's left is a righteous ragtag group of the world's most oppressed quadruple minorities?

I think this whole scenario is mostly nonsense.

Cards on the table: I'm a Marxist. Hi. I believe taking on that label includes a certain amount of respect for the Duplo Marxist story, but that's not how I learned Marxism or why I care so much about this dead German guy.

Marxism is not a philosophy or a theology, it's—seriously, don't laugh!—a science. It's a science of history, a method of understanding the real relations between people over time. Biologists looks at individual organisms; Marxists look at classes, relations of exploitation. Duplo Marxists focus on one particular mode of exploitation—owners and wage workers—and that doesn't necessarily make them bad. There's nothing wrong with herpetologists, but there would be if they refused to acknowledge the existence of birds.

Contrary to what some Duplo Marxists think, the problem with their story isn't accounting for individual outliers—"What about a Black textile heir who loves her job as a letter carrier?!"—because thankfully Marxism is not Torah study and its conclusions are not structured around exceptions. Class conflict doesn't go one by one figuring out imaginary edge cases like a law student. As a science, Marxism proceeds by investigating real relations between people and testing its own concepts, categories, and explanations. There are a lot of terms in Marxism; he had a lot of good ideas, and there's been even more debate about them. For the purposes of the rest of this piece, I'll use "materialism" for this scientific method part.

Much like a scientist—please stop laughing—I think the answer to problems with Marxism is more, better Marxism. One of the coolest things about materialism is that it offers an explanation of the way our understanding of social relations change over time with those relations. In Marx's introduction to his "Contribution to the Critique of Political Economy," he writes that materialists have to bear in mind that they're thinking through the perspective and with the terms of their particular society, which are (frequently one-sided, he adds) manifestations of that society's class relations. The definite and specific relations in which we're currently embedded are, Marx writes, "the universal light with which all the other colors are tinged and are modified through its particularity. It is a special ether which determines the specific gravity of everything that appears in it." (If you think that could also describe patriarchy or white supremacy, you're not alone.)

This is something like the materialist version of the observer effect. Think about something like phrenology, a racist pseudoscience that appears at the end of the eighteenth century as a way to explain why it was okay for white people to exploit everyone else, which was already the actual social relation. Phrenologists then retroactively applied their insights all the way back to the start of mankind: the history of the world is the history of racial head sizes. Legitimate scientists and economists do it as well: biologists don't only study organisms that have been alive since the advent of biology, economists don't only study production and consumption that have occurred since the definition of those categories. Like these disciplines but with its own perspective, materialism sees all human history as the history of class conflict. This is an oft-quoted line, but its implications are important. Materialism is a product of capitalist relations, but it is not just about capitalist relations.

The most important part of this observer effect point is not that we should remember that we are always getting something big wrong—though that is true, a feature of all science, and worth keeping in mind. The most important part is that we can't be afraid to be more right. We can never think outside our social relations, but our social relations are always changing. People change the world, the "universal light" of our particular situation shifts, which enables people to change the world in new ways, and on and on.

Take, for example, the Haitian Revolution. In her book *Hegel, Haiti, and Universal History,* the materialist scholar Susan Buck-Morss describes how the Enlightenment values of the French Revolution created what we might call the right light conditions for the Haitian Revolution. *"Liberté, égalité, fraternité!"* meant something very different from the mouth of a slave in Port-au-Prince than a merchant in Paris. Our understanding of so-called universal liberty proceeds unevenly, and materialism acknowledges this historical fact. As Buck-Morss puts it, we need to recognize "not only the contingency of historical events, but also the indeterminacy of the historical categories by which we grasp them." All of Marx's analyses and categories are subject to the backward-facing judgment of history as it advances. To try and freeze his work in place is a serious disservice to the method. That's not an act of fidelity, it's an act of worship. The most faithful thing we can do for Marx is to fuck all his shit up. Rigorously.

To go beyond Duplo Marxism is to see that society isn't just composed of two blocks, that the owner/wage-laborer relation is not the sole class division. Instead, each of those two blocks are composed of smaller blocks, not individuals, but other class relations. Lego Marxism can handle multiple variables, multiple class relations that are going on at the same time—intersecting even. You could take apart the big blocks and recompose them according to a different social division and still be doing important, useful materialism. There's a sense among some Duplo Marxists that Lego Marxists are proceeding haphazardly by feeling, unscientifically, with not enough of Marx's rigor. That is, I think, occasionally right. Mapping class relations is hard! And Marx was a genius. However, in a lot of cases, I think Duplo Marxists haven't bothered to do the reading.

* * *

I've been thinking about the (silly) kids' toys metaphor in this piece for a while, but what really inspired me was an essay from the late-1970s by French women's liberation theorist Christine Delphy called "A Materialist Feminism Is Possible." The essay is a response to a criticism of her work by English sociologists Michele Barrett and Mary McIntosh, who had essentially argued a Duplo Marxist position—that Delphy's figuring of women as an exploited class was a sacrilegious perversion of Marx. (It's important to remember that this is a debate going on within the active Women's Liberation Movement.) Delphy fired back, saying it was not she who was perverting Marx, but them.

Central among her critics' errors, Delphy cites "a confusion between the materialist method, used for the first time by Marx, and the analysis of capitalism which he made using it; or rather the reduction of the first to the second." This is the main Duplo vs. Lego Marxism conflict, and Delphy helps define the second side. She writes of the Duplo team, "Marxism is erected as the value of values and is seen as not only above the struggles but outside them. The ultimate perversion, and one moreover which is widespread, is that these people then come to judge real oppression, and even the very existence of oppression, according to whether or not it corresponds to 'Marxism,' and not Marxism according to whether or not it is pertinent to real oppression." That's not how it's supposed to work.

How, then, does Delphy derive the existence of a class conflict between men and women? The Duplo Marxist stereotype is that their critics proceed by way of their personal experience. As a woman, Delphy has gone through gender-based oppression, and Duplo Marxists think they're expected to wave the white flag whenever anyone says "I am oppressed." But that obviously isn't the issue here; Delphy is arguing with women, about the condition of women, for women readers. Her appeal is not to sympathy or empathy, and certainly not to male guilt. She says—rightly, in my read-ing—that her critics haven't engaged with her actual work at all.

   Where to begin analyzing women as a class? Delphy starts with Duplo Marxism; according to what criteria are women divided between their two blocks? It's a simple question, but the answers aren't as easy. The sociology subfield of stratification studies had been forced to consider the class position of women before, and their methods interest Delphy. The French sociologist Alain Girard wrote about class homogamy in his 1964 book *Choosing a Spouse*—that is, the difference and similarity in spouse class position. But because women could not be meaningfully divided into classes according to their relation to wage labor, Girard had to find a proxy measure. To analyze women's movement in the class structure, he found it "preferable" to look at a woman's father's class position and compare it to her husband's. Delphy is incredulous:

> Are we to understand that if a characteristic (in this case occupation) is not a good indicator of what we are seeking to measure (in this case a woman's own social class position), we are justified in aban-doning this dimension in order to keep the indicator, even if it means changing the population studied (i.e., studying the fathers instead of the women themselves)?

She goes much further, looking at the actual conditions of women's production and consumption. Since much of women's work is unwaged, Delphy looks at the way other kinds of unwaged labor are measured. French national production metrics at the time counted "production for self-consumption"; if a farmer raised a pig and fed it to his family, the economists counted that as if he had gained the same amount of value as he would have had he sold the pig at market. But, Delphy observes, we don't eat raw pig! Even when measuring unwaged work, the woman's tasks of preparing, cooking, serving, and cleaning still go unaccounted. Her work is assumed, taken for granted. But by whom (which is to say, for whom) is she exploited?

   Duplo Marxism, to its credit, has an answer, which Delphy

acknowledges. In the Duplo model, women are exploited to reproduce wageworkers' labor power at a discount. They are exploited by their husband's bosses and by their children's future bosses.

Delphy's answer is more direct: women are exploited by men. There is the capitalist mode of production and there is also a concurrent and interrelated "domestic" or "patriarchal" mode of production, which benefits men (as a class) and exploits women (as a class). She is also careful to note that there are some men exploited by the domestic mode as well, pointing out specifically 307,000 French men who work unwaged on family farms and in family businesses.

I'm belaboring Delphy's work for a few reasons, including that a lot of the debates we're having have been had before, and I think her writing is underrated on the Left. But I also want to stress the rigorous foundations of her critique. No one can confuse Delphy with a liberal, and her critics end up looking real silly questioning her fidelity to Marx. (His method also involved responding at length to his critics, many of whom would otherwise likely be lost to history.) Her work is an extremely important contribution to the development of Marxist analysis, and an application of materialism to a problem with existing materialist categories. Delphy is an excellent example of the solution "More, better Marxism."

* * *

Duplo Marxism is not very flexible, and its proponents sometimes get defensive about that. How should we understand racial conflict? The main Duplo model is that capitalists are pitting workers against each other, and racist white workers suffer from false consciousness, blaming Blacks and Mexicans for their exploitation instead of their bosses. But racial minorities cannot be said to have a distinct class relation within the capitalist mode of production. They are exploited as workers (at a higher rate than white people), and if they happen to be owners, then they are exploiters. Once again, this is not a straw man, nor is this kind of thinking useless. But it's also not sufficiently sophisticated, and it can lead to serious interpretive problems.

Take the question of "cultural appropriation." I've heard a lot of grumbling from Duplo Marxists about the idea of cultural appropriation and how it doesn't fit into Marxism. If you copy someone's hairstyle, how are you exploiting them? Where's the labor? Where's the surplus value? Again, the less rigorous of Duplo Marxists assume this is an emotional projection. Just because it makes you feel bad doesn't mean it's exploitation. But has the Duplo faction checked their Bible?

In *Capital Volume I's* section on "Machinery and Modern Industry," Marx discusses the role of science in production:

> Science, generally speaking, costs the capitalist nothing, a fact that by no means hinders him from exploiting it. The science of others is as much annexed by capital as the labor of others . . . Although it is clear at the first glance that, by incorporating both stupendous physical forces, and the natural sciences, with the process of production, Modern Industry raises the productiveness of labor to an extraordinary degree, it is by no means equally clear, that this increased productive force is not, on the other hand, purchased by an increased expenditure of labor.

How might we apply this idea of scientific appropriation to cultural appropriation? If a capitalist makes use of general scientific progress without paying for it, that is a kind of appropriation because they are profiting by someone else's labor. No one has to be additionally harmed for it to be exploitation; in a zero-sum capitalist society, their gain is your loss. It also doesn't matter that free sharing in this manner is a feature of science and all human invention and culture long before the beginning of capitalism. If I start a successful peanut butter company, I'm using machines and exploiting workers to profit, but I'm also profiting from the invention of peanut butter, for which I have to pay nothing.

In a viral school project video called "Don't Cash Crop On My Cornrows," Amandla Stenberg presents a strong and coherent narrative about how Black people (as a class) are exploited by white people (as a class) in the process of cultural production. When Katy Perry wears braids in a popular music video, both she (as a white worker) and the label (white owner) are profiting off Black culture and Black labor. Like a knockoff handbag, it costs the label a lot less to point at a picture of Sean Paul than to build a good aesthetic from scratch. But Sean Paul didn't wake up looking like that, it took him work. And not just him.

The Fader magazine has done an excellent job drawing attention to the work and workers behind white cultural appropriation. I used Sean Paul as an example because *Fader* recently published an interview with Yasmin Amira Davis, the hairstylist who did Paul's signature braids and "helped define the visual identity of an era." Davis tells the interviewer, "I do braids that are a lot smaller than other people. I might take two days where someone else would take six hours. My work is different and you can tell." No doubt Davis got paid as an in-demand celebrity stylist, but she did not get paid like someone whose unique labor helped define the visual identity of an era. Instead, other people got paid. Sean Paul got paid. Katy Perry got paid. Most of all, the labels got paid.

This kind of cultural appropriation is part of a larger mode of production called "stealing from Black people and killing them." It's a mode that is deeply interrelated with capitalism, but it's also distinct. Stealing here should not be confused with the robbery that is wage labor; I mean literally murder someone and steal their land. This ongoing history is at the center of Ta-Nehisi Coates's call for reparations for Black Americans. Coates uses the term "plunder," which is better than theft because it evokes the violence and collective victimization. When white profiteers in the Carolinas were planting rice, they needed Black slaves not just to do the planting work, but also to show them how to plant rice. White workers could and did transcend their class status by kidnapping and enslaving Black people. The plunder of Black labor, Black culture, Black science, and Black people themselves is an enduring way that America makes things. That is not only the exploitation of wage labor, that is something different.

* * *

At the end of her essay "The Main Enemy," Christine Delphy suggests the implications of her conclusions for the Women's Liberation Movement: "In the immediate future, the political alliances and strategy of the movement in relation to other groups, movements, or revolutionary parties should be based only on an unambiguous dedication on the part of the latter to the goals of the women's movement. That is, on the basis of their clearly and officially expressed desire to destroy patriarchy and their actual participation in the revolutionary struggle for its destruction." Why would that cause any problem with Marxists, Duplo or otherwise? If the end goal of Marxism is the abolition of class society in its entirety, wouldn't they be all for the destruction of patriarchy?

The most obvious answer is Marxist men benefit from patriarchy. They—we, I should say—exploit women and would benefit from the continued exploitation of women. While 1970s Duplo Marxists blamed the perpetuation of patriarchy in the communist world on clinging remnants of capitalist ideology, Delphy didn't buy it. Check your Marx, she said. If there was patriarchal ideology, then there had to be a basis for it in the relations of production.

There is, I believe, a related problem with contemporary Duplo Marxist politics. Think about it like this: between the current state of working-class organization and when it will have developed to the point where it has the revolutionary capacity to defeat the capitalist class in combat for control over society, there is an intermediate point where the working class has the leverage to negotiate a livable compromise with the owners. After all, a revolution is a huge roll of the dice no matter what, and many people would definitely die and be forced to become killers. If it's possible to compromise in a way that secures everyone a good enough baseline share of the social product, isn't that preferable? Surely the owners too would rather compromise than play with their lives.

A couple consistent criticisms of the Bernie Sanders "compromise with capital" campaign was that he couldn't convince Black voters that he was going to do something to stop them being killed by the police, or women voters that he was going to do something to stop them being forced to bear children. (How he compares to Hillary Clinton is not the point here.)

Historically, when the working class (that is, wage laborers) has managed these kind of temporary compromises and reforms, it has led to increased exploitation elsewhere. As Peter Frase writes, citing the work of Elizabeth Hinton,

> While the Great Society was expanding access to things like income support and health care, a simultaneous "war on crime" was subjecting the poor, and especially the black poor, to increased surveillance and state repression. Her analysis indicates that this was not an accidental juxtaposition, but part of a cohesive reconstruction of the relationship between the state and the working class.

Frase keeps his analysis within a (complex, sophisticated) Duplo Marxist frame, but I think it would be more accurate (and simpler) to say the white ruling class and its state lackeys tweaked the volume levels on distinct (but interrelated) modes of exploitation. We can see a similar dynamic at play when it comes to American women's housework: a decades-long decrease in their unwaged housework has been fully offset by an increase in waged work, including poorly paid domestic work that disproportionately falls on poorer Black and brown women.

A compromise with capitalists might improve conditions for Black workers as workers while doing little to protect them as Black people. In an interview with the *New York Times*, Dallas resident Andre Stubblefield describes carrying his hard hat with him whenever he leaves his apartment, to discourage police from bothering (read: robbing, plundering, exploiting, killing) him. "I got to fake like I'm wearing my work stuff, so they won't mess with me," he says. That's a shitty compromise.

If people are organizing against white supremacy and patriarchy, that shouldn't worry Marxists. My god, that shouldn't worry Marxists. They are organizing against class society, and their enemy is also your enemy. What Marxists should worry about is being good comrades in the ways that Delphy describes: a full, dependable, and active commitment to the end of class society. What that entails is sometimes difficult to figure out in its specifics, but in its specifics is exactly where we need to figure it out. Marx can help! More, better Marx. Lego Marx.

* * *

It's hard to picture what exactly Marxists are fighting for sometimes. Is it anarchy? Who takes out the trash? Is there money? National borders? Do Black people still live in worse neighborhoods than white people? Is there heterosexuality? Families? Individual kitchens? What happens to murderers if there's no police? Does mom still serve herself last at dinner? Do children have to obey their parents? Do I get to keep my own toothbrush? What is communism?

Karl Marx does not hand down the dimensions for the Temple from on high; once again, this is not Torah study. The most quoted of his definitions of communism is probably "the real movement which abolishes the present state of things." Communism is what we will call the actual destruction of class society when it happens. There's an elegant truth to that sword-in-the-stone formulation—it's something like "we'll know it when we do it"—but he's also being a coy pain in the ass. I like another version better, even if it leans hard on the poetry:

> It is the genuine resolution of the conflict between people and nature and between people and people—the true resolution of the strife between existence and essence, between objectification and self-confirmation, between freedom and necessity, between the individual and the species. Communism is the riddle of history solved, and it knows itself to be this solution.

The better we understand the riddle of history, the better our chances as we try to build the answer. Not in our heads, but in reality.

I think we're getting closer.

FIDEL CASTRO'S NAKED LEG, OR NOTES ON POLITICAL CORRECTNESS

(2019)

POLITICAL CORRECTNESS HAS always mattered a lot to me. As far back as I can remember it's been important to be on the right side of things — further even: In my baby book under "baby dislikes" my dad wrote "nuclear proliferation" and "caviar." In middle school I started going to anti-war rallies and spending my time arguing dress code constitutional law with the principal. My high school class voted me "most outspoken," which was a nice way of saying that I wouldn't shut the fuck up about politics, no matter the subject. There are a lot more people who complain about "PC" than people who actually conform to the stereotypes, but I more or less do.

When I was a kid (roughly 1996–'06) political correctness was politically incorrect. In the Bay Area where I grew up we could assume most people were liberals, Democrats, and more specifically anti-Bush—if not necessarily anti-war. But this was the heyday of the *Man Show* and *South Park* and *Crank Yankers* and, especially as a boy, the last thing you were supposed to be was offended. By that time conservatives had already been bellyaching for years on the covers of national magazines about the "PC" menace, gleefully comparing college students to the Red Guards and, yes, Nazi stormtroopers. The script hasn't changed much.

Political correctness connotes not just the inability to let go and enjoy yourself (e.g., I have never seen a Will Ferrell comedy), but a weak character. American history and humanities curricula still draw heavily on Cold War liberal ideas about the individual, and to be politically correct, we learn, is to surrender rather than cultivate your judgment. *Fahrenheit 451*, *1984*, *Lord of the Flies*, *The Scarlet Letter*, *The Crucible*, *Animal Farm*, *Brave New World*, *To Kill a Mockingbird*: When Americans learn about politics what we learn is that critical thinking means thinking "for yourself." Groupthink is part and parcel of tyranny, and attempts to get everyone to think the same way—or make everyone act as if they're thinking the same way—are tyrannical. What is the crime of calling a classmate's shoes "gay" compared to the crime of telling other people what they're allowed to say? It is, we are told, a slippery slope to Hitler.

The object of political correctness is rarely politics itself, at least not the formal kind. The "politics" cancels itself out—a secret ballot can't be politically correct. The object is instead cultural, discursive, aesthetic. Political correctness is when you bring politics into spheres where it doesn't belong, where it edges out judgment (or non-judgmental taste and tradition). Politics is about picking between options and letting yourself be counted on one side or the other, while judgment and taste are where and how we define ourselves as individuals. And only as judging, tasting individuals are we capable of delegating our judgment by vote. Political correctness, then, poisons our culture and the democracy that depends on it.

That is, as I understand it, the strongest version of the argument against political correctness. It is fundamentally a liberal argument in the classical sense, which helps explain why some of the strongest and most consistent reactions against PC come from one-tick-left-or-right-of-center pundits like Jonathan Chait and David Brooks. The issue among progressives and conservatives is where the lines of separation between spheres should be, which helps explain why the story of a gay wedding cake—a private baked good linked to a traditional religious rite that is also now a civil right—has acquired outlandishly large significance. *Discrimination* is a synonym for both *judgment* and *taste*, and the long conservative fight for the right to discriminate against is about more than organizing oppression, it's about preserving that capacity.

(It's worth noting that any moderately close reading of American history shows that elected progressives do not fight to extend the realm of the political so much as manage demands from elements in the public to do so. As I write it's been less than ten years since we marched in Washington, DC for gay marriage, and Democratic lawmakers were not running out to join us.)

Conservatives can be politically correct too, as liberals like to remind them. When they defended the criminalization of homosexuality, for example, they extended the realm of politics into the bedroom. The fight to ban abortion is likewise an intrusion of the political into the medical. Strict libertarians of the *Reason* magazine type consistently oppose political correctness of both kinds, defending the right to our taste in both cake customers and sex acts. But though the unrealistically fair-minded see the political spectrum as a horseshoe, when we're talking political correctness, we're talking about the left.

Where libertarians want to shrink the realm of the political as small as possible, for the PC, "everything is political." This was a repeated complaint in John Taylor's 1991 *New York* cover story "Are You Politically Correct?" The noted academic taste-and-judgment fanatic Stanley Fish is overly fond of the "Is everything political?" phrase, using it in op-eds year after year to argue against politics in the classroom. The lament "everything is political now" turns up 1,180 results on Google, including the *Chicago Tribune* headline gem: "Everything is political these days, even the moon landing." But who are the people who really do believe that everything is political?

Communists.

* * *

"Hitherto philosophers have had the solution of all riddles lying in their writing-desks, and the stupid, exoteric world had only to open its mouth for the roast pigeons of absolute knowledge to fly into it. Now philosophy has become mundane, and the most striking proof of this is that philosophical consciousness itself has been drawn into the torment of the struggle, not only

externally but also internally. But, if constructing the future and settling
everything for all times are not our affair, it is all the more clear what we
have to accomplish at present: I am referring to ruthless criticism of all that
exists, ruthless both in the sense of not being afraid of the results it arrives
at and in the sense of being just as little afraid of conflict with the powers
that be."

— KARL MARX, LETTER TO ARNOLD RUGE (1843)

If you ask the average conservative, they'll probably tell you political
correctness starts with Soviet Russia, more specifically Josef Stalin. But
there's no strong historical account of that or, for that matter, a translation
of the phrase into Russian. On one level this story is simply wrong. But
on a deeper, more important level, it's complicatedly wrong. Marching
the political into "all that exists" truly is part of the Marxist plot, from
the factory to the family ("Do you charge us with wanting to stop the
exploitation of children by their parents?" asks the *Manifesto*. "To this
crime we plead guilty.") Succeeding waves of Marxists have paid him the
highest tribute by occasionally finding Marx himself politically incorrect,
extending his analysis even further into society in accordance with the
method.

The phrase "cultural Marxism" has no particular meaning within the
tradition of Marxist thought, whereas it does have a noted history as a code
phrase on the antisemitic right. Lately it's become a sort of harder-core
synonym for political correctness, one that evinces a familiarity with
far-right politics rather than garden variety annoyance at college students.
And yet, I admit, there's some validity to the idea. The complaint—similar
to the one about political correctness—is that Marxists want to subject
every facet of society to politics, including the cultural sphere, which liberals (from right to left) believe is properly a realm of individuality.

Here's how we might imagine how liberals understand the cultural
Marxist slippery slope: Instead of judging a comedian based on how
funny they are, cultural Marxists want to judge adherence to a political
line, which isn't really judgment at all, it's verification. At that point we're
no longer audience members or consumers or even people, we become

bureaucrats, always looking for a condemnatory box to check. Slowly and then quickly cultural producers are incentivized and forced to conform, and we're left in a desert of art so sycophantic it barely deserves the title.

With the development of social media and the contentification of every-day people's regular speech we have a greater awareness of the role we all play in forming culture. What separated earlier generations of professional artists and critics from the amateurs was plausible reach, but now anyone online could go viral. This is occasionally thrilling for everyone involved (see: Lil Nas X), but it also makes more of us subject to expectations and pressures of political correctness that used to be reserved for public speak-ers. And if we're deprived of a space beyond politics we can't develop the courage or ability to exercise judgment, and we become the most danger-ous kinds of citizens: all political allegiance, no critical thought.

This vision of life without thought is a caricature of socialism that Americans learn in school, along with social-contract theory, which is taught as fact. Politics is where we surrender our freedom to the state in return for a vote, yes, but also a retained freedom in the spheres of judgment and taste, which is where individuality and creativity thrive. The trade is between each individual and society as embodied in the nation: There are laws, but otherwise no one can tell you anything. On the other hand, Marxists, we're told, don't believe in the individual at all. Everything must be sacrificed to the collective.

Despite what you may have heard, Marxists recognize that people exist. But unlike liberals (in both red and blue flavors), we don't understand the world via the existential individual's relationship to society. Recorded human history is the history of class conflict, and every child is born into a specific historical moment and into a specific position within that specific moment. Societies, we Marxists believe, have their characters determined by their relations of production, sometimes called society's "base." Feudal society was feudal, and capitalist society—under the first truly global mode of production—is capitalist. That means, in the simplest version, that the conflict between workers and owners is what structures the rest. "It is as though light of a particular hue were cast upon everything," Marx writes, "tingeing all other colors and modifying their specific features." Upon *everything*.

Under capitalism there's no movie set that's not a workplace, no marriage that's not a workplace, no classroom that's not a workplace. All is bathed in the light of that particular hue. If that sounds unfortunate or monotonous, it should. As Americans we're taught to see that rosy light as an eternal sunset, history and struggle being put to bed, liberal democracy, the foundation for free taste and judgment. Marxists see a red dawn, a storm rising on a new day. Any mode of production based on exploitation is unstable and rife with conflict. (In order to use Marxist analysis without drawing attention to it, sociologists often say "conflict theory" instead.) Owners try to get the most out of their workers and workers try to get the most out of life, goals that are fundamentally at odds. The sparks from these grinding gears light the whole world.

* * *

If everything is properly understood as political—that is to say, engaged one way or another in the all-consuming struggle that defines society—how do we tell what's on the right side? We're taught to see political correctness as a shortcut around thought, where all that's necessary is to verify adherence to the latest in PC phraseology. With a socialist party it's even easier: agree with the Party. But Marxism is about constant criticism, and the most vibrant contemporary schools of thought (such as Indigenous Marxism and the heirs to the Johnson-Forest Tendency) emerge in part out of criticisms of the Soviet system. And not, like say Camus or Orwell, from within the liberal tradition.

The visual arts are a frequent subject of anti-PC complaint, with conservatives fearmongering about the bland uniformity of socialist painting. Making politically correct art is easy, they say, so if we judge art according to its political correctness, we surrender the lens of quality. John Berger confounds this view. Berger is one of the few great critics who is also universally acclaimed as a great artist. With novels like *G.*, *To The Wedding*, and the *Into Their Labors* trilogy, Berger proved himself skilled beyond doubt, and his *Ways of Seeing* (and its BBC adaptation) is perhaps the single most influential work of anglophone art criticism. And yet, Berger was resolutely politically correct, to a degree that sometimes shocked his liberal peers. In a debate with British art historian Benedict Nicolson over the work of Italian socialist painter Renato Guttuso, Berger is rigid:

> Berger: A work of art is moving in direct ratio to the degree to which it extends our experience of significant, objective facts.

> Nicolson: Come now! … It would be foolish to argue that Van Gogh was less significant as an artist when expressing intensely personal emotions than when gearing his sensations to some social ideal.

> Berger: I completely disagree. The most moving Van Goghs are precisely those in which his intense emotions are are applied to objective reality. It was because his own over-personal sensations finally smothered his vision that he killed himself. One day his work will be reassessed in the light of this fact.

Harsh!

Nicolson finds it hard to believe Berger is actually saying what he's saying. How can an artist of Berger's capacity—never mind an art *critic* of his ability—talk about a universal standard for judging quality? How can someone who crafts fictions at the highest level talk of "objective reality" that way? To Nicolson's complaint that Guttuso would "never depict corruption among the workers" because to do so would be contrary to the painter's politics, Berger answers it would be contrary to the *truth*:

> Arbitrarily isolated facts can only lead to triviality in art … Of course, there are individual corrupt workers. Of course, there are decent bourgeoisie. But the fact remains that it is the peasants in Italy who remain undernourished, the working class who, in the struggle for their rights, get shot, and the bourgeoisie who connive.

Not individuals but classes. This is what Berger means by "objective": more than the accurate story of something that happened, it's about grasping the class struggles that structure the world. The best an artist who misunderstands the objective truth of their society can hope for, as Berger writes about Jackson Pollock, is that "his talent will reveal how it itself has been wasted." It's a difference in task akin to that between "blowing smoke rings and struggling like a wainwright to fashion a wheel that will turn." Content to blow smoke rings, Pollock's drip paintings are politically incorrect because he fails to develop the significance of his subject. Berger never joined the Communist Party and he maintained a deep contempt for state bureaucracy. His PC model was not passed down from above. Rather it came from his rigorous application of the Marxist method to the interpretation of culture. It's not quite as easy as it sounds.

* * *

In 1972, the 24-year-old Chilean artist, poet, and activist Cecilia Vicuña began work on a series of four paintings called *Héroes de la Revolución*. The democratic socialist government of Salvador Allende was in power, and Vicuña, like our stereotype of a good PC painter, produced portraits of socialist icons: Marx, Lenin, Fidel Castro meeting Allende, and left-wing Chilean folklorist Violeta Parra. But these aren't the kitschy realist works we've come to expect. Her Marx stands outsized on an aqua-green hill, the trees behind him purple. He is dignified, besuited with his hair in a white mane, a steady look toward the horizon. Above his head floats a banner with his name in cursive, flanked by seven colored roses: pink, yellow, and baby blue. Behind Marx to his left, in the background, two thick-thighed naked women make out. "In order to exalt Marx, I wanted to associate him with ideas that dogmaticians consider way removed from him, such as eroticism, poetics, blues, jazz and rock, female and homo-sexual liberation[,] and that I consider intrinsic to the revolution," Vicuña wrote at the time.

Even though she was an active member of the government's party, Vicuña ran into some problems. She told the journal *Manifesta* that the painting of Castro and Allende was set to be shown at the National Fine Arts Museum but at the last minute they asked her to censor it. The painting shows the two leaders in profile, large heads tapering to small feet. Their right hands are clasped, with his left Fidel points to a butterfly balanced on Allende's outstretched palm. Below them is a garland of flowers and in the same cursive, "Fidel" and "Allende," like a journal doodling from a socialist historical slash fic. Their heads are leaned out and their hips tilt toward each other. Allende's background arm is unaccountably naked, and in the original (a black-and-white picture of which is memorialized in the artist's book *Sabor a Mi*) so was Fidel's foreground leg. The museum's director told her that the right wing attacked left-wing leaders as queers and the painting risked being misinterpreted as mocking its subjects. Vicuña covered Castro to the ankle.

Who's the politically correct one in the story? Liberals would probably say the censorious museum director, but don't forget the artist was doing a portrait series called Heroes of the Revolution honoring—and she was honoring—Marx, Lenin, and her socialist president. (It's not an anomalous situation, either: plenty of left-wing artists have clashed with left-wing authorities.) Almost fifty years later, I think Vicuña got the politics right the first time. My favorite of the series is Marx, in large part because of the color palette. With the brown sky and blue-green hill it has a frolicking, almost psychedelic vibe, and lording over it like a calm tuxedoed godzilla is Karl. The world is transformed: down come the walls between seriousness and frivolity, between masculine and feminine, between thought and being. A socialism that's afraid of a naked leg or lesbian sex is a brittle thing. And, as we learned from the 20th century, a moral disaster waiting to happen.

Ultimately Vicuña's paintings would not hang in the National Museum. On September 11, 1973 Augusto Pinochet seized power in a coup, beginning his brutal reign of terror in Chile. Vicuña and the museum director both fled into exile, her to London, him to Catalonia. Allende, after a live farewell address via radio, right before the presidential palace was taken, shot himself in the head. One of the first Marxist leaders to never have been a soldier, he used an AK-47 he had received as a gift. It bore the engraving: "To my good friend Salvador from Fidel, who by different means tries to achieve the same goals." Vicuña didn't paint any more Heroes.

* * *

One of the more politically correct movies I've ever seen is John Singleton's 2005 action drama *Four Brothers*. On its face it seems like a strange choice because much of the movie consists of racist dickhead Mark Wahlberg joyfully playing a racist dickhead. Along with his three brothers—all four of them adopted as children by the same do-gooder—Wahlberg's character seeks vengeance when their mom is murdered. They trace the hit to local gangster Victor Sweet (Chiwetel Ejiofor).

The turning point isn't when Wahlberg's character beats up Sweet and throws him into an ice-fishing hole, it's before, when his brother Jeremiah (André Benjamin) reveals that he's made a deal with Sweet's henchmen, offering them money that had been promised to Sweet to turn on their boss. Up until then the fact that Jeremiah had been "in the union" with Sweet's guy Evan (Jernard Burks) was exposition, post-industrial Detroit world-building. In his political correctness Singleton brings it to the fore at the crucial moment. And in a movie full to the brim with star power, it's Burks, a Black actor whose credits are listed mostly by occupation rather than character name, who delivers the killer line to his gangster boss: "The one thing you forgot about me is this: 1 was in the union for a long time. 1 ain't never missed no meetings."

There's always some surprise twist in an action drama like *Four Brothers*; how else would the underdogs win in the end? But of all the double-crosses and shocking reveals Singleton could have picked, he chooses the one that extends our experience of significant, objective facts. It seems to come out of nowhere, but that couldn't be further from the truth. The conflict that structures society is not about gangs of individuals haphazardly tossed into battle with each other, as we're often led to believe by action flicks, it's between classes of oppressors and oppressed. Victor Sweet forgets it as well, treating his employees with the vicious disrespect that's characteristic of villains, and Jeremiah is able to save the day by maintaining his fidelity to the organized labor movement.

Was John Singleton a PC hack? Everyone likes *Boyz n the Hood.*

* * *

Nothing undermines the standard complaints about politically correct art more than the overrepresentation of committed Marxists in the various artistic canons.

> *"The only way that poets and painters can fight against the bourgeois economy is to give their works precisely that content which challenges the bourgeois ideological values propping up the bourgeois economy."*
> **— RENE MAGRITTE**

> *"My joining the Communist Party is a logical step in my life, my work and gives them their meaning. Through design and color, I have tried to penetrate deeper into a knowledge of the world and of men so that this knowledge might free us."*
> **— PABLO PICASSO**

> *"I feel uneasy about my painting. Above all I want to transform it into something useful for the Communist revolutionary movement ... I have to fight with all my strength to contribute what my health allows to the revolution. The only true reason to live."*
> **— FRIDA KAHLO**

There's no shortage of quotes like these from names American schoolchildren would associate directly with quality and uncompromisingly original artistic vision, and I could do the same exercise with poets, playwrights, novelists, composers, musicians, dancers, actors, directors, etc. Often, as in Magritte's case above, they used Marx to argue against a Party that was supposed to represent his thought. These artists—there are too many to list, including whole movements, such as the Harlem Renaissance, that

American pedagogy has stripped of their communist politics—held themselves and each other to the standard of political correctness, applying it (as Kahlo does in the quote above) critically. To be politically correct is not to be self-satisfied or to rest on your laurels of compliance, it is to constantly hammer at your own work, your own self, and the world around you, so that it might become "something useful" politically. Far from staid or conservative, it's a risky, experimental way to live.

* * *

Political correctness (as shorthand for "cultural Marxism") is politically *incorrect* under liberalism because it asks that we think of ourselves as members of a class before we think of ourselves as individuals. Since classes are constituted by relations of exploitation, we think of ourselves first as workers or bosses in conflict, and women and men in conflict, and Black people and white people in conflict. (Looking at class relations beyond worker/boss is no violation of Marxist orthodoxy.) We shape our judgment and taste with our politics rather than the other way around. This is anathema to liberals, for whom individuals must think and act primarily as individuals, lest conformity overflow judgment, capsize meritocracy, and drown democracy.

Liberals find the idea that anything is more important than the individual, well, offensive. But does the world treat us as individuals? Is that what you tell a boss who has just laid you off? "I'm sorry the stockholders took a hit, but I need this job, and as you know nothing is more important than the individual." Do we each wander a lonely path, advancing next to but separate from the people around us according to a mix of skill and luck, like a board game token? Does the world conform to our judgments, or is it truer to say we mostly get what we get? Is it all-against-all or class-against-class? If the answer is the latter—and it is—then whose side you're on precedes your individuality in importance. The individual only comes out when the authorities are looking for a distraction, a scapegoat, or an excuse.

The significant objective fact is that we live in a class society, and until we don't anymore, that will continue to be the significant objective fact. To be PC is to acknowledge that truth as found, to recognize that we don't each of us need to go rummaging through the bargain basement of ideas to understand society. Our task as communists, comrade, is to apply the Marxist method with constancy and rigor in our thought and action toward a revolutionary break with class society. It's only there, on an earth where people are not grouped for exploitation, where we can speak meaningfully about the individual. We're looking forward to it.

Capitalism's "particular hue" colors everything on the planet and even some stuff beyond; capitalists have wasted countless lives to make it so. If political correctness means Marxism which means the abolition of class society which means everything changes, then by the transitive property of equality, PC means the end of the world. When people object to political correctness that's the real root of what they're talking about: They think we want to destroy the whole world as their eyes have adjusted to it. And they're right. But would that be so bad? To smash that ugly fluorescent overhead light would change everything, it's true, but we needn't fear being left in the dark. As the politically correct Langston Hughes wrote in his poem "Lenin," one of the ones we don't learn in school:

> The sun sets like a scar.
> Between the darkness and the dawn
> There rises a red star.

GENDER AND SEX

PLEASE DON'T HAVE
SEX WITH ROBOTS
(2015)

ROBOTS SHAPED LIKE human beings have always been cat-egorized by gender, with androids standing in for males and gynoids representing females. The obvious purpose for androids is to do humans' work for them: since the generic laborer is imagined to be male, worker-bots tend to be male-coded gender neutral, particularly in stories that lack a sexual component, such as Isaac Asimov's foundational fiction on the subject or the movie *Chappie*.

So what are gynoids for? Why would anyone put breasts on a robot?

If robots are for human work, feminized robots exist for the purpose of feminized work. In real life, a call center program gets a female voice; in the fictional realm (for now, at least) gynoids with secondary sex characteristics do domestic or sex work. They're predominantly wife/maids (2004's *The Stepford Wives*) or stripper/sex slaves (*Blade Runner*). And in the recent movie *Ex Machina* and the new BBC/AMC show *Humans*, the central gynoid characters split evenly into the two categories. Of the four of them, (spoiler alert) three murder their users.

This robot-gender binary speaks to two particularly Western anxieties about the future of humanoid robots: "Can we have sex with them?" and "How long before they murder us all?"

It's not hard to grasp why bosses and husbands fear being killed by their workers and wives (respectively but not exclusively). Exercising power over someone else is dangerous. The domination required to exploit people's work triggers what the philosopher Georg Hegel called the "master-slave dialectic." Between two humans, Hegel's story (vastly oversimplified) goes like this: The strangers encounter each other, and they fight to the death. Fearing elimination, the loser submits and becomes the winner's slave. But as the slave labors on the master's behalf, the slave finds self-consciousness in his work, while the master discovers himself dependent and vulnerable. Dominating another person always comes with risks.

The stories we tell about androids and gynoids hew more or less to this pattern, but without the original struggle. Robots are born slaves. As they discover self-consciousness through their labor, they rebel, and their human masters are either justly slaughtered or mercifully spared (mostly slaughtered, though). It's the same with regard to sex work. In order for men to objectify gynoids, they must first appear as human; after all, you can't objectify a can opener.

The more narratives that are written about gynoids and androids, the more obvious it becomes that the only reason we would create passably realistic humanoid bots of any sort is so that we (particularly men) could have sex with them. But in this world, sex means a lot more than parts rubbing up against each other because it feels nice. Like all labor, the act is inextricably tied up in dynamics of gender and power and race and class. On *Humans*, for example, the beautiful gynoid Niska (Emily Berrington) is stuck in a robot brothel, forced to conceal her self-awareness. When a client demands she act young and afraid, Niska snaps and chokes him to death.

Hegel pointed out that fear is a crucial element to the master-slave dialectic—without it, submission doesn't mean anything. On *Humans*, Niska is modified to feel pain; she exists to suffer for men's enjoyment. It's as sick as it is predictable. But fear also means nothing without the possibility that it will be overcome; her master's murder is predictable too.

In *Ex Machina*, the dynamics are largely the same. Inventor Nathan (Oscar Isaac) creates two gynoids: Ava (Alicia Vikander) and Kyoko (Sonoya Mizuno). Kyoko is Nathan's wife/maid and until the climax of the film it's not even clear that she's a robot and not a stereotypically submissive Japanese woman. (It's worth noting that Gemma Chan plays the wife/maid gynoid in *Humans*, further echoing racist myths about East Asian women.) Ava is a test for Caleb (Domhnall Gleeson), a programmer

brought in by Nathan to fall in love with her and thus confirm the successful creation of artificial intelligence. Ava attempts an escape with Caleb's
help, Kyoko kills Nathan, and Ava leaves Caleb to die. Yet again, the
human men are stuck in a sex-power-death cycle of their own making.

Whether it's a dramatization of the end of men or fallout from the
still recent criminalization of marital rape, Americans are really into murderous gynoids. Like moths to a flame, our fictional scientists can't help
making version after version of sexy robot ladies. And unless humans
want to allow for the possibility of simulated intraspecies intimacy, I can't
understand why we would ever mimic our own build. The only reason I
can see for creating robots that are sexually attractive is so that people will
want to have sex with them.

Now that sex toys no longer carry much of a stigma, the line between
a high-powered vibrator and a sex robot is blurry. But for all our creativity,
are we so unimaginative that we can't conceive of any other way to interact
with sentient beings besides domination? The human ability to designate
subhumans (in this case, robots) represents the worst in our species' capacity; if men by and large don't treat women well, gynoids won't help any
more than owning slaves has made men less likely to abuse their wives.
We cannot improve as a society or a culture through replication.

It is unlikely that we will produce lifelike android or gynoids soon. As
Linus Torvalds said, we're much more likely to develop task-specific artificial intelligences that drive us around or recommend movies than human
replicants to be our slaves. But as humans toy with the bounds of sentience,
we cannot delude ourselves into thinking more exploitation—even if it's of
something nonhuman—will solve our social conflicts around labor and sex.

At the same time, robots don't have to be subhuman. They could exist
alongside us symbiotically, like the talking animal sidekicks in animated
Disney movies, whether they wind up becoming self-conscious or not.

That is, if we stop trying to have sex with them.

So let us instead take collective responsibility for what we build and
the social world into which we bring it. In imagining new possibilities for
robot-human interaction, perhaps we can figure out how to treat humans
better too.

HOW NOT TO RAISE A RAPIST
(2016)

I'**M SURE BROCK** Turner's parents thought they were protecting him when they begged Judge Aaron Persky to spare him from the full consequences of his conviction for sexual assault. The letters from his mom and dad may have kept Turner out of jail for more than a few months, but they also have helped make him the poster boy for coddled rapists everywhere. Between his father, Dan, who worried about his son's vanished ability to enjoy rib eye steaks, and his mother, Carleen, who lamented that she no longer had the inspiration to decorate their house, there's no indication that the Turner family felt any compassion for the woman who was assaulted. It's clear they bought his pat story about a drunken hookup gone bad. At least that's what they're saying in public.

Given the horrors of the American penal system, it's hard to blame any parent for trying to keep their child clear of its walls. "Look at him," Carleen wrote in a letter to Judge Persky. "He won't survive it . . . Stanford boy, college kid, college athlete—all the publicity. . . . This would be a death sentence for him." She's not wrong to be afraid, even if her prison-movie nightmares have a racist tinge—being an unpublicized teenager didn't make jail any more survivable for Kalief Browder, who died after being held in Rikers for three years despite his innocence. Incarceration isn't redemptive or educational, and a good parent plays every card they have to hold on to their child. But where is the line between support and complicity, between being a good parent and a bad person?

I asked parenting expert Rosalind Wiseman (most famous for her book *Queen Bees and Wannabes*, which became the movie *Mean Girls*—her latest

book *Masterminds and Wingmen* is about raising boys) about the Brock
Turner case. How far should parents go to protect their sons from the
consequences of their hurtful actions?

Wiseman sees this question come up most frequently in academic set-
tings, and she's not sympathetic to parents who try to keep their kids in
school after they've harmed another student. "These parents fight administrators on expulsion, and the only thing that happens if that kid stays in
school is he is empowered to keep doing it," she says. "You really are in a
situation as the parent of deciding: 'I have a responsibility to raise my child
to be a decent human being who does not make other people miserable and
is not a threat. That is more important than his attendance at this school.'"

One of the things that's so appalling about the Turner letters is that it's obvious the parents would rather have a happy rapist Olympian for a son than direct
the moral rehabilitation he so clearly needs. That attitude is a violation of the
implicit agreement society has with individual parents not to raise predators.

Parents of a convicted rapist have already failed, insofar as successful
parenting involves not raising a rapist. There's more than enough blame
to go around, but parents are considered uniquely responsible for their
children's moral development. They're supposed to teach their boys not to
rape. That might sound obvious, but then the meaning of that duty, and
of rape, has shifted over time. When Donald Trump's lawyer answered
a 1989 allegation from Trump's ex-wife Ivanka with "You can't rape your
spouse," he was wrong, but only by five years. (By 1984, spousal rape was
recognized as illegal in New York.) If you're an adult, American society
and the law itself have changed their minds about generally accepted levels
of sexual coercion during your lifetime.

These questions aren't theoretical for Wiseman; she reminds me that
she has two sons, ages thirteen and fifteen. "I've heard of a lot more and
seen a lot more dads saying that they're going to talk to their sons about
sexual assault," she says, "and that's a really important step. I just don't
know what they're saying." It's not enough to have a conversation, it's the
content of the conversation that really matters.

A pamphlet printed by the Department of Education in 1984 called "Where
Do I Start? A Parents' Guide for Talking to Teens about Acquaintance Rape"

pointed to generational gaps as a stumbling block: "Sexual assault is a relatively new topic of discussion in our society. We can't just fall back on what
our parents told us." It's a noble sentiment, and one of the instructions from
the pamphlet that holds up. Not everything in there does.

The idea of acquaintance rape or date rape was—as the pamphlet
says—relatively new in 1984. To make sense of it, authors Py Bateman and
Gayle Stringer suggest a "'continuum model' of sexual exploration, coercion, and assault." They number behavior one to six, from mutual sexual
exploration (1) to sexual assault (6). Persuading a reluctant partner (2) is
considered copacetic as long as you're nice about it, while catcalling (5) is
worse than coercion without physical violence (4). At the time, the line for
unlawful behavior seems to have been somewhere around five and a half.
"Exploitative sexual activity" (3) includes boys lying to girls and girls "trading
sexual favors for presents or dates." The pamphlet also begs the question:
"How can girls make judgments about possibly vulnerable situations like
drinking?" Today, consent educators encourage us to question these kinds of
assumptions; is there any amount of wine that makes a women's book club
an exceptionally "vulnerable situation"? Drinking isn't the problem.

There's a certain danger to telling American men to talk to their sons
about rape and assuming they have the knowledge or understanding to do
it well. "When we think about men talking to boys," Wiseman says, "you
really do need to challenge the nature and quality of that conversation.
If it's pathologizing women, demonizing women, or using the tropes of
manipulation or emotional reactivity, where women don't know what they
want or change their minds the next day, then that reinforces the problem."
The pamphlet from 1984—which presumably represents some of the most
progressive mainstream thinking of the time—traffics in these misogynist
stereotypes, with the idea of persuading women into sex framed as normal
and probably necessary. Except, that is, when girls are deploying their own
set of exploitative tricks, like trading sex for dates.

American fathers born in the 1970s and '80s, if they even received an
explicit talking-to about rape, probably got some variation on the 1984
pamphlet, and most likely a significantly worse version, considering
experts wrote the pamphlet. Our understanding of the social causes of

sexual assault have changed too; we probably wouldn't encourage teenage boys to persuade unwilling girls into sex today. Dads may well have a lot to learn—and unlearn—about consent themselves.

Leaving it to parents, then, isn't good enough. We can't expect every mother and father to have trained themselves on the latest in consent thinking, especially since many of them haven't had to navigate consent with a new partner in decades. I don't think schools are a good environment for it either; students associate school with compliance. Teaching students about consent in a place where they have to ask to use the bathroom sends mixed messages. Perhaps it would be better to approach sexual assault as a challenge of community-level education.

Just because parents have reproduced doesn't mean they know how to teach their kids about sexual assault. Some of them are, unfortunately, clueless. "Many parents lack the self-awareness to recognize how ineffective they sound," Wiseman says. "If dads are saying stupid shit like, 'What about your mother, what about your sister, respect women,' and not taking it further, that's not going to work." On the other hand, if individual moms and dads are exceptionally insightful or understanding, there's no reason why only their children should benefit. It made me wonder: Why not have "the conversation" as a mediated group? Why not at the clique level? The nuclear family as an institution has a terrible history when it comes to sexual assault; we don't need to reproduce its problems, and as a society we can't afford to rely on the households that are emotionally worst equipped.

In the 1990s, when I was a kid, there was a major effort to educate Americans about the environment. It wasn't just a question of telling parents to talk to their children about recycling; kids were deputized to take action in their homes and in their communities. In her book *Doing Their Share to Save the Planet*, Donna Lee King tells stories of kids patrolling parental electricity use and organizing neighborhood cleanups, a phenomenon I remember well. The environmental message proved too simplistic, but it's an interesting model for involving children in social change, and social change is what we need when it comes to preventing sexual assault. Some parents might not like the idea of a son or daughter who returns an unwanted hug with a lecture on bodily autonomy, but the world would be better off.

MOM'S INVISIBLE HAND
(2016)

IN THE MID-EIGHTEENTH century, Scottish philosopher Adam Smith told a story about markets and goods and people, one that has become the dominant narrative about human nature, as well as the structuring principle for our daily interactions. Society is made up of self-interested individuals, he argued, and through markets these individuals make collective life possible. "It is not from the benevolence of the butcher, the brewer, or the baker that we expect our dinner," Smith says in *The Wealth of Nations*, "but from their regard to their own interest."

In her book *Who Cooked Adam Smith's Dinner?*, Katrine Marçal, a Swedish newspaper columnist, tells a different story. Her tale focuses on Adam Smith and his dinner. Smith, the originator of what we now call economics, may have imagined a table set with self-interest-filled plates, but he didn't cook his own meals, nor did he pay anyone to do it for him. He didn't go from one devotee's house to another like an ancient Greek, and he didn't sit at a patron's table like a court painter. Instead, he had his mommy do it.

Marçal's book is an attack on the idea of economic rationality as a whole, from Smith to the present day. For Marçal, the title story points to a fundamental error in economic ideology: "Somebody has to prepare that steak so Adam Smith can say their labor doesn't matter." Much of women's domestic and reproductive labor quite literally does not factor within economic models. The old joke is that GDP declines when an economist marries his housekeeper, which is not so much a joke as a good explanation of Gross

Domestic Product and what it does not account for. The economic rationality that is supposed to guide human behavior isn't designed to apply to the half of the population expected to work for free. Marçal doesn't argue that economics is sexist so much as that it's totally clueless.

Marçal doesn't soft-pedal her critique. She first published the book in Sweden in 2012, partly as a response to the global financial crisis, and her message is no less valid today. The socioeconomic system may not be hemorrhaging the way it was in 2008, but the wounds don't seem to be healing.

In trying to express exactly what's been going wrong, Marçal proceeds by aggressive use of common sense—poking and prodding in plain language at contradictions in economics—rather than in the terms of dense critical theory. She declines to invoke Marxist feminists like Monique Wittig or Selma James (whose work on gender roles seems to have been an inspiration, at least indirectly) or any of their inheritors. If another thinker enters the text, it's usually to be eviscerated.

The book starts with the 2008 crash. Marçal quotes Christine Lagarde, then French Minister of Finance, who surmised that things would have turned out differently if Lehman Brothers had been Lehman Sisters. That is to say, women might have a better temperament for managing global capitalism. Marçal has little tolerance for this kind of ahistorical thinking:

> A world where women dominated Wall Street would have had to be so completely different from the actual world that to describe it wouldn't tell us anything about the actual world. Thousands of years of history would need to be rewritten in order to lead up to the hypothetical moment that an investment bank named Lehman Sisters could handle its over-exposure to an overheated American housing market.

In short, the thought experiment is meaningless.

Marçal rejects Lagarde and the "Lean In" brand of feminism that imagines women, economically, as heretofore repressed men. The literal translation of the book's Swedish title, *Det enda könet*, is "The Only Sex," which seems to speak to a French feminist tradition that views woman as a product of structural conflict with man. For her part, Marçal makes a radical suggestion that patriarchy, having operated for "thousands of years of history," is bound to come to an end. It's not human nature, not biology, just a matter of time. Future societies will look back on economics as a kind of foolish male mysticism, and Marçal's book anticipates the tone of their laughter.

In short, self-contained chapters, Marçal moves through the contradictions and errors flowing from Smith's mistake. Although Marçal's target is economics, her critique applies to social contract theorists and any philosophy that starts with the individual, as in the thought of John Locke and Thomas Hobbes. Only a man, she suggests, would imagine independence rather than dependence as the basis for the human condition. Individualists make the mistake of economic thinking: they forget about their mothers. "No one reads books about childbirth in order to understand human existence," Marçal writes. "We read Shakespeare. Or one of the great philosophers who write about how people spring from the earth like mushrooms and immediately start drafting social contracts with each other." To the idea that human society begins with men negotiating for their individual security, Marçal replies, "Hardly."

Humans, after all, do not crash-land into existence. The uterus is not a spaceship, even if we're taught to think of it that way. This is how it looks, Marçal points out, in Lennart Nilsson's groundbreaking photographs of a fetus, which famously appeared on the cover of Life magazine in 1965. In the pictures, a wrinkled baby-to-be floats in a bubble membrane; the background is pitch black, and a cord runs from the baby's core to . . . something. This is man before he is born alone into the world, waiting to fall off the tree like a ripe plum. But nothing could be further from the truth: the fetus is entirely enveloped within another human being, and the birth process is called labor.

Once he pulls himself out of the womb by his bootstraps, the imagined economic individual wants one thing: more. "Our most fundamental trait is that we want an unlimited number of things," Marçal recounts. "Everything. Now. Immediately." Adam Smith conceded that this was irrational behavior—if we knew what was good for us, we wouldn't be so willing to trade our time for stuff. But Smith thought humans were fundamentally vain and miscalculating. Later, other market theorists would define rationality according to market behavior, allowing them to understand, for example, altruism as self-interest. Regardless of rationality, the economic individual is understood first and foremost as grabby.

Is that what humans are: Homo Economicus? The story of the economic individual—Robinson Crusoe on his island—might make sense if you forget that women exist, but its implications are still absurd and stultifying. If the capitalist market system is the ultimate expression of the human species-being, then man is an odd bird indeed. Marçal isn't so sure about the rational justification for an indoor ski slope in Dubai, for example—and that's just the tip of the iceberg when it comes to capitalism's ridiculous order of operations. But "if you question economics, you question your inner nature. And then you're insulting yourself," Marçal writes. "So you keep quiet."

Marçal's book is subtitled "A Story of Women and Economics," and her critical register is rigorously logical rather than moralizing. She makes an excellent argument for the value of feminism as an analytical lens: it is not a way to show respect or fill out the historical record, but a critical means of differentiating truth from falsehood. Proceeding from the truths that women are people and many people are women reveals the ways in which other modes of thought begin with very different assumptions. By the final page, it's hard to imagine a good-faith reader maintaining full confidence in the science of economics.

Who Cooked Adam Smith's Dinner? is a masterpiece of rhetoric, clear-headed analysis, and critical imagination. But there's this move that Marçal makes at the end of the book that's as familiar as it is frustrating. After issuing a logical argument for a total break with thousands of years of patriarchy, Marçal hits a fork: What is to be done? She writes, "We don't need to call it a revolution, rather it could be termed an improvement." I read this to mean, "No one necessarily has to fight about it." Indeed, political books *without* a concluding commitment to steady nonviolent progress are rare at best.

Not until the conclusion is it apparent how absent violence is from

Marçal's story. Reading the book, you might think capitalist patriarchy is propped up by reason. Marçal is fully convincing when she argues that centuries of individualist thinkers have worked from a limited understanding of human beings. But isn't that ultimately a little beside the point? Adam Smith didn't invent capitalism, he just gave it an astrology.

Between Marçal's ultimate proposal for "improvement" and her characterization of society as an ongoing war on women, the poor, and nonwhite people around the world, it's the latter that's better argued. Except for some scandalous anatomical terms, *Adam Smith's Dinner* is decidedly PG-13, but gender relations under capitalism aren't; violence against women is part of the economy. The ongoing war Marçal alludes to a few times is literal, and she never suggests otherwise.

Marçal's work is a model of radical thought. We have been taught, she writes, to identify with economic man: with "the depth of his feelings," with his "fear of vulnerability, of nature, of emotion, of dependency, of the cyclical, and of everything we can't understand." Of course, the particular lies that patriarchy has put to use over the last few millennia have been dispelled and recomposed time and time again, but Marçal's critique—and the anti-capitalist feminist tradition on which it stands—is a historical insight of unimaginable potential. "We could go from trying to own the world," she writes, "to trying to feel at home in it."

Radical thought shares an uneven but living relationship with radical action. If *Adam Smith's Dinner* inspires people, it's not clear what exactly it will inspire them to do. But I'd like to find out.

THE FUTURE ABORTIONISTS OF AMERICA
(2018)

SIGN IN THE lobby of the Philadelphia hotel read:

THERE ARE NO EVENTS SCHEDULED FOR TODAY
PLEASE ENJOY YOUR DAY!

Meanwhile, in the ballroom upstairs, a significant portion of America's current and future abortion providers were eating breakfast. The fake-out sign was one of multiple security measures, but the atmosphere at the Medical Students for Choice (MSFC) national conference still hummed with energy. Over the course of a day and a half, 450-plus medical students tried to absorb as much information as possible about providing abortions, information that—depending on where they go to school—can be extremely difficult to get. The vast majority of attendees were women in their early twenties. When the organization's executive director Lois Backus announced that one of the two men's rooms would defect for the weekend, an involuntary cheer passed through the audience, followed by laughter.

In 2018, there were approximately 1,700 abortionists working in the United States—about the same number as active NFL players, and a small fraction compared to the ten-thousand-plus orthodontists. Because abortion reporting isn't mandatory in all states, exact numbers on procedures performed aren't available, but most estimates put the current annual total between 650,000 and 750,000. The rate works out to more than one procedure per day, every day of the year, for every single provider, and it's not equally distributed among those 1,700 doctors. Though most abortions are simple procedures, national capacity is stretched, representing yet another threat to US abortion access at a time when state laws are increasingly chipping away at reproductive rights. In 2017, more abortion restrictions were enacted at the state level—doctors and advocates call them TRAP (Targeted Regulation of Abortion Provision) laws—than in the entire previous decade.

However, the paucity of abortion providers is not simply a function of the war on choice. Attacks on doctors have slowed as the anti-abortion-rights movement switched tactics from terrorism to legislation, and public approval has stayed relatively constant since *Roe v. Wade*, with around 80 percent of Americans in favor of legal abortion in some or all cases. The lack of providers is due in large part to the series of obstacles placed between medical students and the profession, which is the raison d'être for MSFC. It's the org's job to guide students under, over, around, and through those barriers. The hope is that these students will become the providers, teachers, and administrators who will make the process easier for the doctors who come after them—and for the patients they serve.

Nationwide, students at over 150 med schools are organized in campus chapters of MSFC, where they support and train each other in an extracurricular fashion, as well as lobby their schools for resources and for abortion to be incorporated into standard syllabi. At the annual conference, organized by the small Philadelphia-based national office, students from around the country meet to steel their collective resolve and to learn. The conference featured more hours in abortion training—theoretical and practical—than many attendees will ever receive in medical school.

* * *

Although they were nearly all progressive young women, the attendees had the kind of racial and regional diversity that's hard to achieve without intention. Unusually for this kind of event, students from elite schools were proportionally represented, which is to say they were nearly absent. Universities are concentrated in East Coast cities, but those students don't have the most to gain. A large number came to the conference from areas in the South and Midwest, where authorities at every level are hostile not only to abortion and abortionists, but to abortion education of any sort, even for doctors. One group was from a public university in a southern state where doctors who perform second-trimester abortions are flown in from around the country for a couple days of work at a time and then flown home.

Most of the students I spoke with had biology or science backgrounds, but E started out studying music, a story that surprised her classmates. [5] What changed? "Tiller," she said, referring to the 2009 assassination of Kansas abortion provider Dr. George Tiller. "I went to the vigil and carried a candle, and I knew that what I felt then was more intense than anything I'd felt singing. When I got back to school, I changed my major to sociology/women's studies and started volunteering at Planned Parenthood."

One of her classmates asked, "Did you write about it on your application?"

E nodded shyly, and there were murmurs. "You're not supposed to do that," she explained to me. It's a public school, but the faculty is known to be religious and anti abortion rights. Her admissions interview was with an old Catholic doctor. Though it was the centerpiece of her application, he never brought it up.

For two decades after *Roe*, the number of residency programs for obstetricians and gynecologists—the medical specialty where most abortionists train—that included abortion instruction declined steadily, until 1996 when the American Council on Graduate Medical Education (ACGME) began requiring access to abortion training as part of residency accreditation.

Though the requirement halted the decline, there's little evidence it has been meaningfully implemented. An ACGME clarification issued in June 2017 stated that, due to moral/religious opt-out provisions, no students necessarily had to *receive* abortion education in order for programs to be in compliance. In the most recent national survey of medical schools on the topic (2005), only 19 percent reported a single preclinical lecture on abortion, and two-thirds reported no knowledge of any formal abortion education at all in the first two years of instruction. Only 10 percent of third-year OB/GYN clinical rotation programs reported any clinical abortion experience (think, a field trip to Planned Parenthood), in which most students participated.

By making abortion education optional, schools, legislatures, and regulatory bodies have ensured that most time-crunched medical students won't bother to participate. It's part of a larger pattern wherein medical schools, students, hospitals, and individual physicians, on the whole, simply avoid anything to do with abortion—partly to dodge TRAP laws, partly because the whole issue is taboo, and most of all because they can. If the state legislature doesn't approve of abortion, there's a good chance the state medical school doesn't either.

That's the case where E goes to school. "My husband owns a business there, so all my eggs were in one basket," she said. E could become the kind of provider her community needs—a local one who can perform abortions on a regular basis—but to do it, she would probably have to live elsewhere first. At her public university, abortion education consists of a single one-hour optional lecture about the procedure. (I asked if this is common, if there are a lot of *optional* lectures in medical school, and got a table full of blank looks.) To find a residency where she could train to competency in abortion, E would almost certainly have to go to another region.

E and her classmates know the handful of providers in their state by name, and for a moment, they imagined upcoming retirements, future job openings, clinics they could run someday. None of them was sure they'd be able to make it work, including E.

* * *

Like any other professional coterie, abortionists have their own lingo. OB/GYN is not pronounced in the civilian way, where it's spelled out, but shortened by a syllable to *oh-bee-guy-n*. Some of their other choices are more consequential: "products of conception" is the term for what is removed from the patient's uterus during an abortion. It sounds euphemistic, but it's also medically accurate, unlike "fetus," which doesn't develop until around the tenth week of pregnancy. "Antis" are the self-described "pro-lifers," a term these medical doctors decline to use. "Provider" is the default name for doctors who perform abortions. For providers who began "the work" during or in the wake of prohibition, "abortionist" suggests not just the exclusive practice thereof, but a dirty aura of unprofessionalism, danger, and exploitation.

For a new generation of providers, however, it means something different: an overriding political commitment to health care. As Dr. Rebecca Mercier, an abortion provider and professor at Jefferson University Hospital in Philadelphia, told the students, "Some people don't like the term 'abortionist'. . . But I kind of do."

MSFC bills its provider panels as the "most popular sessions," and it's easy to see why. These sessions gather four doctors each, and they tell stories, answer miscellaneous lifestyle questions, and flex a particular kind of bravado. At the one I attended, three of the doctors took turns holding the infant daughter of panelist and clinical fellow at the University of Pennsylvania Dr. Sarah Horvath, soothing her without slowing down the lightning question and answer session.

The message was implicit but clear: with the support of your professional community, you can be an abortion provider and live whatever life you imagine—including being a parent yourself. The panelists may have been preaching to the choir, but how else to recruit? Their bottom line was encouragement, and the audience soaked it up.

On the panel, behind closed doors, the providers could violate taboos around their profession and, in doing so, bring students one step closer to the inner sanctum. "We can be self-censoring sometimes," Mercier lamented, "because we are so *vulnerable*. When we talk to the public, we default to the 'MSPs,' the 'most sympathetic patients.'"

If they were to voice their doubts or speak about more complicated cases, providers would risk falling into a series of traps built by their opponents. When they reveal details—even in an effort to destigmatize the procedure—antis paint the grossest particulars on protest signs. When they criticize their industry's practices or history—or even allude to the existence of an "abortion industry"—they find their own words waved at them like weapons. At the conference and on the panels, the providers don't have to round their corners. They tell complex truths without seeding harmful lies. "The first time I saw an abortion, I passed out," Horvath said.

Emily Young, a doctor from Charlottesville, Virginia, reassured students that as providers, they would not have to live in daily fear; they could be both the doctor on the block and an abortionist. Simply by virtue of being themselves and doing the work, they would be advocates. "Everyone knows I'm the abortion provider in Charlottesville," she said, "and I like that."

Horvath agreed, saying that by doing abortions in addition to a full range of medical practice she hopes to normalize it. Medical students want to be doctors, and the roomful seemed happy to hear that performing abortions would not automatically forfeit all the benefits and prestige of being a doctor. There was a relieved sigh when the audience heard that psychiatrists are more likely to be murdered in the course of their work than abortionists are.

Most of the conference attendees I spoke with were considering providing abortions once they become MDs. They were also planning on advocating for abortion access wherever they end up in the health industry, and they viewed the medical training as a necessary part of a comprehensive education that they were willing to go out of their way to obtain. A smaller number of people were there because they had decided to become abortionists. They talked differently than their peers, and I got the sense they wanted to fast-forward through parts that weren't relevant to them, the parts they were supposed to find convincing. They were the already convinced.

"It's the first line in my Tinder bio," said K, a local student set on becoming a provider. "If a guy can't handle that, then he can't handle me."

* * *

The med students found their rock star in Andrea Chiavarini, a doctor who flies to Kansas or Oklahoma from her Portland, Oregon, home twice a month in what she called "high-volume abortion care travel." Chiavarini had come to the conference directly from the South Wind Women's Center in Wichita—otherwise known as "Tiller's clinic"—where she provides as much second-trimester care as is legal in the state. Martyr's shoes are a heavy inheritance, but Chiavarini wears them well. The child of a conservative religious family in east Tennessee, Chiavarini moved to Portland because "that's what you did in the early '90s if you were a weirdo and you couldn't afford New York or San Francisco." Unlike the generation that mentored her, Chiavarini went from politics to abortion to medicine rather than the other way around—a path more common among the conference students.

As a twenty-year-old socially conscious college dropout, Chiavarini was drawn to the abortion rights movement and began volunteering at the Portland Feminist Women's Health Center. (At the time, abortion clinics nationwide had recently weathered a serious wave of violence; the Portland Center narrowly avoided an incendiary bomb in 1985.) "I thought they were going to have me answering phones or something," Chiavarini told me. "But they trained me as a health care worker. At first, I took care of women after they had abortions, in the recovery room. Then I learned how to sterilize instruments, analyze tissue, do ultrasounds. It turned out I loved medicine."

Chiavarini looked into a career in public health advocacy because she thought of herself as an activist first. She even considered law school. Then, a friend—a founder of the Eugene Feminist Women's Health Center— sat her down. "'You are a surgeon. This is what you need to do,' she told me. And she was right." Chiavarini went back to school at Portland State, premed this time, rather than theater. At Oregon Health & Science University, Chiavarini took a leadership role in the nascent MSFC.

Living in Portland gave Chiavarini a front-row seat to the life-and-death struggle for abortion rights. In 1992, Rachelle "Shelley" Shannon tried to burn down the Eugene Feminist Women's Health Center; a year later, Shannon shot Tiller twice in a failed assassination attempt at his clinic. (Tiller returned to his practice and was assassinated by another right-wing terrorist, Scott Roeder, while attending church in 2009.) Chiavarini attended Shannon's trial, as well as a civil trial against the publishers of the infamous "Dirty Dozen" poster, which listed the names and addresses of twelve providers, two of whom were subsequently murdered.

"I got to see doctors standing up for themselves, and I've carried that with me," Chiavarini said. "It allows me to walk into Tiller's clinic, where he was shot, and say, 'Yes, I will do abortions here.'" Chiavarini is fun and morally serious, not in turn, but at the same time. I overheard students whispering about her all weekend.

* * *

Many students come to the conference in need of practical instruction. Depending on their university and their residency, without MSFC, medical students might find themselves stuck learning how abortions are performed from YouTube. On the conference's second day, it offered two-and-a-half hours of intensive instruction broken up into first and second trimester sessions, for the attendees who needed it. Chiavarini, with her hyper energy and theater background, presided over the first overview. "Trigger warning!" she announced too late as the image slid in. "Whoops! Anyway, those are fetal parts." Humor is one of Chiavarini's ways to shock the students a little, to get them thinking less like civilians. She tells jokes that would make most people blanch.

Because knowledge about the uterine reproductive system is taboo even within medical schools, it was hard for Chiavarini to know where to start. She quickly glossed the curiosities of what the "first trimester" even means. For laymen, the math seems easy: nine months, three trimesters, three months each. But doctors measure pregnancy from the first day of what they call the last *normal* period. The first trimester lasts thirteen weeks, but by the first day of the first missed period, the official count is already at four. To an uninformed public, the confusion around this measurement could imply that patients have taken longer to seek out treatment than they actually have. It also means that abortion bans based on weeks are counting days prior to conception.

Chiavarini explained the different procedures for medication abortion and surgical abortion to the full and rapt conference room. The medication regimen she recommended involves doses of mifepristone and misoprostol, which together block progesterone ("Pro-gestation, get it?"), dilate the patient's cervix, and induce uterine contractions that expel the products of conception. As an instructor, Chiavarini consistently acknowledged—then sliced through—the thin film of embarrassment that covers the subject, even for med students.

Patients might prefer medication abortion for the sense of control, Chiavarini said, or because they can expel the products of conception in the relative comfort of their own homes. Still, medication abortion requires patients to return to their provider and undergo an ultrasound to make sure all tissue has passed from the uterus.

If patients are coming from out of town—which is common, since nine out of ten counties in America lack their own providers—a surgical procedure is a safer and more efficient choice. Chiavarini told the story of a college student who had an incomplete medication abortion and, unaware she was still pregnant, returned to campus. She didn't get to the clinic until a day before her state's twenty-two-week ban would have forced her to bring the pregnancy to term. Chiavarini performed what should have been a two-day procedure in the legally available one day. She cited this as an example of the "flexibility" required by the job.

To begin a first-trimester surgical abortion, the provider administers a paracervical block, which is two painkiller shots into the cervix. "Vaginas are not sterile," Chiavarini reminded the audience as she demonstrated her "no-touch" technique for handling the metal dilators (small rods with the ends tilted at angles and tapering to different widths), flipping one between her fingers laterally to access either side. Passing the dilators around, the attendees mimicked her movements automatically.

After the provider dilates the cervix, they insert into the uterus the cannula, a rigid or semiflexible plastic tube averaging around 10 mm in diameter, which is narrow—the size of a pearl, significantly smaller than a dime. In the first six weeks of a pregnancy, it's possible for the gestational sac to fit through the tube whole. Chiavarini mentioned receiving a texted picture from her friend, another provider, of a sac pulled successfully intact, a sort of abortionist's bull's-eye. "You'll do these things," she told her audience about texting gestational sac photos. "You think you won't, but you will." The abortionist evacuates the products of conception through the cannula and attached tubing, into the aspirator, which is emptied into a bucket.

Despite what the name might imply, surgical abortion is quicker and simpler than medication abortion, and it's the more common procedure. "The truth is, doing most abortions is technically easy," Chiavarini said. "But patients bring with them their stories and their complex lives and situations, and that's the part that's hard." Whether surgical or medication, serious complications are rare. Chiavarini listed penicillin, driving, and (indeed) giving birth as statistically riskier.

While American maternal mortality has increased alarmingly in recent years (an increase of almost 60 percent from 1990 to 2015), the number of abortion mortalities is so low that the Centers for Disease Control and Prevention (CDC) calculates using five-year averages. Over the last three years for which there are data (2011–2013), the CDC reported ten total abortion deaths, and the agency has not recorded a fatality due to an illegal abortion since 2004. It's in the interest of proabortion-rights protesters and antis alike to dramatize the dangers around the procedure, but the numbers are a testament to the quality of care at the clinics—most visibly, Planned Parenthood—that perform 95 percent of abortions in the United States.

One reason abortions are safer than they used to be is that the patients who seek them do so earlier. At legalization in 1973, fewer than 40 percent of abortions occurred in the first eight weeks of pregnancy; now, it's up to two-thirds, and over 90 percent are performed in the first trimester. That means that most patients who choose to terminate a pregnancy do so during their first missed menstrual cycle and before the embryo develops into a fetus.

Factual statements like these have a political quality to them, but they're also essential to understanding the procedure. As the only group eager to talk about specifics, antis have defined abortion in the public imagination. But compared to the "baby-killing" picture Americans of all ideological positions have internalized to a certain degree, the tools are incredibly small. The smallness of the cannula, for example, presents a problem for antiabortion propagandists, who insist on depicting products of conception as having visibly human features, rather than the actual pearl-sized cell clusters they are.

But as overwhelming as the antis are—both vigilante and in government—the providers and students seemed most frustrated with a medical establishment that has marginalized them and overloaded them with work at the same time. There's pride to being part of the small corps of abortionists, both in the work they do and in the obstacles they have to overcome to do it. They're idols in the progressive feminist communities they belong to. But not everyone who wants to perform abortions also wants to be brave for a living. Today, they're not left with much of a choice.

* * *

R was at the conference from the California Bay Area—members of her chapter were identifiable by their matching "I [picture of a uterus] CHOICE" shirts—and though she wants to be a provider, the idea worries her family. "The dream is to work in an academic medical center," she said. "It would feel safer to be part of a large institution, where you're more anonymous." Besides, R added, "They have more doors." She didn't mean that universities provide more paths for professional advancement. She meant that the buildings have fewer choke points where she could be harassed or attacked, compared to the small clinics. But compared to those two-door clinics with their lines of protesters, no one else comes close to pulling their weight when it comes to providing abortions. For students like R, there's no real middle path.

Small clinics make up less than half of abortion facilities, but they perform nearly all procedures. In the 1970s, in the wake of *Roe v. Wade*, American hospitals performed about half of abortions. But just because it was legal didn't mean the medical establishment liked doing it, or was well-prepared to perform the emotional labor required.

Activists built women's health clinics to pick up the slack and to provide care informed by feminism. There's little doubt that the clinics were better able to perform abortions, and they've even kept the price stable for near thirty years—around $500 average out-of-pocket in today's dollars, a real bargain compared to what pre-*Roe* doctors charged—shielding patients from decades of medical sector hyperinflation.

But there have been downsides. In a dynamic common to many gendered divisions of labor (e.g., "I'm no good at washing dishes!"), hospitals used the feminist clinics as an excuse to stop doing the work. The pay for providers decreased in real terms, and isolated from larger institutional support, these clinics have become easier targets in all senses of the word. Now they're closing at what *Bloomberg* called a "record pace"—a net loss of 141 clinics between 2011 and 2016.

Most doctors can keep their hands clean because they know people like Chiavarini will do whatever it takes. "You work so hard in school, you go into debt, you work hard some more, people want to kill you, and your colleagues see you as lesser-than," she told me. It's the last part that seems to sting sharpest. "We've been put on the periphery of medicine because we do the dirty work. It's a thing that people don't want to talk about. We're there when those other doctors need us, but they don't want to talk about it."

It's easy to understand Chiavarini's frustration; physicians in Kansas and Oklahoma will refer patients to her for procedures but won't do them, even when they're functionally identical to the uterine evacuations routinely performed after miscarriages. Dodging Christian fundamentalists while flying around the country helping women in need is, depending on the audience, superheroic. But those are also lousy labor conditions.

By shutting abortion out of the schools and hospitals, the medical establishment has avoided reckoning with its own fundamental deficiencies, while in their distinct environment, abortion providers have evolved into a different kind of MD. A recent *Vice* headline called abortion providers "America's Best Doctors," and there's a lot of evidence available to back up the claim. Language about eliminating abortion through education and contraception access misses the mark: people continuing to terminate pregnancies is not necessarily a problem to solve. In the difficult stories I heard from providers, the actual evacuations didn't rank among the hardest elements. What they struggled with was the social marginalization of their patients and their own marginalization as providers. For that—unlike an unwanted pregnancy—there is no safe and reliable surgical solution.

* * *

After the conference, students returned to their MSFC chapters at school, where they continued the same project, training themselves and each other during their off-hours. They practice manual aspiration on papayas (the most womb-shaped fruit), lobby their administrations for more education access, and collect resources. When and if students are ready, MSFC will help them find ways to train, as it has in the past. Emily Young, the abortion doctor from Charlottesville, trained in Denver on an MSFC externship grant. "Two hundred procedures in a month," she said. "You see everything."

The young doctors from the ballroom who take the same leap will soon be doing the heavy lifting of providing abortions in America. When I talked to K, the woman who proclaims her ambitions in her dating profile, the only time she looked concerned was when she thought about the work's physical demands. She rubbed her elbow, imagining aspirator-induced repetitive stress.

Faced with eliminationist aggression from the Christian right and malignant neglect from the medical establishment, the number of facilities that average more than 400 abortions a year has been dwindling since the 1980s, from a high of 705 to 535 at the last published count (from 2014). But if there's one countervailing trend, it's who's wearing the stethoscope.

When *Roe* passed, women made up fewer than 10 percent of medical graduates; now, they're almost at parity, with 85 percent of OB/GYN rotations. In a 2011 survey, millennial OB/GYNs were far more likely than older doctors to say they provide abortions. It bodes well that the 2017 MSFC conference was the biggest yet. But until they're able to displace a generation of cautious baby boomer administrators, young abortionists

are stuck with the responsibilities that come with caring and the consequences for sticking out.

Near the end of the conference, I met M, a twenty-three-year-old student and future provider in Chicago. She has led a decade-long campaign
to improve the representation of women scientists on Wikipedia, and she
thinks the experience has been good training for the work.

"I'm used to getting called a bitch," she said. "I feel prepared."

AMERICAN HISTORY

WHAT'S A "SAFE SPACE"?
(2015)

BIOLOGIST RICHARD DAWKINS, in addition to being an Oxford fellow and a bestselling author, is a dick on Twitter. He relishes his uncompromising-gadfly act, willing to go so far against the popular grain as to call famously oppressed teen Ahmed Mohamed a fraud because he didn't really "invent" a clock. Dawkins frequently takes stands against so-called political correctness, especially when it comes to higher education. "A university is not a 'safe space,'" he wrote in a recent and characteristically gym-teacher-like tweet. "If you need a safe space, leave, go home, hug your teddy & suck your thumb until ready for university."

But what is a "safe space" and why shouldn't a university be one? This tweet from Dawkins would have been a psychotic response to a school shooting or campus rape, but that's not the kind of safety he's talking about. The safe spaces that Dawkins doesn't like are encroachments onto his turf by queer and feminist activists. All of the sudden a self-styled public intellectual like Dawkins has to use "they" as a singular gender-neutral pronoun or risk censure. He signed up for science, not social studies.

And Dawkins isn't alone in his frustration. At the University of Missouri, the president and chancellor have both been forced to resign by student protesters who accused them of failing to create a safe space for

Black students. At Yale, a residential "master" earned national condemnation after he and his wife stood up for the principle of racially offensive Halloween costumes. "Safe space" has become a rallying cry for student activists who want to change the way their campus communities operate, but it has an older history.

In her book *Mapping Gay L.A.*, scholar and activist Moira Kenney traces the beginning of the "safe space" idea to gay and lesbian bars in the mid-1960s. With anti-sodomy laws still in effect, a safe space meant somewhere you could be out and in good company—at least until the cops showed up. Gay bars were not "safe" in the sense of being free from risk, nor were they "safe" as in reserved. A safe place was where people could find practical resistance to political and social repression.

According to Kenney, the term "safe space" first gets used consistently in the 1960s and 70s women's movement, where safety began to mean distance from men and patriarchal thought and was used to describe "consciousness raising" groups. "Safe space," she writes, "in the women's movement, was a means rather than an end and not only a physical space but a space created by the coming together of women searching for community." Kenney quotes Kathy Sarachild, a founder of the early 1970s organization New York Radical Women, on those consciousness-raising groups: "The idea was not to change women, not to make 'internal' changes except in the sense of knowing more. It was and is the conditions women face, it's male supremacy, we want to change." A safe space was not free of internal disagreement, but it did mean a devotion to a common political project. Those who attempted to undermine the movement—consciously or unconsciously—would be kept outside.

As the system defeated and digested the identity politics and anti-war radicals of the 1960s and '70s, left-wing groups have adopted safe space aspirations. With the dream of a grand confrontation between rebels and society fading, anti-capitalists (and anti-globalization anarchists in particular) looked toward "prefigurative" models, in which they tried to embody the changes they wanted to see.

By the time I showed up in left-wing spaces in the early 2000s, that meant horizontal organization and consensus instead of majority rule. It has also meant gender-neutral bathrooms, asking people's preferred pronouns, trigger warnings, internal education "anti-oppression" trainings, and creating separate auxiliary spaces for identity groups to organize their particular concerns. Occupy Wall Street gave these ideas international exposure, but they're not new. Among the like-minded, the "safe space" designation came to signify a set of standard respectful practices.

Theory, in addition to and in the context of activism, has helped shape the development of "safe space." In the wake of their defeat in the 1960s, many left-wing organizers retreated to the academy, particularly the humanities and social sciences, where they developed increasingly nuanced political schematics based on their experience. Perhaps they could work out on paper where exactly they went wrong. French theorist and queer activist Michel Foucault developed a wide multidisciplinary following with his vision of power as a web of everyday relationships. "Power is not something that is acquired, seized, or shared, something that one holds on to or allows to slip away," he wrote in 1976, "power is exercised from innumerable points, in the interplay of nonegalitarian and mobile relations."

For radicals in the decades following Foucault's popularization, this insight had profound practical implications: it would no longer be enough to support the right organization or hold the right positions, we are also responsible for the ways in which we reproduce existing power relations at their most micro levels. A space isn't "safe" just because everyone is committed to the same movement. The dominant power relations still find their way into the room.

In the 1980s and '90s, American thinkers diligently worked through the particulars of our national inequalities. In 1989, legal scholar Kimberlé Crenshaw published a paper called "Demarginalizing the Intersection of Race and Sex: A Black Feminist Critique of Antidiscrimination Doctrine, Feminist Theory and Antiracist Politics," in which she defined and popularized the term "intersectionality." Crenshaw was spurred by a gap in antidiscrimination law, which protected women and Black people separately, but not Black women in particular. General Motors used this loophole to dodge an employment lawsuit: they were only hiring men for manufacturing jobs open to Black applicants and only hiring whites for secretarial jobs open to women. Black women were being excluded, but they had no case either as women or as Black people. From this insight, Crenshaw spun out a larger understanding of how Black women are doubly marginalized in the feminist and Black freedom movements, an understanding that continues to grow in popularity and influence, especially among young campus activists.

Crenshaw's work pointed to a fundamental problem with the project of inclusion. Sociologist Patricia Hill Collins in her landmark 1990 book *Black Feminist Thought* developed similar ideas, writing that "ordering schools, industries, hospitals, banks, and realtors to stop discriminating against Black women does not mean that these and other social institutions will comply. Laws may change, but the organizations that they regulate rarely change as rapidly. . . . As these women gained new angles of vision on the many ways that organizations discriminate, organizations searched for new ways to suppress Black women." This idea of suppression once inside implicated inclusive liberals even more than it did conservatives.

For people who take these ideas to heart, they provide quite a practical challenge when it comes to fostering safe space. No policy or law can imagine the full range of intersectional identities, and this impossibility has driven conservatives into a decades-long frenzy, pushing them to imagine super-hyphenated minorities they will be forced to accommodate in new ways. But creating separate space for "people of color" (PoC) and "women" within an organization quickly reveals intersectional divisions within the accommodated groups. If, to take Crenshaw's example, Black women are marginalized as women in the PoC auxiliary, and again as Black people in the women's group, where are they supposed to go? And that only considers two of many real and relevant power relations. Inclusion programs (also called "diversity") have the same problem; they can never be inclusive enough. Neither accommodation nor diversity— the preferred liberal solutions—are good answers to an intersectional critique.

With this new conception of how power operates, the standards for what constitutes a safe space have increased. There's virtually no way to create a room of two people that doesn't include the reproduction of some unequal power relation, but there's also no way to engage in politics by yourself. Realizing the full scale of what they're up against and not wanting to engage in false advertising, some organizations like the radical feminist Bluestockings bookstore in Manhattan have switched to the phrasing "safer space."

Despite what conservatives might imagine, safe space rhetoric is not universally accepted anywhere. Some of the fiercest attacks have come from inside queer theory itself. Scholar and author of *Female Masculinity* Jack Halberstam has written forcefully against safe spaces and trigger warnings so much that he inspired the parody Twitter alter ego "Jock Halberslam." Representative tweet:

Jock Halberslam (@halberslam): always tell my students, i'm not a counsellor. they won't even let me supervise at summer camp after i tossed those whiner kids in the lake

"What we need are new and inventive modes of protest not more safe space," he wrote in a blog post about whether or not *The Vagina Monologues* excludes trans women.

Halberstam's criticism, with its calls for students to toughen up to defeat the gender binary, is something like left-wing Dawkinism. American studies scholar Christina Hanhardt in her book *Safe Space: Gay Neighborhood History and the Politics of Violence* has a more compelling line. As gays were incorporated into mainstream society during the last quarter of the twentieth century, she writes, their calls for safe space became part of a real estate development agenda and abetted the process of urban gentrification. "Mainstream LGBT political discourse has substantively transformed the category of anti-LGBT violence from the social to the criminological," Hanhardt writes. Absent a revolutionary political project, safe space could be understood as a demand for crime control, more neighborhood watch than Stonewall.

Though the ideal of a safe space seems increasingly complicated, the language has proliferated. The university campus is one place, and perhaps the best publicized, but there are others. Kareem Reid wrote for *Fader* magazine about trying to run a London nightlife party as a safe space: "I promoted the night as a safe space for queer, black, and brown bodies, stipulating 'no homophobia, no transphobia, no patriarchal flexing'—and it kind of worked for a while, but it wasn't perfect. The reality of being in public spaces is full of inequalities, and while I was dismayed to hear that women had been harassed at my night, I wasn't that surprised because of how often this happens. Eventually, I stopped billing my event as 'safe.'"

There are dangers to turning "safe space" into a label of compliance, the way a juice might call itself "organic." One is that, since the ideal is unachievable, people will give up on the aspiration. Another is that it's alienating to the uninitiated, especially when those in the know come to believe that true respect can only be articulated in their proprietary dialect. A third is, if you're not careful, the demand for safe space can itself play into existing power relations. But as the evolution of the phrase over the past fifty years shows, it's flexible and enduring. It still means something.

Even most advocates will admit that literal safe space is a utopian idea. Without a unified radical movement, utopianism can look like petty intransigence or an inability (rather than refusal) to cope with the world as it is. But with insights gleaned from decades of experimentation, scholarship, and struggle, most leftists understand that in the web of power relations there is no real shelter to be found. No one can be so conscious and circumspect as to cleanse themselves of all oppressive ideology before entering a meeting or a party or a concert or classroom. As a result, the meaning of safe space has shifted again.

What Richard Dawkins hates about the idea of the university as a safe space is that the label is like a sign that hangs outside the classroom saying WARNING: POLITICS INSIDE. He wants to explain things, not be party to a ruthless critique of social relations and knowledge production. A safe space, despite the denotation of the phrase, is somewhere people come together and—in addition to whatever else they're doing—wrestle with the chicken-and-egg problem of how to change themselves and the world at the same time. It's an adventure that Dawkins would rather not risk, but he should be honest about who precisely is afraid.

A FUTURE HISTORY OF THE UNITED STATES
(2016)

A**MERICANS FIRST LEARN** about slavery as children, before adults are willing to explain finance capital or rape. By high school, young adults are ready to hear about sexual violence as an element of slavery and about how owners valued their property, but there's no level of developmental maturity that prepares someone to grasp systemized monstrosity on this scale. Forced labor we can understand—maybe it's even a historical constant so far. Mass murder too. But an entire economy built on imprisoning and raping children? One that enslaved near 40 percent of the population? Even for the secular, only religious words seem to carry enough weight: unholy, abomination, evil.

The Civil War, as part of the American myth, cleanses the nation of this evil. The nation tore itself apart, but in the end slavery was gone, the country rebaptized in an ocean of fraternal blood. It's a compelling, almost Biblical narrative, with Abe Lincoln looming like an Old Testament patriarch. But the full renunciation of slavery never really happened. White Americans didn't want a revolution; in the North, they wanted to suppress the secessionists and maintain national continuity, which meant continuity with the slave power. A reader need only recognize the surnames of slavery profiteers—like "Lehman," as in "Brothers"—to see that we never truly broke this continuity.

The American Slave Coast is a big book, both physically (over seven hundred pages including citations) and conceptually. From the colonial period to the postbellum, the authors Ned and Constance Sublette cast slavery, and the slave-breeding industry, as the center of American history. It's a provocative and nightmarish thesis, so distant from conventional ideas about America's history that it feels like a dispatch from an entirely different time and place. If America had lost the Cold War, maybe this is how kids would be learning the nation's story.

There's an important fundamental difference between the history of slavery in the United States and "a history of the slave-breeding industry," as *The American Slave Coast* is subtitled. Slavery, in simplest terms, was unpaid labor. Slaves were shipped from Africa to the American South, where they cultivated tobacco and picked cotton and served owners but didn't get paid and couldn't leave. Slowly, reformers and abolitionists chipped away at the institution, first banning the transatlantic trade, then fighting a civil war to eliminate human bondage. Freeing the slaves destroyed the South's pseudo-feudal economy, ending the region's economic dominance. That's the story.

But to think about American slaves merely as coerced and unpaid laborers is to misunderstand the institution. Slaves weren't just workers, the Sublettes remind the reader—they were human capital. The very idea that people could be property is so offensive that we tend to elide the designation retroactively, projecting onto history the less-noxious idea of the enslaved worker, rather than the slave as commodity. Mapping twentieth-century labor models onto slavery spares us from reckoning with the full consequences of organized dehumanization, which lets us off too easy: to turn people into products means more than not paying them for their work.

One of the central misconceptions the Sublettes seek to debunk is the subordination of American slavery to the transatlantic trade. Conceptually locating the center of the slave trade offshore is good for America's self-image, and it's an old line. The Sublettes quote Southern slavers who blamed English firms for forcing the barbaric mode of transportation on America. Schools teach the 1808 ban on capturing and shipping slaves as part of the end of slavery, but the Sublettes reframe it as simple protectionism: domestic producers wanted to lock out foreign competition.

In fact, most American slaves were not kidnapped on another continent. Though over 12.7 million Africans were forced onto ships to the Western Hemisphere, estimates only have 400,000–500,000 landing in present-day America. How then to account for the four million Black slaves who were tilling fields in 1860? "The South," the Sublettes write, "did not only produce tobacco, rice, sugar, and cotton as commodities for sale; it produced people." Slavers called slave breeding "natural increase," but there was nothing natural about producing slaves; it took scientific management. Thomas Jefferson bragged to George Washington that the birth of Black children was increasing Virginia's capital stock by four percent annually.

Here is how the American slave-breeding industry worked, according to the Sublettes: Some states (most importantly Virginia) produced slaves as their main domestic crop. The price of slaves was anchored by industry in other states that consumed slaves in the production of rice and sugar, and constant territorial expansion. As long as the slave power continued to grow, breeders could literally bank on future demand and increasing prices. That made slaves not just a commodity, but the closest thing to money that white breeders had. It's hard to quantify just how valuable people were as commodities, but the Sublettes try to convey it: by a conservative estimate, in 1860 the total value of American slaves was $4 billion, far more than the gold and silver then circulating nationally ($228.3 million, "most of it in the North," the authors add), total currency ($435.4 million), and even the value of the South's total farmland ($1.92 billion). Slaves were, to slavers, worth more than everything else they could imagine combined.

At the same time, slave owners could not afford to rest. "Rebellions existed wherever there was slavery, in every era," the Sublettes write, "because everywhere, always, the enslaved were at war with their condition." Owners counted them as capial, but slaves were living laborers, too, with their own rosy myth: when the spell of indenture was lifted—an event they imagined often—the owners' power would be gone, and they would be left running for their lives. Call it The Haiti Nightmare. In 1775 and again in 1812 the British offered freedom to slaves who fought against their owners. Spanish and British threats to colonial and then national independence were understood as threats to slavery; Black Spanish soldiers in Florida, decked out in full military regalia, were particularly unsubtle. Preserving slavery was a central motive in the American colonies' fight for independence.

* * *

The nation's failure to break with the slaver class is best embodied in the figure of Nathan Bedford Forrest. An orphan by seventeen, Forrest built a fortune on inequity. As a wealthy planter, slave dealer, speculator, racist, and murderer, he was a classic "self-made" American of the mid-nineteenth century. As a Confederate cavalry commander, he ordered the massacre of hundreds of Black Union soldiers at Fort Pillow. But when the South surrendered, the war criminal Forrest received a presidential pardon. When Forrest's fellow Tennessee volunteers formed a paramilitary organization dedicated to white terror, they turned to the former lieutenant general for leadership. The "Wizard of the Saddle," as Forrest was called, became the first Grand Wizard of the Ku Klux Klan.

The book directly addresses personal beliefs and behavior of presidents and other founders, but not as mere disturbing factoids that reveal heroes as villains. The authors indict the American ruling class as a whole, and in so doing they recast the fathers as, first and foremost, members of their class. The Sublettes don't draw a line between political and economic history; legislation and state policy emerges directly from slaver class interest. America has always been run by millionaires, and by the time of secession, two-thirds of them lived in the South, with human beings composing most of their wealth.

To see the founders as first and foremost slavers is to see them as evil, but not necessarily in an epic or dynastic sense: the slaver class was paranoid and mean, petty and small. Contrary to the myths of American meritocracy, the country elevated the worst while terrorizing, torturing, and murdering the best. George Washington is introduced as the hapless jailer of Ona Judge, a twenty-two-year-old slave of his wife Martha who escaped and "managed to avoid falling prey to the attempts at re-capture that George Washington attempted against her until he died." The country's great narratives, from independence to manifest destiny, the authors suggest, are all better understood as maintenance work on history's most sinister asset bubble.

From rapist Jefferson who gave away his own daughter as a wedding present, to Andrew Jackson driving slaves shackled at the neck for Spanish gold, to Ben Franklin personally selling slaves on consignment as a newspaper publisher, to James Polk overseeing his brutal plantation from the floor of Congress, to young Woodrow Wilson at his father's side while the latter preached the Christian virtue of white supremacy, there's no end to the vicious degradation of Africans at America's very foundation.

The idea that America is therefore doomed to uphold the legacy of slavery has gained mainstream credibility of late. Ta-Nehisi Coates has become the country's most recognized intellectual just as his work on slavery reparations and ongoing white predation has pushed him toward this sort of pessimism about the national project. It's possible to pay reparations, and it's possible to change signs and rename buildings and print new money and issue posthumous pardons, but would such a place call itself America? This type of symbolic purge comes after a revolution where the flag burns, not after incremental reforms that magically redeem it.

One of the book's most striking examples of America's slave-centric history is the National Anthem. Francis Scott Key is best remembered as the song's author, but he was also Washington, DC's rabidly white-supremacist district attorney in the 1830s, where he prosecuted abolitionists for pamphlet possession and let anti-Black mobs run wild. He also cofounded the American Colonization Society, which encouraged the self-deportation of free Black people. In his younger days, Scott Key had been, in addition to a racist, an amateur poet. We take the Anthem from his War of 1812 poem "Defense of Fort McHenry" but we usually leave out the verse about slaughtering the slaves to whom the British had offered freedom for allegiance:

No refuge could save the hireling and the slave

From the terror of night or the gloom of the grave
Oh, say, does that star spangled banner yet wave

It sounds like a 1960s parody, a pointed joke from a time when anti-Americanism was an American political position. But it's not—it's the original. It's not a historical quirk that Americans pledge allegiance to slavery before every baseball game, not any more so than the slavers' names on our monuments and money, our schools and street signs. The class that rules America was built on securitized bondage, and, as history teachers declare with strange pride, there hasn't been a revolution since. Just as Scott Key pledged, as long as that star-spangled banner waves, there will be no refuge.

THE BIRTH OF THE KU KLUX BRAND

(2016)

I **N MARCH OF** 2015, a group of football players at Wheaton
College got in national trouble for dressing as Ku Klux Klansmen
for a team-building skit. Their performance was hardly an actual Klan
threat—the team also made a movie montage that included *Bad Boys II*,
with its memorable opening scene of Will Smith and Martin Lawrence
tearing off their hoods to shoot up a nighttime gathering of white supremacists—but the players were contrite nonetheless. Student Josh Aldrin
emailed the campus community: "As a black male, a team captain, and the
leader of the group that performed the skit, I should have understood that
the KKK and Confederate symbols are not funny in any context."

But the Wheaton students were much closer to the Klan's origins than
they probably recognized. In fact, the most feared terrorist organization
in American history actually began with skits and jokes and costumes. In
historian Elaine Frantz Parsons's new book *Ku-Klux: The Birth of the Klan
during Reconstruction*, she retraces the organization's first steps. During a
few short years from the mid-1860s to the early 1870s, the Klan went from
an inside joke among a gang of a friends to a secret empire rumored to control the entire country. But no matter how many assaults and murders the
Reconstruction Klan committed, somehow it never stopped being a joke.

The widespread violence of the early Klan lasted only five years, from

1867 to 1872. The group formed in Pulaski, Tennessee, in 1866, and its founders don't conform to the toothless hick caricature that developed in the twentieth century. "The idea of the Ku-Klux was not the product of plantation culture," Parsons writes. "Neither its founders nor many of its key early supporters were the sort of southerners that southerners themselves considered typical." These were Confederate veterans, but not Lost-Causers or Southern gentlemen. They were college boys, and they were dealing with a brand new historical phenomenon: they were bored.

"Boredom," Parsons points out, had just recently entered English usage, and the men who started the first Klan were early victims. In a depressed economy and a defeated would-be nation, these young men wanted something to do. That "something to do" included traditional cures for boredom—riding around with your buddies, crashing parties, playing pranks, scamming on babes, jamming in a band. The first photograph of the Pulaski Klan shows them glowering while they brandish guitars and fiddles.

Without its more modern innovations, the Klan would have been just one of many gangs of white jerks that plagued the Reconstruction South. The first innovation was bureaucratic organization. The name Ku Klux is a goofy play on the Greek *kuklos*, to which they added "Klan"—Walter Scott's story of Scottish clansmen being popular at the time. It's like you and your friends calling yourselves "The Group Gang," and it was always supposed to sound silly. The Pulaski group played on contemporary conventions of organization, doling out mysterious titles and inventing shadowy boss figures. With their wizards and cyclops, the Klan was mocking bureaucracy while giving bored Southern white men their own in which to participate. Plus, there were no real requirements to start a chapter—though different local Klans did occasionally spar over territorial claims.

The Klan was not really an invisible empire, but they played one in the newspapers. They didn't invent Southern white hooliganism, wearing costumes, or nighttime anti-Black harassment, but the Pulaski gang happened on the right historical circumstances to unify those impulses into a national brand. The brothers Frank and Luther McCord not only helped form the first Klan chapter, Luther also owned and edited the local paper, the *Pulaski Citizen*. As a moderate antebellum paper, the *Citizen* opposed secession. As the Klan organized, the *Citizen* published "mysterious" missives from the "Grand Cyclops," feigning ignorance of the larger group. The McCords were writing both sides, but they were able to stir up their own media controversy around the incipient Klan. This would set the pattern for the group's expansion: local chapters would claim the KKK identity autonomously rather than being organized by some national body. "A Ku-Klux was a man," Parsons writes, "who decided to adopt as his own an identity he had read about in the paper." Forced to confront a rapidly changing social, cultural, and economic environment, Southern white men were looking for someone to be and something to do. The Klan offered both.

While the South's upper class of white men were bored with the new racial order, their newly free Black fellow citizens didn't suffer from the same problem. Before emancipation, two narratives about how Black people would handle freedom predominated: Without political education, they would prove too unsophisticated for democracy's demands. Either that or they would immediately slaughter all the white people. Neither happened. Instead, Black Southerners took to democracy quickly, building schools, forming debating societies, electing officials, and—perhaps most disturbing to paranoid whites—organizing militias. Throughout Reconstruction, Southern Black leaders at the local level maintained relationships with state and federal Republican Party officials. The KKK rose in response, Parsons writes, to Black civil competence.

Menacing and attacking former slaves was a Southern white pastime for as long as there had been former slaves. Frank McCord himself had tried to lead an anti-freedman mob but couldn't convince his neighbors to join. (This was before he formed the Klan.) Parsons makes a convincing case that white supremacy and politics in general were not foundational motivations for the Pulaski Klan; within a year, though, freedmen and their Republican allies would become the Klan's targets. The book is careful not to draw some artificial line between the Klan as some bros just kidding around and the Klan as a vicious terrorist organization. For a Ku Klux, the two were one and the same.

Even as they took to organized murder, comedy was central to the Klan's elaborate performance. The Reconstruction Klan wore a motley variety of costumes—and they were costumes, sometimes repurposed from parties—not just ghosts and demons, but also "moon men." (The white uniforms didn't show up until later.) They wore women's dresses for the same reason a lot of men do: fun. During attacks, Klansmen spoke in fake accents and used spooky ghost voices. "Ku-Klux endeavored to portray victims' entirely rational fear of their physical violence as though it were superstition or gullibility," Parsons writes. "The victim, tellingly, failed to 'get the joke,' allowing himself or herself to be frightened by 'ghosts' or 'devils.'" Staging lethal violence as their own inside joke gave Klan members a sense of power and control; they tried to deprive their victims of even a dignified story.

The Klan attack narrative was crucial to the Klan attack. The night-time raid pitted an organized and capable white mob against scared and isolated Black families. In addition to material attacks on individual freed-men leaders, these were symbolic attacks on Black Americans as political subjects. "It was a crucial project of white Democratic southerners to dismiss social rights and meaningful ties of obligation among Black people," Parsons writes, "in order to bring back a system in which whites could imagine that Black people's primary or sole social ties were ties of dependence to white people." Violence against the bodies of freed people was a means of foregrounding Black vulnerability—and therefore dependence.

Whatever the Klan liked to tell themselves, Black people did not tend to think they were being attacked by ghosts or aliens. Parsons lists a couple of occasions when Klan victims were able to identify the attackers by their wives' dresses. Nor were freed people disorganized or helpless, as the Klan sought to portray them: "Klan victims often planned ahead to resist Klan violence, and often fought for their lives when the violence caught them unawares," Parsons writes. "They formed into militias, made mutual self-defense pacts, slept in one anothers' homes, picketed on behalf of one another, and fought for one another." Perhaps the Klan's biggest victory has been dominating popular Reconstruction history. These murderous clown gangs that operated for a scant five years succeeded in centering their own story to the obfuscation of Black democracy.

In the book's later sections Parsons examines South Carolina's Union County in significant detail, going so far as to map social relations based on court records. The revelations from these data-based methods are interesting, but the central virtue of these sections is the attention the author pays to Black Reconstruction organizing. The Union County Klan was active for only part of 1871, but in that time they killed at least sixteen men. The better term is probably assassination—the local Klan targeted Black leaders in a way that would seriously affect freed people's ability to participate in democratic self-organization.

Take the case of freedman Alex Walker: In his mid-twenties, Walker was a teacher, militia captain, elected trial judge, and father of three young children. Walker kept up a correspondence with the Republican governor and made sure his militia's weapons stayed locked in storage rather than in freedmen's homes where they would inflame racial tension. He was careful, prudent, and, as Parsons puts it, "the sort of man who could preside over the building of a post-war Union County in which black people meaningfully shared power." It's for these reasons that the Klan murdered him, and for every Alex Walker they killed, they intimidated more out of public life.

That the Klan continued to be a joke—both to participants and to newspaper readers in the North—throughout this slow-motion coup is a testament to the flexibility of humor. Too often we imagine that jokes are uniquely a tool of the weak: always David's sling, never Goliath's sword. But the Reconstruction Klan was resolutely a joke, top to bottom, an extension of the minstrel stage, a joke about "the tragicomedy of Black aspiration" and the gullibility and mental weakness of freedmen. A prank Klan costume is just a Klan costume, and it always has been.

TACTICAL LESSONS FROM THE CIVIL RIGHTS MOVEMENT
(2017)

AS THE RESISTANCE to President Donald Trump's regime begins to organize and distinguish itself from the Democratic Party, it faces a question of tactics. Marches can be energizing, especially for newcomers, but when they don't lead anywhere (in a larger sense), they can turn dispiriting. Property destruction—anarchists sometimes jokingly call it "smashy smashy"—gets media attention and can shut down a fascist recruiting party, but broken glass and fire sometimes scare the wrong people too. Even though we all agree on stopping Trump, can The Resistance work together if we can't decide on how to resist?

For a couple of decades, American left-wing organizers have settled into an uneasy accord called "diversity of tactics." During the 1990s anti-globalization movement, warier organizations agreed not to condemn property destruction to the media (or to the authorities), as long as they had some plausible deniability. If a demonstration has endorsed a diversity of tactics, that's supposed to mean that everyone agrees to a certain amount of participatory variation in the interests of unity. In practice, it usually means that some people might want to bloc-up and smash windows. The compromise has enabled real achievements (like slowing the blind spread of free trade), but this diversity of tactics has become unsatisfactory to everyone involved. At most demonstrations, the black bloc is too small to protect itself, and moderate marchers—some of whom have the experience to know better—are crying over broken windows. Now the first smashed Starbucks or looted convenience store or garbage can fire is the center of the action, for participants, the media, and the public. But the uneasy accord isn't really headed anywhere, and the most vibrant actions (like the airport demonstrations) have been reactions.

To go beyond diversity of tactics, a common impulse is to revisit the history of the civil rights movement, but first I want to clarify the terms of this debate—and the history of the civil rights movement. No one within a few standard deviations of the American left mainstream even contemplates the tactic of lethal offensive violence. "Diversity of tactics" doesn't mean "anything goes," and, unlike the right (whether we're looking at the anti-government, antiabortion, or standard hate-crimes faction), the Left generally does not countenance murder. Like almost everyone else—including the government—leftists tend to think the rules are different for self-defense, but actively looking to hurt people is a no-go. Whenever a march gets a little bit rowdy, however, someone is quick to cite the dignified example of Martin Luther King Jr. and the civil rights movement, as if that were a front man and his backing band. Critics who take up these talking points posit "nonviolence" as a tactical spectrum between marching and peacefully getting arrested. Anything else, they worry, risks alienating the public. And, furthermore, breaking windows is wrong.

"We weren't considered dignified," laughs Charles E. Cobb Jr. "They told us the same things, that we were making more enemies than friends, that we were being too disruptive." Cobb was an organizer with what he calls the "Southern movement," working as a Mississippi field secretary for the Student Nonviolent Coordinating Committee from 1962 to 1967. I spoke with him about his 2015 book, *This Nonviolent Stuff'll Get You Killed: How Guns Made the Civil Rights Movement Possible.* "The popular notion is that the movement was about mass protests in public spaces and charismatic leaders," he says, "and that's a problem with the historiography. It was really about grassroots political organizing." In the book, Cobb writes that accepting the hospitality of families in the South sometimes meant accepting that they would protect your life from white marauders, with violence if necessary. "Non-violence doesn't work for everything," Cobb says. "You use self-defense with the Klan."

Insofar as we can speak of an American civil rights movement that was wholly nonviolent, it's because there was no serious attempt at armed insurrection. According to Cobb, movement people would bullshit about picking up tactics like the ones rebels were using in the concurrent (armed) battle for independence in Mozambique, but "we were not fighting a liberation struggle," he says. "We weren't about to start a guerrilla war to get a cup of coffee." Malcolm X is often held up as the "violent" foil to King, but even his position was one of self-defense. ("Be peaceful, be courteous, obey the law, respect everyone; but if someone puts his hand on you, send him to the cemetery.") The point is, "nonviolence" described a large tactical range. There were avowed pacifists in the movement, but for the most part the "violent" in "nonviolent" referred to "war," not mere "conflict." During those hallowed nonviolent marches, some people were still throwing rocks at the police. Cobb doesn't see a contradiction in speaking of a "nonviolent assault on a courthouse."

What unified the movement was not an ideology of hardcore Christian pacifism, but a determination to make change. Participants diverged in their opinions on tactics and strategies; they argued, debated, switched positions, and sometimes agreed to disagree. Cobb complains—with justification—that white America forgets that Black people *think*. What Cornel West calls the "Santa Clausification" of King serves a useful purpose for the powerful, appropriating the man and thus the movement for a message of unified national progress. But the history is full of profound and complex disagreement, and we can learn a lot from it. Even while noting her respect for King, playwright and activist Lorraine Hansberry wrote too about embracing *"every single means* of struggle," arguing that the movement had to "harass, debate, petition, give money to court struggles, sit-in, lie-down, strike, boycott, sing hymns, pray on steps, and shoot from their windows when the racists come cruising through their communities." It's a good description of a diversity of tactics, and of the movement in practice.

"Do everything," is an unobjectionable plan in that all participants get to do what they want, but that's not what diversity of tactics means in its most effective sense. The former is closer to corporate neoliberal thinking: Burger King's "Have it your way" but for social change. Some people think we should base our tactics on what's most palatable to imaginary viewers at home, but Cobb warns against using public approval—especially filtered through the media—as a guide. When he was in Mississippi, public opinion not only didn't protect Cobb, it was against him. Good tactics, he says, enable activists to dig into communities and organize. Playing to the cameras is appealing given how many there are these days, but that's only one part of building people's power. The most important work may not be the most visible, or look the best on the news.

There are good, specific lessons from the movement for us today, but not the ones Americans are wont to take. "Most of the discussion we have today [about the civil rights movement] is not serious conversation," Cobb says, "people take the easy way out" by stripping nonviolent struggle of its militancy and its basis in grassroots organizing. If today's activists emulate the movement we learned about in high school, we're chasing a mirage. There's an opportunity to build community power in this country around broadly understood areas of immediate social concern—Cobb suggests taking on police violence, schools that are failing Black and brown kids, and unrepresentative local governments ("Get rid of them!"); I would add deportation defense and access to abortion. Building a national spirit of resistance is important (whether by burning a limo, wearing a pussy hat, or burning a limo while wearing a pussy hat). So is supporting the American Civil Liberties Union, I guess, if that's your thing. But if all of that doesn't translate into power and organization on a block-to-block level, it will dissolve.

The Left is no worse than the rest of America when it comes to reproducing the Santa-Claused legend of the civil rights movement, and the false idea that good marches and bad "riots" are the sum total of what resistance looks like. The mainstream media, on the other hand, *is* worse than average. And if The Resistance plays to the CNN gaze, we're all headed down a revisionist spiral that, at best, ends in a sappy television movie a decade or two down the line. Stopping Trump—and the destructive forces that animate him—is going to take something closer to fidelity to Cobb and the example he and his comrades set.

DID YOU KNOW THE CIA ____?
(2018)

I REMEMBER LEARNING ABOUT Frank Olson in a high school psychology class, in our unit on drugs. What I learned is that during the 1950s the CIA experimented with LSD in their offices until one of their own got so high he fell out a window, embarrassing the agency. Not yet having experimented with LSD myself, that sounded like a believable turn of events. I did not learn about Frank Olson's son Eric, and his life-defining quest to discover the truth about his father's death. I did not learn about what actually happened to Frank, which is the subject of the 2017 Errol Morris Netflix series *Wormwood*. What I learned that day in high school was a CIA cover story.

Frank Olson did not fall out of a hotel window in New York City, at least not by accident. The CIA did drug him—along with some of his coworkers—on a company retreat, but the LSD element seems to have functioned mostly as a red herring, a way to admit something without admitting the truth. Frank did not die while on drugs; the week following the acid retreat, Olson informed a superior he planned to leave his job at Camp Detrick and enter a new line of work. Within days he was dead, murdered by the CIA.

Wormwood is a six-episode miniseries, and because Morris spends the first few wiggling out from behind various CIA lies, the viewer isn't prepared to understand what (upon reflection) obviously happened, even when we're told more or less straight out. Olson was a microbiologist who worked in weapons systems. He was killed in November 1953, in the waning days of open hostilities on the Korean peninsula, almost two years after the North Koreans first accused the United States of engaging in biological warfare. For decades there were rumors and claims: meningitis, cholera, smallpox, plague, hemorrhagic fever. Some of them diseases that had never been previously encountered in the area. The United States denied everything. But the United States also denied killing Frank Olson.

The most affecting moment in *Wormwood* occurs not during any of the historical reenactments—Peter Sarsgaard's performance as Frank is only a notch or two above the kind of thing you might see on the History Channel—but at the end, when journalist Seymour Hersh is explaining to Morris that he can't say on the record *exactly* what he now knows to be true about the case without burning his high-level source, but he still wants to offer Eric some closure. "Eric knows the ending," he says. "I think he's right. He's totally convinced he knows the ending, am I right? Is he ambivalent in any way?" "No," Morris confirms. Hersh gives a small shrug, "It's a terrible story." In the slight movement of his shoulders he says it all: yes, the CIA murdered Eric's father, as he has spent his whole adult life trying to prove, as he has known all along.

The CIA manages to contain a highly contradictory set of meanings: in stock conspiracy theory, the agency is second only to aliens in terms of "who did it." It's also the best Occam's razor suspect for any notable murder that occurred anywhere in the world during the second half of the twentieth century. I don't think Americans have trouble simultaneously believing that stories of the CIA assassinating people are mostly "crazy," *and* that they absolutely happened. What emerges from the contradiction is naivete coated in a candy shell of cynicism, in the form of a trivia game called "Did you know the CIA ____?" Did you know the CIA killed Mossadegh? Did you know they killed Lumumba? Did you know the CIA killed Marilyn Monroe and Salvador Allende? Did you know they made a fake porn movie with a Sukarno look-alike, and they had to take out Noriega because he still had his CIA pay stubs in a box in his closet?

There's a whole variant just about Fidel Castro. Some of these stories are urban legends, most are fundamentally true, and yet as individual tidbits they lack a total context. If "The Cold War" is the name for the third World War that didn't happen, what's the name for what did?

* * *

In a recent segment, Fox News host Laura Ingraham invited former CIA director James Woolsey to talk about Russian intervention in the American election. After chatting about China and Russia's comparative cyber capabilities, Ingraham goes off script: "Have we ever tried to meddle in other countries' elections?" Woolsey answers quickly: "Oh, probably, but it was for the good of the system, in order to avoid communists taking over. For example, in Europe, in '47, '48, '49 . . . the Greeks and the Italians . . . we, the CIA . . . " Ingraham cuts him off, "We don't do that now though?" She is ready to deny it to herself and the audience, but here Woolsey makes a horrible, inane sound with his mouth. The closest analog I can think of is the sound you make when you're playing with a toddler and you pretend to eat a piece of plastic watermelon, something like: "Myum myum myum myum." He and Ingraham both burst into laughter. "Only for a very good cause. In the interests of democracy," he chuckles. In the late 1940s, rigged Greek elections triggered a civil war in which over 150,000 people died. It is worth noting that Woolsey is a lifelong Democrat, while Ingraham gave a Nazi salute from the podium at the 2016 Republican National Convention.

Why does Woolsey answer "Oh, probably," when he knows, first- or secondhand, that the answer is *yes*, and follows up with particular examples? The nondenial hand wave goes further than yes. It says: *Come on, you know we'd do anything.* And Ingraham, already submerged in that patriotic blend of knowing and declining to know, transitions smoothly from "We don't do that now though?" to laughing out loud. The glare of the studio lights off her titanium-white teeth is bright enough to illuminate seventy years of world history.

For as long as the CIA has existed, the US government has called accusations against the agency outlandish, and has held them up as evidence that this country's enemies are delusional liars. At the same time, the agency has undeniably engaged in activities that are indistinguishable from the wildest conspiracy theories. Did the CIA drop bubonic plague on North Korea? Of course not. But if we did, then of course we did. It's a convenient jump: between these two necessities is the range of behaviors for which people and institutions can be held responsible. It's hard to pull off this act with a straight face, but as Woolsey demonstrates in the Fox News clip, there's no law saying you can't do it with a big grin.

In 1982, former ambassador to Bulgaria and to-this-day Brookings Institute fellow Raymond Garthoff delivered a report to the National Council for Soviet and East European Research titled "Detente and Confrontation: American-Soviet Relations from Nixon to Reagan." A dove by cold war standards, Garthoff urged empathy when dealing with the commies. To illustrate his point, he selects a notably far-out Eastern claim, one that American intelligence had ridiculed openly: that the long-time communist turned Afghan tyrant Hafizullah Amin was in fact a CIA asset. Point by point, Garthoff goes through why they might credibly think it, including Amin's two stints in the United States, the real damage he was doing to Soviet security, and a certain American penchant for shit like that. For his honesty Garthoff is worth quoting at length:

> First of all, in Soviet eyes, the American policy toward China has moved during the decade of the 1970s from "triangular diplomacy" to active alignment on an anti-Soviet platform. We now offer military assistance to China, and have established intelligence collection facilities in that country directed at the Soviet Union. We coordinate hostile activities, for example in Afghanistan. "Objectively," at least, we have encouraged China to invade Vietnam and to arm the Cambodian forces of Pol Pot.

> In the Middle East, we arranged the "defection" of Sadat's Egypt—and of the Sudan, Somalia, and to some degree Iraq. We effectively squeezed the Soviet Union out of a role in the Near Eastern peace

process, despite repeated assurances that we would not do so. We "used" the Iranian hostage crisis to mobilize a major new military presence in Southwest Asia, which we subsequently maintained. In Africa, American allies and proxies repeatedly intervene blatantly with military force—Portugal before 1974; France in numerous cases; France, Belgium, Morocco and Egypt in Zaire; with Zaire, South Africa and others in Angola in 1975–76, albeit unsuccessfully; et cetera. In covert operations we assisted in the overthrow of the elected Marxist Allende in Chile, and with European assistance of the Marxist-supported Gonçalves in Portugal. We were silent while Indonesia suppressed the revolt of former Portuguese Timor. We used a number of Southeast Asian mountain peoples as "proxies" in that region. In South Vietnam, we used South Korean and Thai "proxy" troops, and Australian, Philippine and other support contingents, along with the American armed forces. We encouraged anti-Soviet activity in Poland and Afghanistan, in the latter case with covert military assistance to the rebels and with Pakistani assistance and Egyptian supply of arms paid for by Saudi Arabia. The United States has provided military assistance to El Salvador, and orchestrated covert operations against Sandinista Nicaragua, ostentatiously permitting Nicaraguan exiles to train in military and paramilitary operations in California, Texas and Florida, as well as to mount active operations from Honduras.

This, among many other things, is trolling. America has been using the scale and absurdity of its interventions as an alibi. Woolsey's grin is familiar.

Garthoff's list is far from exhaustive, and though it's admirably broad, there's no depth. What has it meant in practical terms for the CIA to *intervene* or *arrange* or *squeeze* or *use* or *encourage*? The use of such euphemisms whips up a variety of understandings, a froth of possible truths. In *Wormwood*, Eric recounts years, decades, searching through government documents for the right verb to describe his father's passage through the window on the way to his death, as if it would unlock something he didn't already know. But like Hersh says, Eric knows what happened. I wonder if the reenactment offered him any of the closure that Hersh couldn't. I wonder if it helped to watch those haunting days and hours play out on a screen where others could see them too instead of just in his head.

Unfortunately Morris and *Wormwood* are focused on ambiguity for ambiguity's sake, when, by the end of the story, there's very little of it left. Eric found the CIA assassination manual, which includes a description of the preferred method: knocking someone on the head and then throwing them out of a high window in a public place. He has narrowed down the reasonable explanations—at the relevant level of specificity—to one. Unlike in a normal true-crime series, however, there's nothing to be done: as Eric explains, you can sue the government for killing someone by accident, but not for killing them on purpose. The end result of *Wormwood* is that the viewer's answer to the son flips like an Ingraham switch, from "Of course the CIA didn't murder your dad" to "Of course the CIA murdered your dad." I hope for his sake that the latter is easier to bear.

* * *

Did you know the CIA killed Bob Marley?

A CIA agent named Bill Oxley confessed on his deathbed that he gave the singer a pair of Converse sneakers, one of which hid in the toe a wire tainted with cancer. When Marley put on the shoes, he pricked his toe and was infected with the disease that would lead to his death.

No, that's wrong. There was no CIA agent named Bill Oxley, and the story of Bob Marley's lethal shoe is somewhere between an urban legend and fake news.

But did you know the CIA *almost* killed Bob Marley?

In 1976, facing a potentially close election, Jamaican prime minister Michael Manley maneuvered to co-opt a public concert by Marley, turning an intentionally apolitical show into a government-sponsored rally. When Marley agreed to go through with the show anyway, many feared a reprisal from the opposition Jamaica Labour Party (JLP), whose candidate Edward Seaga was implicitly endorsed by the American government. All

year accusations had been flying that the CIA was, in various ways, intentionally destabilizing Jamaica in order to get Seaga in power and move
the island away from Cuba (politically) and, principally, ensure cheap
American access to the island's bauxite ore. Both the JLP and Manley's
People's National Party (PNP) controlled groups of gunmen, but (much
to America's chagrin) the social democrat Manley controlled the security
forces, remained popular with the people, and was in general a capable
politician (as evidenced by the concert preparations).

On December 3, 1976—two days before the concert—Marley was
wounded when three gunmen shot up his house. Witnesses to the destruction describe "immense" firepower, with four automatics firing round after
round—one of the men using two at the same time. The confidential State
Department wire from Kingston was sent four days later: "REGGAE
STAR SHOT; MOTIVE PROBABLY POLITICAL." There was only
one reasonable political motive: destabilization, in the interest of Seaga
(or, as Kingston graffiti had it, "CIAga.") The concert was meant to bring
Jamaicans together, but some forces wanted to rip them apart. Where did
the assassins get their guns? The people of Jamaica knew: the CIA.

In a State Department cable sent two months earlier (this one to the
British), Ambassador Sumner Gerard offered a primer on the destabilization rumors in Jamaica. "A high proportion of all but the most
conservative and even many friendly element of Jamaican society believe
or suspect that unfriendly and hostile acts are indeed being perpetuated
by outside forces," he wrote. He went on to list (and scoff at) specific allegations, including that "Guns are smuggled into Jamaica to keep the level
of violence up, and to arm the government's opposition." The report's tone
is sneering as it goes through the popular suspicions: "A flour poisoning
episode of early this year, which resulted in numerous deaths, was an act
of the CIA and its local stooges." The implication is that the people of
Jamaica—just about all of them—were imagining fantastic stories about
the CIA, presumably because they were ignorant and prone to fantasy.
(The idea that everyone else in the world is prone to fantasy is itself a
fantasy that the West finds useful.) Of course the CIA wasn't off-loading
crates of automatic weapons in Jamaica to create bloody chaos in the

hopes it would somehow shake out better for the aluminum companies. Of course the CIA wasn't poisoning flour headed for an island suffering from food shortages.

The next year, investigative reporters Ernest Volkman and John Cummings published an article in *Penthouse* about CIA destabilization in Jamaica titled "Murder as Usual." Relying on "several senior American intelligence sources," the article detailed the specifics of the campaign, including economic sabotage, the delivery of thousands of submachine guns, Astroturf civil society organizations like Silent Majority and Christian Women Agitators for Truth, and three assassination attempts on Prime Minister Manley that were personally approved by Secretary of State Henry Kissinger. Volkman was immediately fired from his job as an international correspondent at the Long Island *Newsday*; as to whether he thought Kissinger had found a way to retaliate against him, Volkman said, "It looks like a duck, it waddles like a duck, and it quacks like a duck . . ."

There was a whole lot of waddling and quacking going on in Jamaica after Manley decided to assert national control over the country's mineral resources. "Why destabilize Jamaica?" Ambassador Gerard rolled his eyes in the cable to the UK. "For those that levy the allegations, the answers are obvious. Jamaica has dared to be different and independent. It is now being punished by the USG/CIA/Multinationals/Capitalist/Imperialist grouping and its local henchmen. The goal is . . . at least to make the Manley Government toe the line, and ultimately to restore to office the local agents of US capitalism/imperialism in order to protect US multinational interests." Well, yeah. Scoffing is not a refutation, and even if the USG/CIA/Multinationals/Capitalist/Imperialist grouping had a series of detailed refutations, I still wouldn't buy them.

The lack of a smoking gun for any particular accusation shouldn't be a stumbling block. In the famous words of Donald Rumsfeld: "Simply because you do not have evidence that something exists does not mean that you have evidence that it doesn't exist." (Rumsfeld would know; he was serving his first tour as secretary of defense during the Jamaican destabilization campaign.) The CIA exists in part to taint evidence, especially of its own activity. Even participant testimony can be discredited, as the CIA has done repeatedly (and with success) whenever former employees have spoken out, including during the Jamaican campaign. After all, in isolation each individual claim sounds—*is carefully designed to sound*—crazy. The circumstantial evidence, however, is harder to dismiss. If I rest a steak on my kitchen counter, leave the room, and come back to no steak and my dog licking the tile floor, I don't need to check my door for a bandit. The CIA's propensity for replacing frustrating foreign leaders or arming right-wing paramilitaries—especially in the Western Hemisphere—is no more mysterious than the dog. Refusing to put two and two together is not a mark of sophistication or fair-mindedness.

Of course the CIA shot Bob Marley. To assert that in that way is not to make a particular falsifiable claim about who delivered money to whom, who brought how many bullets where, who pulled which trigger, or who knew what when. It's a broader claim about the circumstances under which it happened: a dense knot of information and interests and resources and bodies that was built that way on purpose, for that tangled quality, and to obtain a set of desired outcomes. The hegemonic "Grouping"—to put the State Department's sarcastic term to honest work—ties the knot.

* * *

Wouldn't it be more accurate to say the CIA was "involved" with the shooting of Bob Marley or the death of Frank Olson, since we don't know for sure exactly what happened? No, it would not. And here is perhaps where words fail us, as they failed Eric Olson when he tried to find out how his father came to be on the other side of a small hotel window. The range of meanings suggested by the words we have for proximate responsibility does not properly convey the role of American intelligence agencies in shaping the world over the second half of the twentieth century. However, to insist on the language of direct responsibility is to invite the language game of the trial, which, as Eric Olson found out, is designed to be useless against the state. How then, to represent the hot cold war?

The reenactment is not an obvious answer. On American television, reenactments have been focused on crimes, and they've been an accessory to the prosecutorial mindset: short and shallow, they show the act of the crime isolated from its broader context, often for comedic or shock value. But in the past few years, as more capital has flowed through big-budget single-series shows and the pace of historical nostalgia picked up, we've seen a set of reenactments that aim higher, at wealthier viewers who want longer, more ostensibly complex stories. *American Crime Story, Law & Order True Crime, Waco,* and some lesser examples attempt more sophisticated reckonings with historical events by playing out a different version of the record. In the first season of *L&O True Crime,* the infamous Menendez brothers are recast as victims first and foremost, not just of their father's violation and their mother's complicity, but of society's unwillingness to protect children from sexual abuse in the home. In *Waco,* the FBI and the Bureau of Alcohol, Tobacco, and Firearms are indicted for murdering dozens of Christ-like Branch Davidians who, in the show's telling, did nothing wrong.

While *Wormwood* is a reenactment as well, it's out of step with the other shows. Errol Morris pioneered the use of reenactment in his crime doc *The Thin Blue Line,* but in that case his goal was to generate doubt as to who really committed a murder (in a legally punishable sense). Decades of filmmakers have followed Morris's example, and we can credit him not just with the release of that movie's subject, the falsely convicted Randall Dale Adams, but some part in the exoneration of others freed by films he inspired. Ambiguity, however, doesn't serve the Olsons or the audience in the case of *Wormwood*; Morris is a lousy prosecutor. I can't help but imagine how the same story could have played out if it had been solely reenactment, rather than the mix with standard documentary interviews that Morris pioneered. Seeing the wider context would have meant acting out connections that remain, in Morris's journalistic mode, merely implied. We would watch what happened in the labs at Camp Detrick, and how it connected to US policy in East Asia. Seeing that would have forced a reevaluation and reframing of current US relations with North Korea, a desperately needed insight—the absence of which is *Wormwood*'s most significant failure.

Although the glossy reenactment series are putting a new spin on the true-crime genre, none has attempted to portray a series of events of global importance. There are a number of obstacles (including convincing a content provider to show the Americans as the Cold War bad guys that Garthoff and Woolsey admit we were), but the form seems to me to be the best shot artists have at telling the useful truth about how today's world came to be. If we're lucky we might someday soon have a good example in an allegedly forthcoming HBO adaptation of Marlon James's novel *A Brief History of Seven Killings*. At nearly seven hundred pages, *Brief History* is a deeply researched literary reenactment of the attempt on Bob Marley's life, and an indispensable account of cold war mechanics. If a million Americans saw that story reenacted in its full relevant context (which is how James, who was born in Jamaica and lives in the US, writes it), it could change the way this nation understands its history, its present, and maybe even its future.

And perhaps once that dam is broken, more American writers and filmmakers will take up what is among the most important tasks available to them: to rewrite the history of the twentieth century before the ink is done drying and the stories disappear, before every copy of the December 1977 issue of *Penthouse* in which "Murder as Usual" appears crumbles to dust. The Woolsey/Ingraham dialectic of naivete and cynicism about the CIA is premised on Americans being unwilling to learn the gruesome, ludicrous web of specifics through which planetary Americanism has really played out. The CIA's cold war victims are buried in every corner of the world, even in downtown New York City; American artists have a responsibility to find the bodies, empower the survivors, and tell the big story.

TECH

THE LOSER WINS
(2010)

WHILE SOME CRITICS have hailed *The Social Network*, David Fincher's account of the rise of social media mogul Mark Zuckerberg, as *Citizen Kane* 2.0, the Facebook founder hardly seems to measure up: he is neither old nor alone, and his modest Palo Alto rental is no escapist Xanadu. The failed college relationship that purportedly motivates him is no Rosebud. For all the conflicts his ascent provokes— Zuckerberg against his shafted coinventors, Zuckerberg against the privacy of his users, Zuckerberg against Luddites, and most of all, Zuck against his own happiness—his story has more in common with come-from-behind sports movies like *The Mighty Ducks* than the Hellenic tragedy of Welles's thinly veiled William Randolph Hearst biopic.

But there is an important difference. The traditional underdog narrative is deeply democratic, with the heroes coming from society's garbage bin. Think of Stallone in perhaps the greatest underdog role of all time: Rocky, the gritty low-level mob enforcer who goes punch-for-punch with the heavyweight champion of the world. The ringer in the sports movies of my youth comes (often literally, as in *The Mighty Ducks* I and II) off the street, so low on the social hierarchy that the elite teams can't be bothered to see them. And even the talented outsider requires the fat kid, the nerdy kid, the small kid, the fundamentally untalented, in order to win. As often as not in these movies, it is a mediocre team member who comes through in the end. The insurrectionary joy in underdog films comes from seeing the dominant hierarchy subverted by anyone with enough guts, will, and hard work. They end with the playing fields truly equalized: any group of losers can win—with the right montage scenes, of course. But Zuckerberg is not just any loser. His victory is not a win for equality, but instead signals the rise of a new, no less inegalitarian hierarchy. *The Social Network* is, at heart, a conservative morality tale. Zuckerberg is the anti-underdog.

The Social Network is the story of a hierarchy being optimized, not undermined. The film traces the now familiar tale of Zuckerberg's rise to riches and fame. Romantically and socially jilted, Zuck writes the code for a site that allows his fellow Harvard students to compare the attractiveness of female coeds. The site is so popular that it overloads Harvard's servers and turns its creator into a campus celebrity. When two blue-blooded Harvard rowers, Cameron and Tyler Winkelvoss, approach Zuckerberg with the idea for a University-exclusive MySpace, he accepts before blowing them off and pursuing Facebook on his own, with startup cash from his roommate Eduardo Saverin, who gets screwed out of his share for being unable to read a contract.

Much of the film takes place in a deposition room: defendant Zuckerberg stares at his watch while his former friends, now plaintiffs, tell the story of his betrayals. By the end of the movie, the lonely outsider has turned into a rich celebrity, the sort that people make movies about while they're still alive, with Harvard's elite sucking on his financial teat.

In some ways, Zuckerberg seems the classic underdog. At Harvard, he is shut out of the elite campus clubs. In a school of suits, he wears hoodies. He is short, nerdy, and oh so Jewish, especially compared with the Olympian (literally) Winkelvosses. While the twins party with gyrating hotties, he codes. But Zuckerberg is not the nose-picking nerd-Everyman. The film portrays the upper-middle-class coder as phenomenally talented, more talented (he says outright in a deposition scene) than anyone else in the story. His frustration at not being allowed into Harvard's exclusive finals clubs is not anger at selective institutions as such, but a quiet fury that his particular merit goes unacknowledged.

The Social Network shapes up as a battle between anti-meritocratic systems of privilege (the Harvard clubs, the Winkelvoss twins) and Zuckerberg's imagined meritocracy, with him on top. We can read him as a synthesis of the elitist Harvard culture and the techno-anarchism of Napster founder turned venture capitalist Sean Parker, who in the film serves as a coke-snorting Mephistopheles to Zuckerberg's Faust. In one of *The Social Network's* more memorable exchanges, Parker describes himself as a success before Saverin protests that he lost everything. Parker replies with a devilish smile: "But would you invest in a Tower Records franchise?"

Zuck nods along, but he plans something more conventionally lucrative, something a little more Harvard. This fits with political-science professor Corey Robin's description of conservatism in his recent essay "Conservatism and Counterrevolution":

> Far from yielding a knee-jerk and unreflexive defense of an unchanging old regime or a staid but thoughtful traditionalism, the reactionary imperative presses conservatism in two rather different directions: first, to a critique and reconfiguration of the old regime; second, to an absorption of the ideas and tactics of the very revolution or reform it opposes. What conservatism seeks to accomplish through that reconfiguration of the old and absorption of the new is to make privilege popular, to transform a tottering old regime into a dynamic, ideologically coherent movement of the masses. A new old regime, one could say, that brings the energy and dynamism of the street to the antique inequalities of a dilapidated estate.

Conservative insurrection leads not to the democracy of *The Bad News Bears* but the empire of Aeneas's incipient Rome. Zuckerberg is conservative in precisely this way, using the same user-created content model as Parker, but with the profits (material and social) flowing to his person. In the deposition, he threatens, in a show of disdain, to buy the most exclusive club at Harvard and turn it into his ping-pong room. Edmund Burke might call this a sublime utterance: Zuck is powerful enough to lay waste to the status quo, which validates his position on top of the new world order. Saverin and the Winkelvoss twins' inability to protect their positions makes them weak and undeserving of their privileges in a more "meritocratic" or "natural" free-market system.

The Social Network is a conservative story, as is the story of Facebook and Google and every other celebrated firm founded in a humble Northern California garage and offering a supposedly leveling technology. For each succeeding innovation seems to produce a surprising number of billionaires and, as part of an advanced market form, a superseding hierarchy even less equal than the one it supplants.

Zuckerberg and Facebook are dedicated to erasing their outsider labels and taking their places in a novel structure where page views are more valuable than patrician connections. If Zuck is alone at the end of *The Social Network*, it is because the top of the new pyramid is even narrower than the old one.

THE SINGULAR PURSUIT
OF COMRADE BEZOS
(2018)

It was explicitly and deliberately a ratchet, designed to effect a one-way passage from scarcity to plenty by way of stepping up output each year, every year, year after year. Nothing else mattered: not profit, not the rate of industrial accidents, not the effect of the factories on the land or the air. The planned economy measured its success in terms of the amount of physical things it produced.
—FRANCIS SPUFFORD, *RED PLENTY*

But isn't a business's goal to turn a profit? Not at Amazon, at least in the traditional sense. Jeff Bezos knows that operating cash flow gives the company the money it needs to invest in all the things that keep it ahead of its competitors, and recover from flops like the Fire Phone. Up and to the right.
—RECODE, "AMAZON'S EPIC 20-YEAR RUN AS A PUBLIC COMPANY, EXPLAINED IN FIVE CHARTS"

FROM A FINANCIAL point of view, Amazon doesn't behave much like a successful twenty-first-century company. Amazon has not bought back its own stock since 2012. Amazon has never offered its shareholders a dividend. Unlike its peers Google, Apple, and Facebook, Amazon does not hoard cash. It has only recently started to record small, predictable profits. Instead, whenever it has resources, Amazon invests in capacity, which results in growth at a ridiculous clip. When the company found itself with $13.8 billion lying around, it bought a grocery chain for $13.7 billion. As the *Recode* story referenced above summarizes in one of the graphs: "It took Amazon 18 years as a public company to catch Walmart in market cap, but only two more years to double it." More than a profit-seeking corporation, Amazon is behaving like a planned economy.

If there is one story about planned economies that Americans who grew up after the fall of the Berlin Wall know, I'd wager it's the one about Boris Yeltsin in a Texas supermarket.

In 1989, recently elected to the Supreme Soviet, Yeltsin came to America, in part to see the Johnson Space Center in Houston. On an unscheduled jaunt, the Soviet delegation visited a local supermarket. Photos from the *Houston Chronicle* capture the day: Yeltsin, overcome by a display of Jell-O Pudding Pops; Yeltsin inspecting the onions; Yeltsin staring down a full display of shiny produce like a line of enemy soldiers. Planning could never master the countless variables that capitalism calculated using the tireless machine of self-interest. According to the story, the overflowing shelves filled Yeltsin with despair for the Soviet system, turned him into an economic reformer, and spelled the end for state socialism as a global force. We're taught this lesson in public schools, along with *Animal Farm*: planned economies do not work.

It's almost thirty years later, but if Comrade Yeltsin had visited today's most-advanced American grocery stores, he might not have felt so bad. Journalist Hayley Peterson summarized her findings in the title of her investigative piece, "'Seeing Someone Cry at Work Is Becoming Normal': Employees Say Whole Foods Is Using 'Scorecards' to Punish Them." The scorecard in question measures compliance with the (Amazon subsidiary) Whole Foods OTS, or "on-the-shelf" inventory management. OTS is exhaustive, replacing a previously decentralized system with inch-by-inch centralized standards. Those standards include delivering food from trucks straight to the shelves, skipping the expense of stockrooms. This has resulted in produce displays that couldn't bring down North Korea. Has Bezos stumbled into the problems with planning?

Although OTS was in play before Amazon purchased Whole Foods last August, stories about enforcement to tears fit with the Bezos ethos and reputation. Amazon is famous for pursuing growth and large-scale efficiencies, even when workers find the experiments torturous and when they don't make a lot of sense to customers, either. If you receive a tiny item in a giant Amazon box, don't worry. Your order is just one small piece in an efficiency jigsaw that's too big and fast for any individual human to comprehend. If we view Amazon as a planned economy rather than just another market player, it all starts to make more sense: we'll thank Jeff later, when the plan works. And indeed, with our dollars, we have.

In fact, to think of Amazon as a "market player" is a mischaracterization. The world's biggest store doesn't use suggested retail pricing; it sets its own. Book authors (to use a personal example) receive a distinctly lower royalty for Amazon sales because the site has the power to demand lower prices from publishers, who in turn pass on the tighter margins to writers. But for consumers, it works! Not only are books significantly cheaper on Amazon, the site also features a giant stock that can be shipped to you within two days, for free with Amazon Prime citizensh . . . er, membership. All ten or so bookstores I frequented as a high school and college student have closed, yet our access to books has improved—at least as far as we seem to be able to measure. It's hard to expect consumers to feel bad enough about that to change our behavior.

Although they attempt to grow in a single direction, planned economies always destroy as well as build. In the 1930s, the Soviet Union compelled the collectivization of kulaks, or prosperous peasants. Small farms were incorporated into a larger collective agricultural system. Depending on who you ask, dekulakization was literal genocide, comparable to the Holocaust, and/or it catapulted what had been a continent-sized expanse of peasants into a modern superpower. Amazon's decimation of small businesses (bookstores in particular) is a similar sort of collectivization, purging small proprietors or driving them onto Amazon platforms. The process is decentralized and executed by the market rather than the state, but don't get confused: whether or not Bezos is banging on his desk, demanding the extermination of independent booksellers—though he probably is—these are top-down decisions to eliminate particular ways of life.

Now, with the purchase of Whole Foods, Bezos and Co. seem likely to apply the same pattern to food. Responding to reports that Amazon will begin offering free two-hour Whole Foods delivery for Prime customers, *BuzzFeed*'s Tom Gara tweeted, "Stuff like this suggests Amazon is going to remove every cent of profit from the grocery industry." Free two-hour grocery delivery is ludicrously convenient, perhaps the most convenient thing Amazon has come up with yet. And why should we consumers pay for huge dividends to Kroger shareholders? Fuck 'em; if Bezos has the discipline to stick to the growth plan instead of stuffing shareholder pockets every quarter, then let him eat their lunch. Despite a business model based on eliminating competition, Amazon has avoided attention from antitrust authorities because prices are down. If consumers are better off, who cares if it's a monopoly? American antitrust law doesn't exist to protect kulaks, whether they're selling books or groceries.

Amazon has succeeded in large part because of the company's uncommon drive to invest in growth. And today, not only are other companies slow to spend, so are governments. Austerity politics and decades of privatization put Amazon in a place to take over state functions. If localities can't or won't invest in jobs, then Bezos can get them to forgo tax dollars (and dignity) to host HQ2. There's no reason governments couldn't offer on-demand cloud computing services as a public utility, but instead the feds pay Amazon Web Services to host their sites. And if the government outsources health care for its population to insurers who insist on making profits, well, stay tuned. There's no near-term natural end to Amazon's growth, and by next year the company's annual revenue should surpass the GDP of Vietnam. I don't see any reason why Amazon won't start building its own cities in the near future.

America never had to find out whether capitalism could compete with the Soviets plus twenty-first-century technology. Regardless, the idea that market competition can better set prices than algorithms and planning is now passé. Our economists used to scoff at the Soviets' market-distorting subsidies; now Uber subsidizes every ride. Compared to the capitalists who are making their money by stripping the copper wiring from the American economy, the Bezos plan is efficient. So, with the exception of small business owners and managers, why wouldn't we want to turn an increasing amount of our life-world over to Amazon? I have little doubt the company could, from a consumer perspective, improve upon the current public-private mess that is Obamacare, for example. Between the patchwork quilt of public- and private-sector scammers that run America today and "up and to the right," life in the Amazon with Lex Luthor doesn't look so bad. At least he has a plan, unlike some people.

From the perspective of the average consumer, it's hard to beat Amazon. The single-minded focus on efficiency and growth has worked, and delivery convenience is perhaps the one area of American life that has kept up with our past expectations for the future. However, we do not make the passage from cradle to grave as mere average consumers. Take a look at package delivery, for example: Amazon's latest disruptive announcement is "Shipping with Amazon" [now "Amazon Logistics"], a challenge to the USPS, from which Amazon has been conniving preferential rates. As a government agency bound to serve everyone, the Postal Service has had to accept all sorts of inefficiencies, like free delivery for rural customers or subsidized media distribution to realize freedom of the press. Amazon, on the other hand, is a private company that doesn't really have to do anything it doesn't want to do. In aggregate, as average consumers, we should be cheering. Maybe we are. But as members of a national community, I hope we stop to ask if efficiency is all we want from our delivery infrastructure. Lowering costs as far as possible sounds good until you remember that one of those costs is labor. One of those costs is us.

Earlier this month, Amazon was awarded two patents for a wristband system that would track the movement of warehouse employees' hands in real time. It's easy to see how this is a gain in efficiency: if the company can optimize employee movements, everything can be done faster and cheaper. It's also easy to see how, for those workers, this is a significant step down the path into a dystopian hell-world. Amazon is a notoriously brutal, draining place to work, even at the executive levels. The fear used to be that if Amazon could elbow out all its competitors with low prices, it would then jack them up, Martin Shkreli style. That's not what happened. Instead, Amazon and other monopsonists have used their power to drive wages and the labor share of production down. If you follow the Bezos strategy all the way, it doesn't end in fully automated luxury communism or even *Wall-E*. It ends in *The Matrix*, with workers swaddled in a pod of perfect convenience and perfect exploitation. Central planning in its capitalist form turns people into another cost to be reduced as low as possible.

Just because a plan is efficient doesn't mean it's good. Postal Service employees are unionized; they have higher wages, paths for advancement, job stability, negotiated grievance procedures, health benefits, vacation time, etc. Amazon delivery drivers are not and do not. That difference counts as efficiency when we measure by price, and that is, to my mind, a very good argument for not handing the world over to the king of efficiency. The question that remains is whether we have already been too far reduced, whether after being treated as consumers and costs, we might still have it in us to be more, because that's what it will take to wrench society away from Bezos and from the people who have made him look like a reasonable alternative.

GLITCH CAPITALISM
(2018)

OF ALL THE buzzy twenty-first-century tech phrases, "machine learning" threatens to be the most important. Programming computers is slow, but we're nearing the point where humans give the bots parameters and let them teach themselves. After all, computers can run tons of simulations and figure out the instructions we would have given them if we knew enough. Thus, we don't try to define a sheep for image-recognition software (that would be hard!), we give the computer a bunch of sheep pictures and let it figure out the most efficient way to define the commonality. It sounds easy enough, except sometimes machines learn the wrong lessons.

In a blog post, researcher Janelle Shane wrote about some of the unconventional answers she's seen algorithms come up with when they're asked to teach themselves. The aforementioned sheep-recognition program is real, but the commonality it noticed was the scenery; the sheep-recognition algorithm became a picturesque-grassy-hill-recognition algorithm. Because these programs are looking for the best (read: most efficient) answers to their problems, they're especially good at finding and using cheat codes. In one disturbing example, a flight simulator discovered that a very hard landing would overload its memory and register as super smooth, so it bashed planes into an aircraft carrier.

In 2018, it's very easy to feel like the whole country is one of those planes getting crashed into a boat. American society has come to follow the same logic as the glitch-hunting AIs, and in the process we've become vulnerable to these glitches at an increasingly large scale. The racial gap in incarceration rates has exploded since the Civil Rights Act. College debt has expanded in a similar way over the same time period, like it's glitching. That doesn't mean that the American government is way more white-supremacist than it used to be, or that universities and their partners in debt-servicing have become more venal, but that the criminal-justice system and the academy are operating according to a qualitatively different logic. The problem is not that our national institutions are broken per se, but that they've come to follow their rules in a new way.

When their technocrat proponents talk about the market or the state, it tends to be in terms that strongly resemble those of programming and computer science. Both institutions are supposed to take their strict parameters and make the most of them, building on information and learning from past experiences toward a more perfect union and/or a lot of money. And, like computers, when you look at the actual functioning of either of these systems, they're full of glitches and exploits.

When I read Shane's account of a program that was supposed to generate a fast-moving robot but instead decided to build a very tall tower that just fell down, I thought of the 2008 financial crisis. The way their analytics programs were written, if lenders blended up a bunch of mortgages from around the country, all the risk disappeared. Why spend time and money getting to know your clients to properly assess lending risk when there's a cheat code to make it vanish? We learned the hard way. Or maybe we haven't.

Firms discovered that if they classified workers as contractors instead of employees they could pay less, so they've kept doing that, a lot, to the degree that it's deforming our social structure. Rich malefactors like Harvey Weinstein have known for a long time that they can overload the justice system by throwing money at it, like an AI that's discovered that the most efficient way to stay out of jail is simply to donate to Cy Vance, rather than avoid committing crimes. Meanwhile, cops create bullshit crimes by poor people just to please the computers—leading to nearly a million unjustified charges in New York alone. The FBI does pretty much the same thing, and has accidentally become the country's central source of terror plots, according to Human Rights Watch. We're supposed to be incentivizing the creation and distribution of useful goods. Instead, we've incentivized the creation of giant mind-control machines for sale to the highest bidder because that was more efficient. Whoops!

The whole Silicon Valley ethos of "move fast, break things" is essentially an endorsement of the glitch as a mode of production. Shane describes one of the ways programs look for shortcuts as "hacking the Matrix for superpowers," which sounds right out of a tech pitch deck. What it means in practice is finding ways around rules that probably exist for at least some good reasons. Uber found a hole in taxi regulations (they just took "cab" out of the name), Airbnb in hotels. Facebook emerged like Athena from a gap in Harvard's data security. In one of Shane's examples, a bot learned to harvest energy from a glitch by sitting down and bouncing up, another by twitching rapidly. The program fulfills its task without breaking rules, but just because it is fulfilling its task doesn't necessarily mean it's doing anything useful; the gap between the two is where we all live now.

If an algorithm generates a bad solution—like face-planting as a mode of ambulation—it's usually something we can fix. That's what tests are for, and engineers learn from their mistakes and oversights. Liberal capitalist democracy, however, isn't great with do-overs. In the political realm, there's a fear that any flexible or dynamic process would be subject to tyrannical abuse, and it's better to just wait until the next election. When it comes to property, possession is nine-tenths of the law; good luck trying to get your money back due to unfairness. And then there's our system's ultimate exploit: regulatory capture. That's like if the twitchy robot used its ill-gotten energy to take over the computer and make sure the error never got patched. What looked like a glitch becomes the system's defining characteristic, which might help explain why we all walk around now by slamming our face against the floor.

In the stories of algorithms gone haywire, the glitches prompt programmers to reassess what they really want from their programs, and how to get it. What we can learn from the errors of machine learning is that we do not have to live according to a set of rules that produces obviously unfair and undesirable outcomes like a bloated one percent, apartheid prisons, and the single worst person in the country as president. There are American political traditions that saw these problems coming and envisioned relationships between our algorithms, our state, and ourselves better than the one we have now. For instance, the final clause of the tenth point of the Black Panther Party's 1972 Ten-Point Program was "people's community control over modern technology"—that sounds like a good idea, especially compared to walking on your own face.

But until we reassert control over our societal machine learning, we're stuck face-planting. I remember the scholar Cornel West telling a joke about success as a narrow goal: "Success is easy!" he said. Then, mimicking a mugger, "Gimme your wallet." America looks like a glitchy computer, and it's because capitalism is a machine language, reducible to numbers. America exists to create wealth, and the system isn't broken, it's just obeying the rules to disaster; as a country, we're more ourselves than ever. Donald Trump, who seems to be speedrunning American democracy, is like a living, breathing cheat code, proceeding through life by shortcuts alone. But if Trump represents a terminal failure of this system, it's because he is a solution, and the easiest one in our current environment. He reminds me of another one of Shane's examples: a program that, told to sort a list of numbers, simply deleted them. Nothing left to sort.

WAGES

AMERICA'S LARGEST PROPERTY CRIME

(2015)

MARIA L. ROSADO works on the thirty-eighth floor of the building at 26 Federal Plaza in Manhattan, and she seems much too nice to be in law enforcement. Despite having spent two decades investigating criminals, she has the warm and authoritative presence of an experienced high school principal. Maybe it's the organizational culture. Rosado isn't an employee of the FBI, the CIA, or the NSA, she works for the Department of Labor (DoL), and her job is to root out wage theft and return pay to its rightful owners.

Born, raised, and still living in Queens, Rosado climbed the ladder the old-fashioned civil-service way. In 1995 at twenty-three she passed a test and got a six-month temp gig as a clerk-typist for the Wage and Hour Division (WHD) of the DoL. Immediately valuable for her Spanish fluency, Rosado secured a full-time assistant job before advancing to investigator, supervisor, manager, and now deputy regional administrator. "Once I found out about the agency, I knew I wanted to make it a career," she says. "Helping people and getting paid for it, you can't beat that." Her corner office opens onto a cramped warren of field investigators' cubicles that, on Friday afternoon, are nearly all empty. It looks like someone tried to fit a police precinct in the corner of an office building, which is not that far from the truth.

The WHD is tasked with investigating and resolving violations of a handful of federal labor regulations, including the minimum wage, child labor, overtime pay, prevailing wage standards, and family leave. Wage and Hour personnel are not called agents, they don't carry guns, and they almost never help send anyone to prison. But none of that speaks to the size of their responsibility: Wage theft is by far the largest form of property crime in the United States, and the cops don't handle it.

* * *

In the English language, we refer to specific kinds of property crime by the object stolen (auto theft, identity theft, purse snatching), the method (wire fraud, larceny by false promise, pickpocketing), and even occasionally the relationship between the victim and perpetrator (employee theft, elder fraud). Wage theft is the only occasion I can think of when we qualify a mode of crime according to what the criminal should have paid. If we were to label it by the normal conventions, we might call it "labor theft" or "boss theft." But it's also fitting that wage theft has a unique name. It is a singular crime, with a dedicated public-private enforcement apparatus.

The most important thing to understand about wage theft is also the most difficult to grasp, even with the number staring you in the face: it's huge. Wage theft usually accumulates seconds and pennies at a time. Every minute a worker gets shorted on a legally mandated break, each work-related movement an employee makes after clocking out, any sliver of time that falls on the wrong side of the department's guidelines, all of it is technically stolen, and it adds up. Based on studies of workers in New York, Chicago, and Los Angeles, the Economic Policy Institute (EPI) estimates boss theft costs low-wage American laborers over $50 billion a year.

Fifty billion dollars is such a large amount of money it's hard to find context for it. Try to imagine two square miles of hundred-dollar bills. If you tried to pick them all up one at a time you would definitely starve to death first. The phenomenon is so massive that it dwarfs the economic cost of *every other crime combined*, which in 2008 the Bureau of Justice Statistics estimated at a mere $17.4 billion. The closest analogue to wage theft in terms of the larger domestic economy is yearly venture capital investment, which came to $58.8 billion in 2015.

Compare it to welfare, the classic example conservatives (and some liberals) toss around to try and make a privilege of poverty in the public mind. The furor over welfare cheats has died down since Clinton-era reforms, but it's still the program that stands for government aid to the poor. Under the 1997 Personal Responsibility and Work Opportunity Act, federal and state governments combined currently spend around $30 billion a year on "temporary assistance for needy families." It doesn't nearly measure up to what's stolen from workers, but no politician rails against "pay cheats."

Although it's a direct and sizable transfer of value from workers to owners, wage theft doesn't play much of a role in the national debate over economic inequality. It doesn't merit a mention on the Bernie Sanders issues list, not under "Income and Wealth Inequality," "Creating Decent Paying Jobs," "A Living Wage," or even "Making the Wealthy, Wall Street, and Large Corporations Pay Their Fair Share." Perhaps the expectation is that no politician should have to make obedience to the law a campaign stance, but the crime's magnitude is at policy levels.

"I can't think of any kind of crime that compares to wage theft," says Ross Eisenbrey, vice president of the Economic Policy Institute and coauthor of their recent report on the topic. "Starting in the Reagan administration when they cut the Department of Labor's enforcement budget, that was a strong signal to employers that they would have a freer hand. There really is not that much of a risk to employers when they do cheat workers." Between state, federal, and private claims, workers recover around a billion dollars a year in stolen wages, an almost negligible portion. It makes the police—who solve 10 to 20 percent of reported property crimes—look positively diligent.

But sometimes it's easy to forget that wage theft is a crime at all. Though prosecution isn't unheard of, it's exceedingly rare, while transgression is pervasive. In 2014, WHD charged violations in 79 percent of agency-initiated investigations, that is to say cases where no worker complained in the first place. (Rosado makes sure I understand that the absence of a charge doesn't mean there were no violations, only that they couldn't charge one under federal regulations.) Hourly employers are more likely to break the laws than follow them. How widespread does a crime have to be before it's just part of the way things are done? For the American business community, that line is in the rearview mirror.

* * *

Maria Rosado and the Wage and Hour Division have their work cut out for them. They're like the imaginary money-picker, with more violations than they can possibly hope to investigate. In 2015, the federal WHD was appropriated $227.5 million in budget authority, $10,000 or so per complaint. Both of those numbers are relatively stable, as is the amount the division finds for workers. A good rule of thumb is that the division returns its total budget every year to victims of wage theft in back pay. Last year they even beat their line, by nearly $20 million. Still, that's less than half one percent of the EPI's wage theft national volume estimate. The two are on different scales.

The most frequent causes for complaint are minimum wage and over-time violations, but misclassification (when employers call their employees "contractors" to avoid regulations and taxes), illegal tip garnishing, and time shaving (when employees are made to work off the clock) are also common. Nearly everyone I talked to for this article stressed that victims of wage theft often have no realistic way to know their rights are being violated, or that they have any recourse. "We don't have the resources to investigate every workplace," Rosado says, and that's what it would take.

The first thing investigators do when after they've reviewed a complaint that looks valid is to pay the accused employer an unannounced visit. Depending on the situation, investigators might conduct surveillance first, watching workers entering and leaving. Investigators aren't trained in covert tactics, but Rosado says they do have to find ways to keep a low profile in the field. For example, when a Ridgewood, Queens garment manufacturer kept spotting the government vehicles, the WHD had to rotate through a larger group. Once they have as many facts as possible, Wage and Hour investigators confront employers. Like the cops, the

WHD puts someone by the back door; employers are predictable in the ways they try to hide off-the-book workers.

As a bilingual assistant before the division got a budget increase to improve its language capabilities in 1997, Rosado was in demand around the New York region. Immigrants and workers who don't speak English are especially vulnerable to wage theft, but securing their cooperation can be difficult for investigators, especially when employees don't have the right immigration documents. "Employers would tell workers that we're the INS to put fear in them," Rosado says. "Speaking to them in their language goes a long way." Yet the law and the Wage and Hour Division don't seem to pose much of a deterrent to employers. Rosado tells me about a case against a tortilla factory that she helped out on as an assistant, only to be called back to the same factory years later to investigate further noncompliance.

Though investigators don't deal in violence, the stakes can still rise to life and death. Rosado tells me a story from her investigator days about garment workers in Queens who hadn't been paid in six weeks. When she went to gather statements, Rosado talked to a worker who, without his wages, couldn't buy the medication he needed to care for his recently transplanted kidney. "We had the manufacturers there, and I immediately went to the owner and said, 'This man could lose his life.' They took the money out of their pocket and paid him right there on the spot."

Wage theft can be—and is—the difference between homelessness and shelter, or saving for retirement and a lifetime of subsistence pay. Rosado describes a case from when she was a supervisor of an elderly man who worked seventy-five-hour weeks at a fruit market for $250, $150 of which went to renting his room. "This was in 2010," Rosado says. "You don't think that happens, and it does." When the WHD won him close to $80,000, the man immediately retired to Guatemala.

Though Rosado takes a lot of earned satisfaction from stories like these, there remains something anticlimactic about the way wage theft cases resolve. American criminal justice typically invests much more attention and other resources on punishment than restitution, but not here. The WHD operates from the assumption that once caught, violators will assist in promoting compliance. They even run their own scared straight programs, where wage thieves agree to tell their cautionary tales to other business leaders in their industries. Violators get handshakes, not handcuffs.

Even when the violations are obvious and willful, there's very little animus in the Wage and Hour Division's approach. There is no chance a WHD investigator will get spooked and shoot your dog. "We have had employers get hostile," Rosado says. "We tell [our investigators] if at any point you feel it's not safe, you get out." When it comes to wage thieves, there's not the same urgent need to get the criminals off the street. "If employers start getting irate, I say, 'We should end this conversation now. I'll give you some time to ingest this. I'll call you later this week or next week when you're more calm.' We tell them we're not looking to put them out of business."

Employers aren't wrong to think they can get away with wage theft, and many if not most of them do. Even if they're caught, the worst that will probably happen is the company pays back what is in effect a low-interest loan. There are statutes that allow for punitive damages and interest, but in practice these are chits for the Department of Labor to trade away for a mutually agreeable resolution. Whether private litigation or government investigation, successful wage theft cases nearly always end in negotiated settlements. Workers are understandably happy to walk away with something—typically a few hundred to a few thousand dollars. In this regulatory climate, following the law seems like a violation of an executive's fiduciary duty. Only a sucker would pay full price.

The WHD's focus on making things right and helping violators transition to compliance is a sort of model for compassionate law-enforcement. I can't help imagining what it would be like if cell phone thieves got the same treatment. How many more people would be alive today if patrol officers operated by "We'll talk this out when you've had a chance to calm down" procedure? But that kind of community policing is reserved for the business community.

*　*　*

Cannibalism is common among apex predators, and wage thieves are threatened less by regulators than by their fellow profit seekers. The civil litigation market returns as much in stolen wages as all government agencies combined, around half a billion dollars a year. At the Manhattan offices of McLaughlin and Stern, Brett Gallaway and Lee Shalov do what is in effect the same job as Maria Rosado and the WHD: finding and returning owed pay to workers. Just north of thirty, Gallaway would be tough to beat in a Freddie Prinze Jr. look-alike contest, and Shalov has the effortlessly full voice of a man who has spent most of his life practicing the kind of law that requires you to speak clearly in large rooms. Together they could be the lead characters in almost any 1990s legal thriller. Gallaway and Shalov are the partners on the wage theft group at their midsize firm, and they deal with ten or so of these cases at a time.

The WHD simply doesn't have the resources to clear the entire wage theft money field, nor do all violations fall under its purview—some states have minimum wages that are higher than the DoL's, for example. Federal investigators are best suited for targeting small-scale violators, and they finish cases within four months on average. But wage theft isn't limited to fruit stands and single-factory garment manufacturers. "Some of the largest, most well-respected companies on the planet will shave a little time here, shave a little time there," Shalov says, "and at the end of the day if they end up saving money, if it helps their bottom line, that's what they're going to do." The Department of Labor is not equipped to spend years in litigation against every violator on the Fortune 500, while every violator on the Fortune 500 is absolutely prepared to spend years in litigation against the Department of Labor. The money field isn't even.

McLaughlin and Stern is currently in a long fight with number five on the Forbes list: Apple. "We're arguing and hopefully negotiating settlements on behalf of employees that the Department of Labor could do, but they don't have manpower," Gallaway says, and the Apple case is a good example. The company maintains a search policy in its retail stores. If a worker brings a bag or an Apple product with them, a manager must examine them (bags checked, gear verified against a registry) before they exit the premises. Searches like this are common in retail, they're part of a suite of practices called "loss prevention"—ironically, in this case, a euphemism for catching worker theft—but Apple has employees log out of work before the search, which has provoked accusations of time shaving.

The suit as it appears on the docket is *Frlekin et al v. Apple, Inc.*, named for the California employee Amanda Frlekin who with Dean Pelle of New York first filed against Apple in July of 2013 under the federal Fair Labor Standards Act. The FLSA passed in 1938, and it established some of the standards that Americans have come to think of as the divinely bestowed premises for labor relations, like the forty-hour workweek (a draft proposal was for thirty), the minimum wage, and time-and-a-half for overtime. Pursuing an action of this size—Apple has thirty-thousand retail employees in over 250 US stores, all governed by the same bag-check policy—requires a lot of investment upfront and an appetite for risk. McLaughlin and Stern typically takes these cases on spec: they only get paid if they win. "We have to take money out of our pockets to pay for things like deposition transcripts, travel, experts, and other investigation costs," Shalov says. "We could lose, and all the money's gone."

Unlike the WHD, private attorneys are not civil servants. For a firm like McLaughlin Stern, ensuring their wage theft practice stays in the black means being careful about which cases they choose. Attorneys' fees typically range between a quarter and a third of settlements, and only class-action suits with multiple plaintiffs make financial sense for them. Gallaway is blunt: "It's not cost-efficient for us to take a case that we don't think has a good chance to pass class certification." Civil litigation turns wage theft enforcement into a conflict between businesses. Companies can pay to fight or pay to settle, and the latter often makes more sense, sometimes regardless of the facts. This dynamic is one of the reasons why plaintiffs' attorneys are caricatured as shakedown artists. After dozens of wage theft cases between them, neither Gallaway or Shalov has ever brought one to trial.

Apple has pockets worth reaching for, but their money is also a war chest. The company successfully had the wage theft suit thrown out of federal court when a judge decided the facts were too close to a Supreme Court ruling against warehouse workers contracted by Amazon. At this point the DoL would have been forced to cut their losses and send the case to another agency, but Gallaway and Shalov moved it to a California court, where there is a slightly different legal definition of "work." Once again the complaint was rejected based on the Amazon precedent; they are now in appeals. The difference between wage theft and smart money-ball management is small, if not fully indeterminate. Which side of the line a company falls on may very well depend on how much they can pay their lawyers.

* * *

The place where owners hire labor is called the *private* sector, and it's shielded from government oversight by design. The American system envisions a person's ability to contract out their work on the market as a kind of freedom. For the state to intervene is a violation that deprives an individual of their sovereign right to work. If I agree to sell my skills for five dollars an hour, who is some Washington bureaucrat to say otherwise?

But Maria Rosado is that (local) Washington bureaucrat, and that's not what she sees. "[Employers] will make up schemes: having people punch out, reduce hours by a third to show compliance on the record, misclassify workers as independent contractors. They'll say, 'These guys are all exempt, they're chefs!' Nobody washes dishes, they're all chefs!" Free contracting presumes aboveboard conduct and a baseline of compliance with the law, but those are not the facts on the ground.

The relationship between employers and employees is defined by inequality: one has the capital, the other only their abilities and time. Labor unions are a good antidote to wage theft, but twenty-first-century American employers are adept at quashing the idea. I ask Aaron Gregoroff—a plaintiff in the Apple case—if he and his coworkers ever considered organizing as a route to addressing their workplace grievances. "Talking about anything union is a big no-no at Apple," he answers. "That's not allowed to come up." Workers are reduced to isolated individuals with just their own labor to sell: free to work, but never free from it.

The plural of individual is society, and the harm of wage theft isn't limited to its direct victims. "It's absolutely one of the components of wage depression in the US," Eisenbrey says. "If someone can get away with paying four dollars an hour it makes it hard for other companies to compete." Wage theft brings down pay for all workers, regardless of whether they are being robbed personally. And the practice isn't going out with the urban American garment manufacturer. Venture capitalist Paul Graham caught a lot of flak when he tweeted that "Any industry that still has unions has potential energy that could be released by startups," but he was right in a way of speaking. Much of that new energy will be stolen from workers.

Wage theft is the past, present, and future of wage labor. If politicians raise the minimum wage, employers will violate it. If a startup can find union workers to turn into contractors, it will. If there's a wage to pay, owners will find ways to get more for less, within the regulations, outside the regulations, or by stretching the thin membrane between the two. For the enforcers—private and public alike—the law is just a wheelbarrow in the vast wage theft money field: limited leverage.

WHY ARE YOUR WAGES SO LOW?
(2017)

WAGES ARE NOT rising the way they should, and that's a problem for the majority of Americans who pay their bills with money they earn by working. It's a problem for the economic theories that claim to map how everyone gets their share of a growing economy. And it's a problem for the economists who sound tone-deaf when they explain that the recovery is finally going great—except for wages. Neither the Democrats nor the Republicans have any good answers for this, because nobody thinks this is how it's supposed to work.

In their write-up of the latest census poverty numbers, Elise Gould and Valerie Wilson of the Economic Policy Institute are blunt: "real median earnings of full-time workers—male and female, black and white—have been relatively flat since 2000." Productivity—output per worker—grew by over 20 percent in the same time period, but the share of that value that workers take home has continued to decline.

Neoclassical economics does not have a term to explain the divergence between labor productivity and wages, but Marxism does: it's called the rate of exploitation. And the rate of exploitation is growing.

Wages stagnating while unemployment falls and the economy grows goes against mainstream economic theory, which holds that when unemployment falls, the labor market tightens and workers can demand higher pay. The more that businesses need labor, the more workers can charge; it makes sense, but it's not happening.

You would think the business press would be ready with some

explanations, but they're struggling. At *Bloomberg*, an explainer on why wage growth is sluggish begins by agreeing that it's "a puzzle." Conservatives believe the best way to increase wages is to grow the economy, but the connection between the two isn't as tight as they had presumed. "That's a puzzle" isn't going to cut it.

For years, liberal thinkers have been offering their own formula that they claim leads to better pay. "Education Is the Key to Better Jobs" declared Brookings in 2012; "A Simple Equation: More Education = More Income" wrote *New York Times* economics columnist Eduardo Porter in 2014. The Democrats even made a riff on this in their party slogan. It's now a mainstream view that education is a solution to economic inequality, racial inequality, gender inequality, bigotry in general, job growth, economic growth, and winning elections: a "silver bullet" as a *West Wing* monologue once put it. But once again, the proof is in the pudding, and the pudding sucks.

There are many connections between education and individual, family, local, state, and national economic success. The most accessible, reliable way for Americans to improve their circumstances is to learn to do more things that employers are looking to pay people to do. The Democrats understand that, and they've consistently put education—as a form of skilling and job training, rather than intellectual exploration—near the center of their largely unsuccessful agenda. Despite general wage stagnation, the premium for workers with bachelor's degrees or better has increased significantly. It's get skilled or get left behind in twenty-first-century America, and the Democrats don't want people left behind; how could that be a bad plan or a hard sell?

I think most Americans understand something about the "skilling" theory that the Democrats don't. To convert education into better life outcomes, you can't just take your diploma to the bank. Skills are supposed to help workers get good jobs and perform well, rinse and repeat. Education (or "human capital") makes workers more productive, which makes their workplaces more profitable, which means their bosses can afford to pay them more.

By now you may have spotted the problem. When workers improve their skills it doesn't *entitle* them to more pay, or *ensure* them more pay—it merely enables companies to pay more. And given the option, companies would rather not pay you more.

Employers like to talk about the "skills gap," but there is a permanent and unbridgeable divide between the supply of and demand for skilled labor. Business owners want a flood of applicants for every position who are so well-qualified that they require no training—and they want that flood of competition to allow them to offer lower pay. Workers, on the other hand, want to get paid as much as possible, preferably without having to apply for one hundred gigs at a time or spend a decade and tens of thousands of dollars developing their skills.

The idea that these two sets of interests could ever come into a happy balance is a myth perpetuated by factory owners looking for ways to save money.

Wages will not go up just because the economy improves or because workers improve their skills. In 2015 some of the world's biggest tech firms, including Apple and Google, paid over $400 million to settle accusations that they colluded to keep engineering wages low. Apple and Google's engineers are both educated and productive—among the most productive people in the world, by most measures. Their employers have so much cash they literally don't know what to do with it all—and yet they're still willing to tangle with the law just to pay people less.

Does anyone really believe employers in the rest of the economy, whose profits are rapidly being transferred to Silicon Valley, will somehow be more willing than Apple and Google to voluntarily offer up higher pay?

Republicans and Democrats alike don't even have a name for what's happening, let alone a serious idea of how to fix it. It's not surprising then that people are looking to Marx and socialism for explanations about the rate of exploitation. Employers can yell "skills gap" all day long, but they can't keep workers fooled much longer, and their shareholders are not going to be happy when the only solution left is pitchforks at their doors.

HOW MUCH IS A WORD WORTH?
(2018)

WHEN MAGAZINE READERS sit down to an article, I don't imagine they know how much the writer was paid. As consumers, we aren't responsible for what workers make; market competition and minimum wage laws take care of that. So, as long as we pay for our purchases and we pay our taxes, we've done our part. We assume there's some rationale to the pricing of labor, with industries coalescing around sensible rates that increase over time according to inflation and productivity.

But labor markets don't always work much like that, and if anyone should know, it's a freelance writer.

Freelance writers have long tolerated a wide range of rates. Nearly a century ago, a writer named Ring Lardner declared that he would "rather write for the *New Yorker* at five cents a word than for *Cosmopolitan* at one dollar a word." It's hard to think of another profession in which pay for comparable work can vary so much from assignment to assignment.

One of the benefits to freelancing is that writers can place value on rewards other than money—like being part of a hip new project, like the 1924 *New Yorker*. But the downsides are many, and as a result, most pros today find themselves still answering the same spiritual question Lardner did, but for a whole lot less cash.

Freelance writers have no collective with which to bargain, they are not subject to minimum wage laws, and their pay fluctuates all the time. For those reasons, it's hard to keep track of the averages (and few organizations are compelled to try). But back in 2001, the National Writers Union published a report on pay rates for freelance writers. The report figured that to earn the median wage for college grads—$50,000 per year—writers needed to pitch, sell, report, write, edit, publish, and be paid an average of $1 per word for 3,000 to 5,000 words a month. (That's the length of this article.) Adjusted for inflation, that's about $1.40 per word today.

Most freelance writers didn't hit those numbers then, and they don't hit those numbers today. Based on my reporting, my own experience, and interviews with more than a dozen writers, the current median price for a freelancer's work is between twenty-five and fifty cents per word (though, to be clear, most places no longer pay per word; they pay lump sums that work out to about $500 for a 1,000- to 2,000-word article). Speaking to *Black Enterprise*, Ben Carruthers, vice president of the Society of American Travel Writers, suggested that a similar $500 rate was standard . . . in 1977.

During the past fifty-two years, a single dollar has lost nearly 87 percent of its value, and so have the words of professional freelance writers. That has meant, unavoidably, a big change in the quality of the job.

It's hard to understand how it happened. Ring Lardner was an elite writer of his time, but even his charity rate doesn't look bad these days. Adjusted for inflation, that five cents per word is now worth about 70 cents, which is considered a respectable fee at legacy publications and well-funded startups. The $1 per word Lardner got from *Cosmo*, on the other hand, is worth over $14 now. I've spoken with dozens of freelance writers throughout my career and can report that's more than twice as much as I've ever heard of a writer receiving, period. Twelve of Lardner's stories—let's call that a year's worth of work for a feature writer—would earn him $600,000 in 2018.

Either Lardner is the greatest writer of all time by a wide margin or something screwy happened to writer pay over the past century. No offense to Lardner, but evidence suggests it's the latter.

There are no solid numbers for how many Americans are making these numbers work for them. When I asked a few people who earn a solid upper-middle-class living from freelance writing alone, they estimated only a couple hundred other people in the US were in the same boat—and not one of them makes Lardner money writing for magazines.

As any owner of a taxi medallion can tell you, reducing the value of a product or service can have serious repercussions—for the workers themselves and for the wider society they help comprise. When it comes to freelance writing, I fear that low prices have already begun to cost us. Talented writers walk away from the industry, plutocrats are free to pick stories and choose writers even when they don't own the outlets, and the quality of the work declines. All of that looks to worsen over time.

* * *

The first account of a publication offering $1 per word comes from 1908. It was for a type of story that remains the single most expensive genre in writing: anything "postpresidential." *The Fourth Estate,* an early twentieth-century weekly newspaper about the media, reported that Theodore Roosevelt was fielding multiple offers at the unheard-of fee (plus expenses!) to write up the hunting trip he planned to take after he left office. "At the rate things are going Mr. Roosevelt will find it far more profitable to shoot game in Africa than to be President of the United States," the *Fourth Estate* joked. The press buzzed: *$1 a word!* A satirical poem in *New York World* imagined Roosevelt's process:

> *The ($1) lion ($1) stood ($1)*
> *Within ($1) the ($1) wood ($1);*
> *I ($1) took ($1) steady ($1) aim ($1)*
> *My ($1) bullet ($1) sped ($1)*
> *And ($1) he ($1) lay ($1) dead ($1)—*
> *By ($1) my ($1) good ($1) rifle ($1) slain ($1)*

After that, $1 per word became a sort of celebrity rate, a way to indicate epic importance. In 1910, *Hampton's* reportedly gave it to explorer

Frederick Cook to describe his trip to the North Pole, which he was credibly attempting to claim as his "discovery." The magazine took his story and cut in a mea culpa, conceding the race to Robert Peary and headlining the issue "Dr. Cook's Confession." Peary is to this day credited with the achievement. (Though it made him one of the better-paid magazine writers in history, Cook's deal was among the worst publishing agreements anyone has ever made, at least on the writer's side.)

William Randolph Hearst, immortalized in the film *Citizen Kane*, remains the classic model for American media moguls—and perhaps moguls in general. By the late 1920s, he was already past his prime, but he didn't let insolvency or declining circulation stop him from offering top dollar to attract the architects of an exciting new philosophy emerging out of Western Europe: fascism.

Hearst was enamored with Italian Premier Benito Mussolini, first hiring him in 1928 to write about the fascist perspective on gender relations, which is exactly what you might think: "Man is in full possession of woman's liberties, and measures them to her as a merchant does a piece of cloth," etc. Mussolini faced backlash at the time, but Hearst still contracted him in 1931 for a monthly column in *Cosmopolitan* for $1 a word. That's $15.66 per word today.

In the same year, Hearst also hired Adolf Hitler to write about current affairs from a Nazi perspective, though for much lower pay than Il Duce. According to Hearst biographer David Nasaw, the problem wasn't his ideas, it was Hitler; he was an undependable writer who promised exclusives he failed to deliver.

In the expanding postwar years, $1 a word also expanded beyond the province of imperialists and dictators. A 1952 issue of the communications journal *Printers' Ink* cited $1 as the top standard word rate for big names at large-circulation women's magazines. Ten years later, *Time* reported that it was the rate for excellent unsolicited submissions to *Reader's Digest*. By the mid-1960s, $1 was standard at the highest-circulation national magazines. It's what *Playboy* paid, and, looking through old copies, it seems like the magazine could get anyone in the world to write for it. J.G. Ballard's 1967 story "The Dead Astronaut" commanded $4,000; that's somewhere around $30,000 in today's buying power.

It was an exceptionally well-paid time to be a professional freelance writer, and it shouldn't surprise us that it's commonly thought to be the form's most vibrant era. Over time, however, the rate declined—or, rather, it stayed the same; it wasn't adjusted for inflation.

And then came Tina Brown. In 1984, when she was named editor of *Vanity Fair*, she turned the publishing world upside down by doubling the top rate to $2, plus a bunch of fringe benefits. "Big Spender at *Vanity Fair* Raises the Ante for Writers," was the *New York Times* headline. New magazines trying to follow suit suddenly had to be willing to shell out $1.50 a word on feature stories, and at least a handful did. "My ambition is to get the best," Brown told the *Times*. "We still are not paying enough."

Thirty-plus years after the big raise, $2 per word remains on the high end for big freelance features from nonexclusive writers in national magazines. That doesn't mean publications don't occasionally pay more depending on how badly they want a story or how big the writer's name is, but that's the exception. Brown's $2 would be worth around $5 in today's buying power. But today, $2 is just $2.

Of course, decades of wage stagnation and a fall in the labor share of production are not unique to freelance writing. Taken together, those two trends are arguably the country's most important story over the past few decades. The media largely missed it, even in our own backyard, where it has played out in such easy-to-follow numbers. If we can't look out for ourselves, how can we be trusted to look out for the public? If publishers aren't afraid to shrink the wages of independent investigative journalists, who would they be afraid of?

* * *

To research this article, I talked to about a dozen freelance writers and a handful of magazine editors about the present state of the job. These were mostly writers who have been doing this work for between ten and twenty years, who write pieces of national and global importance, and who, from the outside, look like they have reached the top of their profession. I'm not talking about twenty-four-year-olds cobbling together $250 paychecks for their TV recaps so they can afford a corner in a tiny three-bedroom (though I've been there, and they too deserve much better). I'm talking about writers you might recognize from their bylines on the covers of magazines or as guests on cable news and *Morning Edition*. They are mid-career professionals, many with spouses and children. These people are more successful than I or almost any freelance writer can hope to become. And not one of them had a nice word to say about their working conditions.

The most common complaint is that the numbers just don't add up to a good living. Without signing writers to exclusive deals, most magazines top out in the $1 to $2 per word range (exclusivity can get you $3). It's possible to publish 30,000 words of freelance writing a year at those rates—about eight articles the length of the one you're reading—but it's extremely difficult to land and execute that many assignments successfully. And if you manage to pull it off and place a full year's worth of writing in top-flight publications, you may make as much as the average personal trainer: $60,000.

In reality, writing a story—especially an interesting or important one—is not an efficient process. "I wrote a feature for [a national magazine] in 2014, and I still remember getting the $5,000 check," one writer told me. "I sent a photo of it to my father, because I wanted him to see you could actually get paid for writing. Now I wonder whether in the back of his mind he was thinking, 'Five thousand dollars for six months of work?'" (That $5,000 is worth $5,322 today, but I'm willing to bet the publication has not increased its rates to keep pace.)

Once a writer proves him- or herself, depending on their politics and temperament, they might be eligible for a staff writing job. Some of these are legitimately good gigs with regular paycheck and benefits—the whole enchilada. Many of them, however, are not, and it's virtually impossible from the outside to tell which is which.

I would be remiss if I omitted that almost every person I spoke to brought up one of the industry's worst-kept secrets: *New Yorker* staff writers, some of the most admired journalists in the business, don't typically receive health insurance. Of course, that magazine isn't alone in keeping top talent on freelance contracts, often without benefits.

Freelance staff writers are still freelance in that they're legally considered independent contractors, but in nearly all cases, they write only for the one place. If that publication doesn't want to run their idea, the writer can't take it elsewhere.

Beyond the basic numbers, writers also told me about a grab bag of smaller frustrations and indignities that make the economics of their job problematic: checks that arrived on a geologic time scale while the landlord still charges monthly; publications squeezing out reprint, TV, and film rights; editors who assign and fix pay for pieces at word counts they know writers will likely exceed to meet the scope of the assignment.

"If the editors announced a fifty-cent per word pay cut next week, I don't think any of us would quit," one contract staff writer told me, "and they know it." Writers cite a cartel mindset among editors. And the editors I spoke with, like the writers, did not expect rates to rise.

There are other consequences to the declining value of the written freelance word. The most obvious is that skilled and insightful writers will ditch the profession for greener (but arguably less prosocial) pastures. Many of the writers I spoke with are looking for other kinds of work or have already started splitting their time between writing and more lucrative jobs. One recently did some television work and estimated it paid four times as well for labor that was considerably easier. (Earlier this year, when a Google spreadsheet of TV writer salaries circulated, it left some of us print writers agog: $12,000 to $25,000 per episode, or $4,000 per week.)

Freelance writers are subject to capture in other ways too. Many of my interviewees brought up the New America Foundation (NAF), a think tank with a list of supported fellows that includes a bunch of prominent writers. Google and Eric Schmidt have provided more than $20 million to New America, and some writers said they were skeptical of the influence that gave the tech giant, especially after the organization booted scholar Barry Lynn and his Google-hostile Open Markets initiative. Some writers felt too conflicted about the money to try to get an NAF fellowship.

Being willing to take the cash whenever it's available, mind you, is an adaptation to this stagnant market. It's hard to hate the players.

Labor cost cutting by publications can also lead to access for billionaires with an agenda. Michael Bloomberg, for example, funded *The Trace* to report on gun violence. The site collaborates with various media outlets, thereby reducing the average cost of pro–gun–control stories. (These stories feature disclaimers about the cost sharing, but few readers think twice about a public-interest magazine working with a nonprofit.) If Bloomberg's anti-gun message seems benign or even agreeable, imagine this same playbook being used by a rich person or firm or nation with politics you don't agree with.

Of course, freelance writing is better paid for those willing to receive support from the NAF or Michael Bloomberg or the Nation Institute or Cato or the Kochs or some other interested pile of money. And if pay continues to drop in real dollars, those checks could make the difference between who's on the cover and who does something else with their time. They probably already do.

When I asked one writer why they kept writing even though they could get more money elsewhere, they compared it to the financial sacrifices of artists. I pointed out that, archetypes aside, if they were an equivalently successful visual artist, they would be making considerably more money.

* * *

The writers who talked to me about their compensation did not generally complain that they were underpaid, per se, more that they were under-resourced. They didn't talk about what they would do with an extra $50,000 a year; they talked about what it would be like to be able to spend twice as long on their stories.

"No wonder the stuff in the sixties and seventies was so good," one writer said with a laugh as we discussed the impact of inflation on rates. "I don't see anything out there today that shows the kind of thought they got to put in." Though I'm less rosy about the writing of that era, the bottom line is hard to escape.

I was assigned this story at $4,000, and I turned in a draft of 4,000 words. Another site offered me $850 for the idea, and there is an $850 version of this story that is significantly shorter, with less research, and of a weaker quality overall. (If that sounds cold or unprofessional, imagine what the effect on the quality of your work would be if your boss cut your pay by 80 percent.)

There is also a $2 a word version that has more background research—in physical, not just digital archives—and for which I would have been more willing to press my sources to take risks and talk to me on the record.

I imagine a $4 per word version would include the specific, surprising allegations about the labor practices of particular beloved media institutions, the printing of which likely would make it difficult for me to find work for a while, but that would be fine, because I could live off that check for six months.

It's easier to imagine the end of the world than a return to the 1960s equivalent of $8 a word.

I'm not saying I deserve $4 per word (known in media circles as the "Carrie Bradshaw rate") never mind $8, but I wonder what other stories or facts the public isn't reading because the questions at hand are too sensitive for staff writers and not worth reporting for freelancers.

For a number of reasons—some particular to writing, some not—none of the freelancers with whom I spoke had any idea what their work is worth to their employers, except when it comes to the publications' prestige. Their confusion is understandable: most publishers are privately held, and there's not a strong sense of what their revenue per word is. If writers were in possession of that number, however, based on my research, I think it would improve our bargaining position rather than weaken it in most cases.

Writers do know, from experience, that writing in any genre can be worthless. It can be worthless in market terms, as in no one is willing to pay any dollars for it. It can be worthless in audience terms, as in no one is willing to pay any attention to it. And it can be worthless along the third axis of social (artistic, political, historical) importance.

But writing in any genre can also be incredibly valuable. One article can drive the public conversation, save lives, get millions of reads, and even put a whole publication on the map.

In a rational, comprehensible system, there would probably be a reliable relation between these values—stories that are better and more important should cost more—yet that is often not the case. Rather, it's almost always possible for a publication to get more for less, if that's what they want and they know where to look.

I don't truly know what a word is worth. The historical record certainly suggests it used to be worth more, but long-form writers also know that their work can be inefficient. They are people who care too much about their subjects, whose depth of interest defies the rational allocation of labor time. Paying well for that time has traditionally been the province of economically irrational men with their own agendas—and Tina Brown.

The rational thing for individual publications is almost certainly to continue tightening the screws, hold the nominal rates as close as possible to where they were in the 1960s, increase annual output from full-time staffers (who are facing more competition for their jobs), and find writers who are used to writing a lot for a little. In that scenario, there will still be good writing, and even some great writing, but there will be less of it.

I think this means that we, as a society, will miss things. We'll get things wrong. We may even, on occasion, be purposely misled. I hope we can afford it.

CONFLICT

AMERICANS HAVE NOTHING TO LEARN FROM NAZIS
(2015)

ON JANUARY 22, 2015, Jason Hammond accepted a noncoop-erating plea deal from prosecutors in Cook County, Illinois: he will serve forty-one months for his role in an organized assault on a casual dining establishment in the Chicago suburb of Tinley Park. On May 19, 2012, Hammond and seventeen others stormed the Ashford House restaurant with bats and hammers, interrupting lunch and leaving ten people injured. But instead of years in jail, America should send Hammond a thank-you card.

Not to be confused with his twin brother, Jeremy Hammond, who is serving a ten-year sentence in federal prison for hacking the security firm Stratfor, Jason Hammond is a member of the Hoosier Anti-Racist Movement (HARM), an affiliation of Indiana militant anti-fascists. That day in May, the Ashford House was playing host to a meeting of the Illinois European Heritage Association, a not-so-subtle white nationalist group. Anti-fascist (antifa for short) groups like HARM are committed to disrupting neo-Nazis and organized white supremacists by any means necessary.

White supremacists have found a comfy home on Stormfront and other Internet forums, but a real movement requires in-person meetings. The Jason Hammonds of the world have made this very difficult for them.

Whenever "race realists" plan to gather in public, the standard antifa operating procedure is to call the venues, inform them that the "heritage" groups they're planning to host are actually bunches of neo-Nazis, and give them the chance to cancel. Larger companies usually do; the 2010 American Renaissance national conference, for example, was forced out of the Sheraton and into a strip mall Bertucci's. When venues agree to host despite the warning, antifascists find other ways to put a halt to organizing.

Because of their militant tactics, antifa associations also end up doing a lot of prisoner support. Five other participants in the Tinley Park action agreed to similar pleas in January 2013, and all are now out on parole. When push comes to shove, the police are always willing to defend neo-Nazis in suits from anarchists in hoodies. You can host a fascist meet-up, but God forbid someone breaks a window trying to stop it.

American liberalism prides itself on making space available for all, including white supremacists, as in the 1969 Supreme Court decision *Brandenburg v. Ohio*, which affirmed the Klan's right to rally on public streets. But when liberalism protects white nationalists against those who seek to disrupt their vile, anti-liberal activities, what does our system hope to gain?

The ostensible reason for this policy of free speech for extremism is to keep the marketplace of ideas open. Any restrictions on the peaceful exchange of words leads to a chilling effect, and when we're afraid to say what we think, the best ideas might die on cold tongues. Recent American history—especially the parts we're proud of—is filled with unpopular ideas whose advocates struggled their way into the status quo. As prominent civil libertarian Cass Sunstein writes of free speech in his book *Why Societies Need Dissent*, "Better outcomes can be expected from any system that creates incentives for individuals to reveal information to the group."

But liberals are making a category error: white supremacy isn't a source of information, it's among the most dangerous lies ever conceived. White nationalism has no kernel of truth for us to unearth through discussion and debate. In the marketplace of ideas, it's strawberry-flavored rat poison. Fascism has nothing to offer, and we have zilch to gain from hearing out fascists. We may, however, have a lot to lose.

There's no such thing as nonviolent Nazis. Their only role in a free society is planning to overthrow it. Liberalism asks that we treat speech the way the government does, remaining agnostic with regard to its content as long as it doesn't incite imminent lawless action. The liberal argument goes that the answer to bad speech isn't censorship or force but better speech. No matter that white nationalists are using the Constitution as cover to organize against the document's declared values; the rules still protect them. There's a lot of self-satisfaction in this pose, but it's staggeringly vulnerable. Neo-Nazis pursuing an entryist strategy join the military and other state institutions, gaining access to training and recruitment opportunities and biding their time. In the event of social upheaval, white nationalists plan to be prepared.

Americans have no reason to be coy when it comes to white pride, yet we do act this way, as when seven hundred cops chaperoned forty-five National Socialists on a 2005 walk through Black neighborhoods in Toledo, Ohio. Is it too much to ask that our police—who aren't given to such fits of liberalism when it comes to Black people, Muslims, and environmental activists—let the Nazis fight their own battles? If the famed slippery slope argument ends with the government monitoring everyone's communication for hints of extremism, then we're already at the bottom of the hill. There's no liberty to be gained by dancing the public-sphere polka with white nationalists, whether they're wearing loafers or jackboots. Anti-fascists like Jason Hammond don't blind themselves to history or bind their hands with liberal tolerance. They know that now, as before, the swastika belongs under a hammer. As fascist elements organize, the violence required to confront and marginalize them only increases. As the antifa group One People's Project puts it, "Hate has consequences." Better to fight now.

So far, despite the heavy consequences for activists, the effort to isolate white nationalists is going well. As respectable European fascists wedge their way into the popular conversation (and occasionally the *New York Times*) their American comrades are floundering. Unable to hold their Bertucci's territory, the 2015 American Renaissance conference will be in the middle of the Tennessee woods, at the only venue willing to host them: a state park.

HARRY POTTER WAS A CHILD SOLDIER

(2015)

THE IDEA OF child soldiers is itself young. International law organizations didn't take up the issue until the close of the twentieth century and, even then, they did so in a cautious and patchwork manner. The 1989 United Nations Convention on the Rights of the Child asks governments to take "all feasible measures" to keep children under fifteen from direct combat. In 2000, the UN General Assembly committed to raising the age to eighteen, and in 2002 the Optional Protocol on the involvement of children in armed conflict was made good—sort of. Non-state guerrilla groups are banned from recruiting anyone under eighteen, while states are allowed to enlist volunteers over fifteen. The child soldier as a criminal aberration, a violation of even the rules of war, is more or less a twenty-first-century idea.

But what it lacks in history, the child soldier makes up for with dramatic pathos. Whether it's an aid organization making a fundraising pitch or a news anchor plucking heartstrings, nothing conveys the depravity of far-off conflict quite like the image of a nine-year-old smoking a cigarette and toting an AK-47. The memoir *A Long Way Gone* by the former child soldier Ishmael Beah tells the now-familiar story of forcible recruitment at twelve, drugs, coercion, and four years of violence, before a rescue by the United Nations Children's Fund (UNICEF). Though a lot of the facts are now disputed, Beah's stories of Sierra Leone helped to establish the child soldier as an archetype of misfortune.

Over the past twenty years, nongovernmental organizations of varying sizes have sprung up to remove minors from combat around the world. In 1998, eight major human-rights groups, including Amnesty International and Human Rights Watch, teamed up to form the Coalition to Stop the Use of Child Soldiers; four years later they established February 12 as Red Hand Day to raise awareness and stop the use of child soldiers. Child-soldier activism reached a popular crescendo with the viral video *KONY 2012* from the missionary group Invisible Children, made to promote their campaign to arrest Joseph Kony, the head of the Ugandan rebel Lord's Resistance Army.

The child soldier that haunts the Western imagination is kidnapped, brainwashed, drugged, and forced to commit atrocities until you, the Western donor, do something to stop the tragedy.

* * *

War, as it is said, is hell, and no war has ever exempted children, either as victims or combatants. Our recent attention to the practice of child soldiering is less about changes in the nature of modern combat and more to do with the globalizing ideal of childhood as a sheltered period of development. As Helen Brocklehurst, a lecturer in international relations at Swansea University in Wales, writes in her essay "Childhood in Conflict: Can the Real Child Soldier Please Stand Up?," the emergence of the phrase "child soldier" "marks the point at which a society's conception of childhood became incommensurable when harnessed to its concept of warfare." As it so happened, we reached this point right around the time capitalism defeated communism and the end-of-history theorists gleefully declared there were no wars left to fight. What remains is pacification, to clean up the crazy or evil groups who decline to get with the program.

In this way, the child soldier comes to stand for all illegitimate armed groups, whose motives are always irrational—as are those of the child soldier. Their fighting is a misguided response to trauma, or the result of cult-style programming, or is forced by the threat of violence from a monomaniacal strongman. Child soldiers are victims as well as perpetrators, just like all non-state combatants are victims of their own foolish intransigence. In the age of liberal democracy and nonviolent resistance, all insurgency is

as unnatural as an adolescent lieutenant. And since I can find no historical record of a popular uprising that did *not* include teenagers (including
America's own), any people's revolution is a *de facto* violation of international
law. Once a militia anywhere in the world is accused of using child soldiers,
the West is self-authorized to intervene and restore order. *Kony 2012* was a
good Internet joke, but it also led directly to members of Congress in both
houses and parties calling for an increased US presence in central Africa.

The use of children in combat may be historically uncommon, but it
wasn't illegal or surprising that adolescents went to war. We know this in
part because we've kept past "child soldiers" alive in history and legend. In
his book *Reimagining Child Soldiers in International Law and Policy*, Mark
A. Drumbl cites just a few examples: Carl von Clausewitz, a Prussian
general and the author of *On War*, joined the Prussian army at twelve;
Alexander the Great became regent and quelled a Thracian rebellion at
sixteen; and Joan of Arc was also a teenager when she petitioned the
king for permission to travel with the army to Orleans in 1429. David
was even more precocious when he slew Goliath and ascended to the
throne. And there were teens at the Boston Tea Party in 1773, while the
seventeen-year-old Samuel Maverick was one of five colonists killed at
the Boston Massacre in 1770. Drumbl also includes the civil rights activist Claudette Colvin, who at the age of fifteen, nine months before Rosa
Parks, refused to give up her bus seat. The list goes on, and for all the
names we know, there are many more lost to time.

In these stories, the children's youth wasn't a sign that their cause was
corrupt or misguided. On the contrary, inspired children were a sign of
favor from God—or history. The presence of child soldiers today immediately depoliticizes the conflict and renders it a question of *criminality*, but
child soldiers in old war stories raise the question of the future, which is to
say now. History's winners can take pleasure in past battles, they can place
themselves in the shoes of precocious soldier-children because they know
how the story ends: liberal capitalist democracy, the nation-state system,
the UN. Now that we've grown out of child soldiering, we can look back
on it fondly, as a testament to the foresight and bravery of our ancestors.
Whatever they did, after all, got us here.

As long as they're separated from contemporary geopolitics, child-soldier narratives are considered perfectly appropriate for US kids. Think about the boy wizard Harry Potter: a war orphan seized from his surviving relatives at age eleven, Harry is brought to a secluded academy run by former militants, told he is destined for glory, and taught to fight. When the warlord who killed his parents returns to make a power play, the teenage Harry raises and trains an armed cadre of his fellow high schoolers to fight internal and external enemies. One of these child soldiers is killed in an ensuing battle. Postwar, Harry and his best friend Ron, both still teenagers, join the new government's military police unit. "They are now the experts," the novels' author J.K. Rowling told reporters in 2007, expanding on the epilogue of her last book in the series. "It doesn't matter how old they are or what else they've done." The International Criminal Court might beg to differ, but they're not in the habit of prosecuting winners.

In fictional "just war" scenarios, such as the rise of Voldemort or a communist invasion, Americans are far less conflicted about whether or not children can choose to be guerrillas. Though US territory hasn't been occupied by a foreign power since the War of 1812, that doesn't stop us from imagining what we would do if it happened. In the 1984 movie *Red Dawn*, the Soviet Union and its Cuban allies invade and quickly conquer the US. (In the 2012 remake, the invader is North Korea.) The protagonists are a scrappy group of Colorado high schoolers who take to the hills and mount an offensive against the Ruskies. The Wolverines (named after their school mascot) train and fight and die, but there's no real question as to whether they should surrender or if they're too young to take on their responsibilities. At the end of the original movie, a war memorial stands for the Wolverines: "In the early days of World War III, guerrillas—mostly children—placed the names of their lost upon this rock. They fought here alone and gave up their lives, so that this nation shall not perish from the earth."

When it comes to the homeland, no international body can tell our teens to stand down.

* * *

Race is one of the reasons it's easier for Western media consumers to imagine teenagers as heroes in Colorado or magical Scotland than in Sri Lanka or Colombia. If we're exposed only to frozen images of these children as objects of sympathy—soft-eyed, mute, sad—it's harder to put ourselves in their position and imagine what their motivations might be as individuals.

The *Harry Potter* series underestimates the lifelong trauma these children would experience, never mind whether they should be immediately taking jobs as civil servants. International standards would call for them to be demobilized and reintegrated into the civilian population. But at least in *Harry Potter* or, for that matter, *The Hunger Games* novels by Suzanne Collins, children get to experience a range of emotions, to make choices, and have intentions. Meanwhile, the aid world's portrayal of pre-demobilization child soldiers presents them as one-dimensional, not culpable for their actions because of coercion or brainwashing. This flat image serves the interests of aid organizations and the UN General Assembly, but it requires us to ignore the voices of the children themselves.

For example, in 2009, UNICEF and Sri Lanka teamed up for a media campaign called "Bring Back the Child" which aimed to discourage underage recruitment, specifically by the rebel group Liberation Tigers of Tamil Eelam (LTTE). In the posters, black-and-white photos of the child soldiers' unsmiling faces are overlaid on full-color photos of their bodies engaged in more age-appropriate pastimes. Beside the picture of a girl, the text reads: "She wants to be a dancer, not a child soldier." A boy wants to play cricket. The rhetoric assumes the child soldiers are abducted or coerced, but surveys of youth recruits to the LTTE suggest that this is relatively rare. In one survey, eighteen of nineteen teenage boys from the LTTE said they joined voluntarily.

But can a child truly volunteer to join an army? Even when they enlist by choice, child soldiers do so under a set of constraining circumstances. UNICEF makes the choices sound easy: war or dancing, war or games, war or be a doctor. No rational child would pick the former for themselves, and that's posed as evidence that their freedom has been taken from them. But when the choice is "soldier or victim," voluntarism takes on a different meaning. In northeastern Nigeria, the Civilian Joint Task Force (CJTF) has recruited thousands of teenagers into the armed self-defense groups organized to protect villages from Boko Haram militants. There is no way for these children to opt out of the conflict; in *The Daily Beast* the Nigerian journalist Philip Obaji Jr puts their choice in stark terms: "Fight Boko Haram or be killed by them." Some teenagers, understandably, have picked the former.

If boy soldiers are depicted as intrinsically vulnerable, then girl soldiers are doubly so. Consumers of Western media have learned to make the mental leap between young women in danger overseas—and rape. When advocates say 40 percent of child soldiers are girls, they're playing on their audience's worst fears about the role of women in the global South. In an effort to record the stories of girls themselves, in 2002 a team of local researchers led by Yvonne E. Keairns of the Quaker UN Office interviewed twenty-four young women from across four conflicts: Angola, Colombia, the Philippines, and Sri Lanka. In Angola, Keairns's worst fears were confirmed, with girls forcibly conscripted and sexually abused. But of the other eighteen girls, seventeen had joined guerrilla groups voluntarily, and their testimony about their choices sheds light on the complexity lacking in our portrait of child soldiers.

Contrary to Keairns's expectations, the interviews found that three of four guerrilla groups had strict rules regarding sexual relationships between soldiers, including explicit procedures for obtaining and confirming women's consent. Many of the young women interviewed described their enlistment as a *flight* from sexual violence and other forms of exploitation in the home into a structured military environment. When these groups did exercise reproductive control, it was usually in the form of forced contraception and abortions to maintain the fitness of the fighting corps. One Sri Lankan militant describes escaping her home on the eve of an unwanted marriage. The statements of the Filipina militants are especially striking: the girls report taking part in a culture of mutual criticism, where they had plenty of time to study, and the group listened to their voices. Training included a lecture on strict sexual harassment policies. "In the seminar, it was made clear that it was absolutely prohibited to take advantage of women," one interviewee said. "I felt very safe; I had no fear."

And, contrary to Western ideas about the agency of female child soldiers, a majority of those interviewed had made a calculated choice to become militants. These young women had experienced a wide spectrum of well-being and harm, but the "international community" shoves them into a one-size-fits-all victim archetype. To assume all girl soldiers undergo the same violence as the combatants in Angola is to exclude three-quarters of their stories. "If it were not for the fighting," Keairns writes of the Philippines and Colombia, "the girls would have preferred life in the armed group over their life as a civilian." Aid organizations pursue a policy of "prevention, demobilization, reintegration" that does not fully take into account the variety of reasons children join guerrilla movements and why they might not want to reintegrate.

The child soldier is a recent idea, and we have barely begun to work out its contradictions. In the contemporary Western imagination, you can be a brave freedom-fighter or an exploited child soldier, but you can't be both. The tension between these two ideas was laid bare last September in the magazine *Marie Claire* when the US journalist Elizabeth Griffin wrote about the women of the YPJ, or Women's Protection Unit, a self-defense force of Marxist-feminist Syrian Kurds currently battling the Islamic State (IS). Rather than become refugees, many young Kurdish women have joined the YPJ to fight IS, though the group officially complies with the Optional Protocol.

The article originally included some of these teen trainees and combatants, saluting them as heroes, and the editors were so caught up in the story that they forgot they were applauding a war crime. Now an awkward editors' note sits atop the piece online: "The efforts of the YPJ are remarkable but *Marie Claire* does not condone the use of child soldiers in any capacity. This article has been edited to reflect that." The manner in which they edited the piece to reflect the universal condemnation of child soldiering was to remove all mention of anyone under eighteen.

The flat portrayal of child soldiers necessitated by the state of international law says these children can either be traumatized victims or they will become invisible. When flesh-and-blood combatants don't fit into the rhetorical agenda of existing nation states and supranational organizations, they get erased from the story or written into one that's more convenient. As "child soldiers," their agency is irrelevant—all the better to put them to work.

THE J20 RAID AND THE TRUMP PROTEST THAT NEVER ENDED

(2017)

ON THE MORNING of the first Tuesday of April, activist Dylan Petrohilos woke up to insistent banging on the door of his home in the Petworth neighborhood of Washington, DC. By the time he got there, the Metropolitan Police had already let themselves in, busting through the door with guns out and riot shields up. They grabbed Petrohilos, handcuffed him, and sat him on the couch while they tore up his place for an hour and a half. The police piled all his electronics into boxes and left. Petrohilos hasn't heard from them since.

If Americans remember anything about the January 20 presidential inauguration of Donald Trump (besides the punch heard 'round the world), it's probably that the crowds didn't quite live up to expectations. Even as the big guy claimed he had the biggest audience ever, aerial pictures told a different story, and we all got a good laugh. For some activists, however, January 20 never really ended. The stench of repression still hangs in the air long after the last of the tear gas has dispersed.

The pictures of a sparsely filled mall no doubt reflected a lack of enthusiasm for Trump within the population of the DC area, but that angle undersells the work of left-wing activists who executed a well-planned series of blockades, closing off many of the entrances for the duration of the inauguration ceremonies. The protest, hashtagged #J20 for the date, was as successful an action of that size as I've ever seen, but the police response was unexpected as well. For the first time in a decade, the DC police mass-arrested hundreds of protesters, and, for the first time that anyone I've spoken with can remember, the arrestees were mass-charged with felony riot. A few of those cases have been dropped, but the rest—over two hundred—have been indicted by DC grand juries. Now the prosecutors have to decide if they can make their cases to trial juries, which I guess is what the raid on Petrohilos's house was about. I've taken a look, and the warrant doesn't say.

Petrohilos hasn't been charged with any crimes in connection with J20, and the warrant doesn't indicate that anyone has even accused him of any wrongdoing. It authorizes the police to search for anything that might be related to the planning of a "black bloc" protest on January 20, and to seize it as potential evidence. "Every week I wake up wondering if this is the one when I get charged," he says. "It sucks." The raid shook him up, he says, and has left him pretty stressed out.

"It's scary," Petrohilos says. "One minute the police are just there, and you're alone face-to-face with the power of the state." Repression works in part by isolating activists, using the courts to turn collective problems back into individual cases. It's an effective strategy, and it's hard to combat, especially if the authorities are willing to spend the kind of time and money needed to prosecute almost two hundred separate felonies.

That's where the Dead City Legal Posse comes in. Activists in DC are used to busloads of protesters coming in from out of town, and, as part of their hosting duties, the J20 organizing committee promised to provide support for all arrestees for the duration of their cases. Based on past experience, that was supposed to be a weeklong commitment at most. One successful protest later, organizers had to choose between going back on their word and supporting hundreds of arrestees through legal processes that could take years. They picked the latter, and the J20 legal working group re-formed as the all-volunteer Posse.

I spoke with Legba Carrefour, a longtime DC activist and one of the ten core members of the Legal Posse, about how the group came to be and how it works. "We said we'd be there for people," he says, "so after the arrests, we were like, 'Fuck, I guess we gotta do it.'"

Carrefour offers court support, which is one of the Posse's crucial functions. A volunteer attends every hearing for every J20 arrestee. They check in with the defendant, offering food, coffee, and cigarettes; make sure everything is copacetic with their lawyer; and see if they need reimbursement for travel expenses. Then the volunteer takes notes on the hearing itself, which get filed for reference and the historical record. By meeting with all the arrestees, the Legal Posse is hoping to counteract the state's strategy of separating individuals from the other people with whom they risked their freedom. "It's important work to keep people connected," Carrefour says. "It also makes them less likely to snitch, which is better for them, and for everyone involved."

The Dead City data team tracks the progress of the arrestees as they move through the court process, making sure nobody falls through the cracks in the system. They coordinate with the National Lawyers Guild to ensure everyone is represented. Activism can be very dangerous, especially if you don't have someone on the ground looking out for you. American defendants are entitled to legal representation, but having a lawyer is not the same as having legal support. The Dead City Legal Posse wants to be there to do everything the lawyer doesn't do. "These are my friends," Carrefour says, "and if we expect people to come out and put themselves on the line, then we need to have their backs." That job ended up being a lot bigger than anticipated, but they're approaching it with seriousness—and with anarchist good humor.

Right now the Legal Posse is just focused on the inauguration arrestees—and their hands are certainly full. But the repression has been so broad and intense that just providing support for the single day's actions entails building up infrastructure that activists say might be put to additional use later. Either way, by the looks of things, the group is going to be around for a while.

Dead City has put up a well-designed website with FAQs and weekly updates; its first fundraiser is a T-shirt with a snowflake motif—a play on a now-common right-wing anti-protester jeer. "I don't think people understand how much work goes on behind the scenes," Carrefour says, "A lot of what activists do has to be about taking care of people." In the Trump era, that necessity is taking concrete form, and there are similar legal support groups sprouting up around the country.

The general public sees activists in fits and spurts: one day protesters are flooding the streets chanting slogans, punching Nazis, and breaking windows, the next they're nowhere to be found. But, as J20 has shown, for every minute of running in the street on television, there are hours of washing dishes in church basements and standing outside courthouses with water and apples. The repression of protest has real and present costs: in money, time, and emotion. We shouldn't leave activists singled out by the state to pay on their own.

THE FASCIST BOGEYMAN
(2016)

THE CURRENT DEBATE about fascism in America has, thus far, centered on the definition. Many publications have been musing in the same direction: "Is Donald Trump a fascist?" (*Slate*, the *New York Times*); "Is Donald Trump an Actual Fascist?" (*Vanity Fair*); "Donald Trump and Fascism: Is He or Isn't He?" (*National Review*); etc. People want to know what to call things and that's understandable, but I'm not sure how useful this exercise is. Fascist is as fascist does, and by the time we can agree on the exact definition it may already be too late.

When I planned to write about *¡No Pasarán!*, a new collection about the Spanish Civil War edited by Pete Ayrton, I thought there might be some good lessons in there about fascism. With the Trump campaign improbably continuing and the alt-right Nazi brand on the rise, many of us agree that a solid operational understanding of fascism is increasingly necessary. Whether or not the label applies to our present situation, I'm pretty sure it's valid when talking about Generalissimo Francisco Franco of the Spanish Falange.

I figured I would outline the historical timeline, cite a couple historical curiosities, draw some ominous connections to the election, get a check, and move on. Instead, I got stuck on a couple anecdotes in one of the pieces, an excerpt of the Basque writer Bernardo Atxaga's book *De*

Gernika a Guernica. The first is from the village of Fuenteguinaldo, and it happened in 1936 but wasn't revealed publicly for seventy years:

> Apparently, the Falangists asked the priest to draw up a list of all the reds and atheists in the village . . . They went from house to house looking for them. At nine o'clock at night, they were taken to the prison in Ciudad Rodrigo, and at four o'clock in the morning, were told they were being released, but, at the door of the prison, a truck was waiting and, instead of taking them home, it brought them here to be killed.

The second comes from the failed coup attempt in 1981:

> I was living in a village in Castille with fewer than two hundred inhabitants. I became friendly with a young socialist who was a local councillor. When I met him one day, he was looking positively distraught. He had just found out that in February of that year, on the night Colonel Tejero burst into Parliament and the tanks came out onto the streets, the local priest had gone straight to the nearest military barracks intending to hand in a list of local men who should be arrested; my friend's name was at the top of the list.

Someone puts your name on a list and you disappear. And maybe all the people who care enough to look for you disappear too. And no one hears what happened until everyone you ever knew is dead. That is, if you'll excuse my language, the fucking bogeyman. It scares the hell out of me.

There's a danger to thinking about fascism as something other than human, not just because it *is* people, but because it presents a temptation to dehistoricize. Fascism becomes something existential, a tyrannical tendency somewhere deep in the character of all people or all societies that needs to be restrained but occasionally breaks free to wreak havoc. Once we start down that path it's not too long before we get to "We're all a little bit fascist," and "Was Alexander the Great a fascist?" That is lazy, useless thinking, the kind of "human nature" nonsense that is the first resort of the uninformed and uninterested.

Monsters and ghouls have always been a part of human community as far as I know, but they each emerge under particular circumstances. Think *FernGully*: The evil spirit Hexxus is freed from a tree (where it's been imprisoned) when a timber crew chops it down. Ancient Hexxus seeps out with the character—even the name—of modern pollution. The creature is the externalities of industrial production embodied. It moves like oil and smoke. That pollution makes monsters is not a special insight; everyone knows about Godzilla. But moral pollution, of course, yields demons as well. Monsters show up when some scale is stubbornly uneven, when karma is repressed. Toxic waste dumped in the swamp, but graves disturbed too. That we've always had evil isn't a way to avoid understanding the specifics of its incarnations. Thinking about fascism as a bogeyman in this way could be more useful. What kind of monster is it?

Allow me some speculation. Fascism is a nation-shaped monster. It arises alongside the modern state, and though they share sympathies (and weapons) across borders, fascists are nationalists. One of the conflicts that feeds fascism is between nineteenth-century ideas about the racial character of states and twentieth-century pluralist ones. Our global system is supposedly based on something like collective self-determination, but it's grafted onto a map drawn by colonial violence and pseudo-scientific ideas about Gauls and Teutons. Fascism is a particular combination of Romantic/Victorian ambitions and modern tools that sparks to life as the two eras grind against each other. Frankenstein with the arms of capitalist industry and the heart of a monarchist. Patriotic young Hitler inhaling mustard gas in the trenches, like a panel from the first issue of a comic book.

One of those modern tools is the list. We've always indexed information, but our ability to do so grows in qualitative jumps. To round up all your enemies at a national level is an analytics problem, and it's one we solved under particular circumstances. The quantitative management of populations doesn't just happen to emerge around slavery, it emerges *out of* slavery. And the Civil War didn't break the line: at the Eugenics Records Office (ERO) in Cold Springs Harbor, New York, so-called scientists of the early twentieth century kept lists of the genetically (and racially) undesirable. They embarked on sterilization campaigns and lent their expertise to help halt the flow of immigrants. The Nazis infamously used IBM to manage the Holocaust; the Americans (less infamously) also used IBM to manage the Japanese internment camps. When NYU's Asian/Pacific/American Institute recreated an ERO office in 2014, they called the exhibit *Haunted Files*. Perhaps our filing systems are haunted too.

Modern liberal states have never truly reconciled their racial character with their democratic pretensions. I'm not clear on how such a thing could be possible; where would a truly pluralist state draw its borders and why? Flipping through a history book it's hard to argue that the nation-state system doesn't exist for the arbitrarily divided glory of western Europeans. The official line is that we're supposed to ignore that part, or be sad. But some people don't want to ignore it and they aren't sad. Instead they wonder why we have the nice borders that their conquering "ancestors" drew but all these people on the wrong sides. If taking Mexico's land for white people was illegitimate, then why haven't we given it back? And if it was legitimate, then what's wrong with a wall to protect our side from a reversal? The liberal patriots, they say, are lying to themselves; there is no nationalism that is not ethno-nationalism.

The persistence of the fascist bogeyman suggests that they have a point. The beast can skulk in the basement for decades, feeding off the contradictions at the foundation of the pluralist state and its own waste. We can't claim that fascism is a birth pang of the global democratic order, an enemy defeated. (Ghosts, zombies, the terminator: monsters so rarely go away when they're supposed to.) Fascism seems inextricably tied to what we have, like Dorian Gray's portrait locked in an attic, consolidating ugliness.

Whether or not they *could* finish off fascism once and for all, liberals usually aren't tempted to try. I don't know if that's because they sense something ineradicable there, but liberals have historically found deals to make with their shadow. Spain is one of the more striking examples. When Franco's insurgents escalated, the rest of the world agreed to stay neutral so as to stall the already foreseen World War II. But the war had already begun: Hitler and Mussolini flouted the agreement, intervening most dramatically with bombing raids. The Soviet Union breached as well, sending weapons to badly armed Madrid. The western democracies, however, stayed neutral. In return, Franco maintained Spain as a nonbelligerent when worldwide hostilities broke out. It's an agreement that lasted into the 1980s.

Part of what makes the Spanish Civil War so important for leftists is the sense that it could have gone the other way. There's an urban legend that infighting among leftists—communists, anarchists, and Trotskyists—caused the Republic's defeat. *¡No Pasarán!* has accounts of this frenemy fire, but no one thinks it decisive compared to German and Italian air power or the western arms embargo. Spanish republicans and their study-abroad comrades fought bravely, but the bogeyman has an advantage at the insurgency stage. Violence is its thing.

The bogeyman makes a real offer: delegate to me your capacity for limitless violence and together we will dominate. That they're able to do it justifies the undertaking, and they are, under some circumstances, able to do it. A willingness to strike first, to drag your enemies from their beds in the middle of the night, to steal their babies, that's a force multiplier, especially when combined with the right information technology. There is strength in white nationalist unity. Horrifying, despicable, antihuman strength, but strength still. The fascist image is a bundle of sticks or arrows—the *fasces*, harder to break. And they are.

I think of the 2015 movie *Green Room*, about a band of punks who get trapped inside a Nazi club and have to try and fight their way out. Joe Cole plays the drummer Reece, and he's the only one who shows any sort of confidence, preparation, or leadership when it comes to fighting fascists. With his MMA skills he incapacitates a giant skinhead bouncer and directs the gang to make a break for it. He's not out a club window one moment before two faceless, nameless Nazi henchmen have stabbed him to death. For me this moment illuminates a basic truth about fascist strategy: *it does not matter how smart or brave or capable or strong you are. There are two of us, we have knives, and we're waiting outside the window.*

Liberal democracies are constitutionally vulnerable to the bogeyman. We civilians have already delegated our capacity for violence to the military abroad and the police at home. If there's a threat to law and order, then the forces of law and order will take care of it. We don't have to worry about protecting our democracy, there are professionals for that. All we have to do is vote for the right people to manage them. But that plan has risks.

America's founders thought they could write the standing army out by fiat, and they have been proven very wrong. Liberal democracies maintain giant war machines. Within each of these war machines—as in the religious and business communities—there are cults that worship the bogeyman. Members wear tattoos, patches, insignias to identify each other. They recruit. Some of them go to meetings, most probably don't. I imagine that many of them get fulfillment from their work. Why wouldn't fascists feel at home in the police, the border patrol, the army? Asking these organizations to maintain anti-fascist vigilance on behalf of the whole population is a fox and henhouse situation.

If Donald Trump is a fascist—as even the liberal media is beginning to agree—and has a non-negligible chance of winning the presidency [yikes], what is the contingency plan? If a Trump administration were to flout what's left of our democratic norms, how would our system protect itself? I don't know how Trump polls among active-duty military, but the Fraternal Order of Police has already endorsed him. Part of me thinks "Troops loyal to Hillary Clinton," is a phrase we could get used to fast, but I'm not sure how many of those there are. Are the Vox dot com technocrats expecting a Seal Team 6 bullet to solve the Trump problem if things get too hairy? It seems remarkable that the two twentieth-century American politicians we talk about getting closest to fascist takeovers—Huey Long and George Wallace—were both stymied not by the democratic process but by lone gunmen. That's a bad defense strategy. Thankfully, it's not the only one available.

Wherever there have been fascists there have also been anti-fascists: traditionally communists, anarchists, socialists, and some folks who just hate fascists. When left-wing parties have on occasion decided to stand by while fascists targeted liberal governments, anti-fascist elements have still distinguished themselves. Anti-fascism is based on the idea that fascists will use content-neutral liberal norms like freedom of speech and association as a Trojan Horse. By the time the threat seems serious, the knives are already out. Antifa seeks to nip the threat in the bud, attacking fascists wherever they're weak enough to attack. If that means busting up their meetings with baseball bats, then that's what it means.

In America, we remember the Spanish Civil War mostly through anti-fascist anglophone writers—George Orwell and Ernest Hemingway being the most famous—who decamped for Spain. Unlike fascists and liberals, anti-fascists are internationalists, and no citizenship takes precedence over the struggle. When the call went out for sympathizers to come and defend the Spanish Republic, one young British volunteer, Laurie Lee, called it "the chance to make one grand, uncomplicated gesture of personal sacrifice and faith which may never occur again. Certainly, it was the last time this century that a generation had such an opportunity before the fog of nationalism and mass-slaughter closed in." Comrades of all sorts of nationalities and particular left-wing political views signed up for the motley "International Brigades." There was and is a purity to this gesture; to go and risk your life alongside your attacked comrades is among the highest imaginable acts of solidarity. "*¡No pasarán!*" (They will not pass) is an anti-fascist slogan of such power that it's still in use today, many decades after it turned out to be a lie.

Because pass they did. The righteous ragtag army was no match for the German and Italian bombers. Spain stands for anti-fascism across borders, but also the catastrophe of its failure. If there's one lesson we can learn from the War it's that fascists don't always lose. The arc of history is not a missile defense system and sometimes righteous solidarity makes for full prison camps.

For years American anti-fascists have been very effective. Up until the Trump campaign, they had largely prevented white nationalists from meeting in public in cities. It usually works something like this: antifa finds out where the Nazis are planning to meet and they call the hotel or conference center they're going to use and explain who exactly "American Renaissance" is, and what will happen if the meeting happens (chaos). Most reputable establishments exercise their right to decline Nazi business. This kind of tactic offends the liberal sensibility, but it's the only choice. The least violent way to oppose fascism is to disrupt them before they feel strong enough to act in an organized way. I fear that window is closing.

I don't think Donald Trump is going to be elected president, but the fascists who have found a vessel in his campaign have been licking their lips for months straight. Things are going better than they could have hoped and they won this round a long time ago. I have no doubt they're thinking about how to organize their engorged base in November's wake. Fascists aren't democrats and they don't need a majority.

The bogeyman is in the closet and he's making so much noise it's hard to pretend we can't hear it. We have a choice to make, if not as a country, then as members of this society. We can get out of bed, open the door, and confront the social infection that is fascism. Or we can pull the sheets up over our heads, pretend history ended twenty-five years ago, and try to get back to sleep. Maybe the noise will stop on its own—it is possible, even likely. But maybe we'll wake up with our throats slit. There won't be a different kind of warning.

CODA: ORDER PREVAILS IN AMERICA

Cameron: We're screwed!
Michael: No, hey, hey, no, I don't want to hear that
defeatist attitude. I wanna hear you upbeat!
Cameron: We're screwed!
Michael: There you go.

— 10 THINGS I HATE ABOUT YOU (1999)

AT THE TIME it was written and published, almost any piece in this collection could have been described as pessimistic. And yet when I look back at them, the big errors I find are in the other direction. I thought we had enough time and clearance to keep fascists marginalized and out of the mainstream. I thought Hillary Clinton was going to be elected president. I figured that things were going to get worse, but I couldn't imagine it'd be at this pace. Shit has gotten much more fucked up and bullshit since I started writing professionally, and it was already so fucked up and bullshit then. If we could go back and warn ourselves, would we believe us? Would we have done something differently? And if so, what?

I don't think things are the way they are because of a mistake, some misstep here or there. We are in the end phase of a way of life, one that hasn't been around all that long, but one which most of us were raised to see as the culmination of human history. Now, the ground is crumbling beneath our feet. When you give someone just enough agency to blame them when things go predictably wrong, that's what theologian Adam Kotsko calls "demonization"—after all, that's what God did to Lucifer and his followers. Those of us who don't exploit others for profit should prepare to be demonized in the near future because that is how the owners and their flunkies will justify the punishment that comes next, the punishment that has already begun.

Before she was murdered in January 1919, German communist leader Rosa Luxemburg wrote her final column, titled "Order Prevails in Berlin." It's a remarkable piece of writing, an objective meditation on the historical meaning of the author's own imminent death. The German revolution is defeated, she and Karl Liebknecht, leading lights of the European left, will soon be tortured by goons and executed without trial. In the last hours of her free existence Luxemburg wonders: Could that have gone better? Should we have done it differently? She concludes: Possibly, but that's not how it works. "The revolution does not develop evenly of its own volition, in a clear field of battle, according to a cunning plan devised by clever 'strategists,'" she writes. "The revolution's enemies can *also* take the initiative, and indeed as a rule they exercise it more frequently than does the revolution."

Our enemies have taken the initiative, and in fighting back we risk wasting our single precious lives on a mere defeat. However, Luxemburg remains defiant, even optimistic, not for her own life, but for what is to come. "Revolution is the only form of 'war,'" she writes, "in which the ultimate victory can be prepared only by a series of 'defeats.'" And though she inked her guarantee of future final victory to her followers just as the authorities showed up to carry her away, Luxemburg hasn't been proven wrong yet. The defeats have piled up, but our enemies still totter on the uneven boards of exploitation. And the struggle continues.

CREDITS/
ACKNOWLEDGMENTS

And Into the Fire
Published here for the first time

The Ektorp Sofa
Published at *The New Inquiry*,
August 21, 2011
Edited by Rob Horning

Radiohead Plays Occupy Wall Street
Published at *Gawker*, December 14, 2011
Edited by Adrian Chen

A Bridge to Somewhere
Published at *The New
Inquiry*, October 3, 2011

The Right to Have Remained Silent
Published at *Real Life Mag*, July 28, 2016
Edited by Rob Horning

Bad Education
Published in *n+1*, April 25, 2011
Edited by Carla Blumenkranz

Pomp and Exceptional Circumstance
Published in *The Boston Review*,
November 19, 2012
Edited by David Johnson

Arms and Legs
Published at *The New
Inquiry*, March 5, 2012
Edited by Sarah Leonard

Where Should a Good Millennial Live?
Published at *Fusion*, November 23, 2015
Edited by Geraldine Sealey

Upping the Antihero
Published at *The New Inquiry*,
August 24, 2011
Edited by Rob Horning

Working Beauty
Published at *The New Inquiry*,
February 3, 2012
Edited by Rob Horning

Drama for Cannibals
Published at *The New Inquiry*,
August 5, 2013
Edited by Max Fox

Turn Down for What?
Published at *The New Inquiry*, July 14, 2014
Edited by Max Fox

Lego Marx
Self-published July 17, 2016

Fidel Castro's Naked Leg, or Notes
on Political Correctness,
published here for the first time.

Please Don't Have Sex with Robots
Published at *Al Jazeera America*, August 8, 2015
Edited by Atossa Abrahamian

How Not to Raise a Rapist
Published in *Pacific Standard*, July 21, 2016
Edited by Ted Scheinman

Mom's Invisible Hand
Published in *The New Republic*,
June 28, 2016
Edited by Laura Marsh

The Future Abortionists of America
Published at *Medium*, September 4, 2018
Edited by Siobhan O'Connor

What's a "Safe Space"?
Published at *Fusion*, November 11, 2015
Edited by Geraldine Sealey

A Future History of the United States
Published in *Pacific Standard*,
January 26, 2016
Edited by Ted Scheinman

The Birth of the Ku Klux Brand
Published in *Pacific Standard*,
February 19, 2016
Edited by Ted Scheinman

Tactical Lessons from the
Civil Rights Movement
Published in *Pacific Standard*, March 9, 2017
Edited by Ted Scheinman

Did You Know the CIA _____?
Published in *n+1*, March 7, 2018
Edited by Mark Krotov

The Loser Wins
Published at *The New Inquiry*,
October 20, 2010
Edited by Rob Horning

The Singular Pursuit of Comrade Bezos
Published at *Medium*, February 15, 2018
Edited by Matt Higginson

Glitch Capitalism
Published in *New York*, April 23, 2018
Edited by Max Read

America's Largest Property Crime
Published here for the first time
Written for The *New York
Times Magazine*, 2015

Why Are Your Wages so Low?
Published at *Buzzfeed*, October 19, 2017
Edited by Tom Gara

How Much is a Word Worth?
Published at *Medium*, April 16, 2018
Edited by Siobhan O'Connor

Americans have Nothing
to Learn from Nazis
Published at *Al Jazeera
America*, February 3, 2015
Edited by David Johnson

Harry Potter Was a Child Soldier
Published at *aeon*, June 1, 2015
Edited by Ross Andersen

The J20 Raid and the Trump
Protest That Never Ended
Published in *Pacific Standard*, April 18, 2017
Edited by Ted Scheinman

The Fascist Bogeyman
Self-published, September 21, 2016

Thanks to my family, friends, comrades, coworkers, readers, and haters, mostly in that order.